Tainted Breeze

Tainted Breeze

The Great Hanging at
Gainesville, Texas
1862

Richard B. McCaslin

LOUISIANA STATE UNIVERSITY PRESS
Baton Rouge and London

Copyright © 1994 by Louisiana State University Press
Manufactured in the United States of America
First printing
03 02 01 00 99 98 97 96 95 94   5 4 3 2 1

Designer: Laura Roubique Gleason
Typeface: Janson Text
Typesetter: G & S Typesetters, Inc.
Printer and binder: Thompson-Shore, Inc.

Library of Congress Cataloging-in-Publication Data

McCaslin, Richard B.
    Tainted breeze : the great hanging at Gainesville, Texas, 1862 /
Richard B. McCaslin.
       p.   cm.
    Includes index.
    ISBN 0-8071-1825-7 (hard : alk. paper)
    1. Hanging—Texas—Gainesville—History—19th century.
  2. Gainesville (Tex.)—History.   3. Texas—History—Civil War,
  1861–1865.   I. Title.
F394.G15M33   1993
976.4′533—dc20   93-15835
                                                            CIP

The paper in this book meets the guidelines for permanence and durability of the
Committee on Production Guidelines for Book Longevity of the Council on Library
Resources.∞

To hear a Northern man crying out Union, Union,
Methinks I hear the bugle blast of the robber chief.
To hear a Southern man cry out Union, Union,
Methinks I snuff Treason on the tainted breeze.
—Austin *Southern Intelligencer*, July 13, 1859

Contents

Illustrations

Acknowledgments

There is no way to thank all of the people who aided me in the completion of this book, but my affection and respect for all of them compel me to try. If anyone is omitted, please accept my humble apologies and anonymous gratitude. None of these people are to blame for any errors in this volume; I claim all as my own in the sincere belief, as a friend once told me, that there are no perfect books, only published ones.

This work began in the History Department of the University of Texas at Austin, and developed under the meticulous supervision of L. Tuffly Ellis, my mentor and my friend. Terry G. Jordan of the Geography Department at that institution also strongly influenced this study, as did Randolph B. Campbell of the University of North Texas, who was the first to introduce me to the riches that can be found among the local records of Texas. I owe all of these men a debt of gratitude that I can never repay.

I would like to thank the library staff of the University of Texas, especially those at the Eugene C. Barker Texas History Center; they did their utmost to provide me with a wealth of material, as did the archivists and curators for the Austin History Center and the Texas State Archives, both in Austin, and the Morton Museum in Gainesville, Texas. I would especially like to thank Margaret Hayes, former director of the Morton Museum, whose initial assistance breathed life back into a flagging project. Financial support was provided by the History Department of the University of Texas at Austin, the Dora Bonham Foundation, the Daughters of the Republic of Texas, and the Colonial Dames of America. Without the help of all these people, this work would never have been completed.

Many individuals have contributed immeasurably to this project through their friendship. It would be difficult, if not impossible, to list all of them without inadvertently leaving someone out. As I do not wish to hurt anyone's feelings, I will simply convey my heartfelt gratitude to them anonymously. They know who they are.

Finally, I wish to thank my wife, Jana, not only for lending her support through the many nerve-wracking years of college and postgraduate struggle to become established—that would be reason enough, of course—but also for handing me a dusty pamphlet from a shelf in the back room of an Austin bookstore and asking if it interested me. It was an old copy of the Texas State Historical Association reprint of Thomas Barrett's memoir of the Great Hanging, and it certainly did catch my attention. Jana may well have had cause to regret handing me that tract, but she has been gracious enough not to say so and to encourage me while I developed this project based upon it.

Abbreviations

AGR	Texas Adjutant General's Records, in Archives Division, Texas State Library
Amnesty Files	U.S. Department of War, Adjutant General's Office, Case Files of Application from Former Confederates for Presidential Pardons 1865–1867, in Record Group 94, National Archives
BTHC	Eugene C. Barker Texas History Center, University of Texas at Austin
CSR	U.S. Department of War, Compiled Service Records, Confederate States of America, in Record Group 109, National Archives
GOR	Texas Governor's Office Records, in Archives Division, Texas State Library, Austin
LC	Manuscript Division, Library of Congress
OR	*The War of the Rebellion: A Compilation of the Official Records of the Union and Confederate Armies* (130 vols.; Washington, D.C., 1880–1901)
SWHQ	*Southwestern Historical Quarterly*
TSL	Texas State Library, Austin
UNT	Archives Division, University of North Texas Library, Denton
UT	University of Texas at Austin
WTHA Yearbook	*West Texas Historical Association Yearbook*

Tainted Breeze

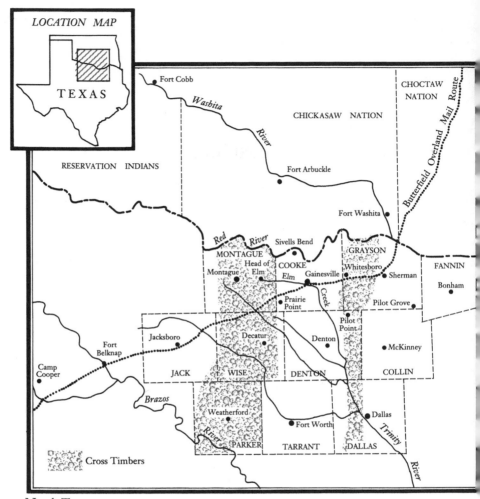

North Texas
Map by Bobbie Young

Introduction

Texas militia during the early morning hours of October 1, 1862, scattered through a handful of counties that lay along the Red River, arresting more than two hundred suspected Unionists. In Gainesville, the seat of government for Cooke County, vigilantes executed at least forty-two of these prisoners for conspiring to commit treason and foment insurrection. Few of the victims had plotted to usurp Confederate authority, and most were innocent of the abolitionist sentiments of which they were accused, but their pleas made little difference. There were others who were lynched in neighboring Grayson, Wise, and Denton counties, but the Great Hanging claimed the most lives in Gainesville, the community most closely identified with the atrocity in subsequent accounts.

The Great Hanging climaxed several years of escalating vigilante action against persons accused of fostering disorder on the North Texas frontier, which lay along the Red River from Fannin County to Montague County, north of Dallas. This groundswell reflected the extralegal violence erupting throughout the antebellum South as southerners attacked those who they feared would endanger them by disrupting the established pattern of society, particularly abolitionists. Dickson D. Bruce has observed, "Antebellum Southerners craved order and a stable, secure, community life." Unfortunately, they believed that most humans were dangerously passionate beings—especially the potentially rebellious slaves—and thus that their society was insecure. Most of the time they resolved this conflict by observing "tightly constricted formal procedures" that dominated antebellum southern social relations. When those failed, southerners were quick to resort to violence as the most efficient method for achieving security through the maintenance of the customary social order, as evidenced by the frequency

1

of vigilante movements and of individual clashes during the antebellum period.[1]

Southerners who lived on the frontier, like the settlers in Cooke County, were more likely to resort to violence than residents of established communities for the simple reason that their society was more insecure. Not only did they have to live with the ever-present fear of slave insurrection, every southerner's nightmare, but they also were frequently attacked by hostile Indians, against whom homesteaders often had to defend themselves without effective aid from the government. The barbarities inflicted by each faction upon the other reinforced the familiarity with violence that was inherent in slavery, facilitating decisions for violent actions. Furthermore, the population was highly mobile, with newcomers arriving every day. In places where many of them came from the Upper South and Midwest, as in Cooke County, rumors of abolitionism began to fly and insecurity mounted. In the absence of well-established legal institutions, this tension frequently led to vigilantism. All too often, a North Texas settler later admitted, "when men were caught in any act of extreme violation of the law and good order," a "rope and some convenient tree" were used "to dispatch business."[2]

The vigilantes in Gainesville, like those elsewhere in the South, were initially conservative. Led by the economic and political elite among the populace, they resorted to illegal actions as the only viable method available for the maintenance of lawful order. This contradiction they reconciled through a strict adherence to formalism. While it is true that they could call upon a European tradition of organized social violence, they invoked instead the precedent of the American Revolution. It was the revolutionary generation that had extended the concept of social violence to include killing, and had even inserted the word *lynch* into the American lexicon, though it was not until later that it became synonymous with *hang*. American revo-

---

1. Dickson D. Bruce, Jr., *Violence and Culture in the Antebellum South* (Austin, 1979), 12, 39, 65–66, 93–94, 98, 111, 130; Bertram Wyatt-Brown, *Southern Honor: Ethics and Behavior in the Old South* (New York, 1982), xii, xv, 15, 19, 364–65, 369, 436; David W. Meinig, *Imperial Texas: An Interpretive Essay in Cultural Geography* (Austin, 1969), 49.

2. David J. Eddleman, "Autobiography of the [?]" (Typescript in UNT), 24; John Hope Franklin, *The Militant South* (Cambridge, Mass., 1956), 26–31, 36, 68–69, 70–71, 76–79; Richard M. Brown, "Historical Patterns of Violence in America," in *Violence in America: Historical and Comparative Perspectives*, ed. Hugh D. Graham and Ted R. Gurr (New York, 1970), 67–68, 156; Eddleman, a slave owner from Kentucky, moved to Pilot Point in Denton County during the fall of 1856 after residing for two years in adjacent Collin County.

lutionaries also provided vigilantes with the ideological and philosophical justification of popular sovereignty. Those in Cooke County, as elsewhere, observed the propriety of voting on each step, and honored the spirit of law and order by permitting the accused to testify before a jury, to examine witnesses, and to employ legal counsel. The editors of a nineteenth-century collection of essays on prominent westerners recalled this propriety in an article on James G. Bourland, a leader in the Great Hanging, when they defended his acts as being like those taken against Tories, and just as necessary.[3]

After the mysterious assassination of William C. Young, who had played a vital role in maintaining some lawful propriety in the prosecution of the accused, an overwhelming desire for vengeance negated much of the concern for formalism: the Citizens Court, as it was called, was reorganized, no more witnesses were called, and the jurors elected to hang a larger percentage of prisoners. Slavery—specifically the concern of slaveholders for both their property and their security—had a tremendous influence on this escalation of violence. The jury convicted only on a majority vote, but most of the jurors as well as other principals in the Citizens Court were slave owners, while all but one of those they condemned were not. Allegations of abolitionism significantly reduced the possibility of mercy for a prisoner, especially in the hysteria that pervaded Gainesville after Young's death. The intervention of a few officials and state judges brought an end to the slaughter, but not before the violence had spread far beyond Gainesville.[4]

3. Richard M. Brown, *Strain of Violence: Historical Studies of American Violence and Vigilantism* (New York, 1975), 4, 45–49, 56, 59–61, 93, 109; Michael Feldberg, *The Turbulent Era: Riot and Disorder in Jacksonian America* (New York, 1980), 74, 90–91; Bruce, *Violence and Culture*, 87; Charles Tilly, "Collective Violence in European Perspective," in *Violence in America*, ed. Graham and Gurr, 4–31; John R. Ross, "At the Bar of Judge Lynch: Lynching and Lynch Mobs in America" (Ph.D. dissertation, Texas Tech University, 1983), 16–21, 76–78; John H. Brown and William S. Speer, eds., *Encyclopedia of the New West* (Marshall, Tex., 1881), "Texas," 233–34. The question of whether humans are violent by nature or acculturation is best left to sociologists and psychologists, but it is evident that the participants in the Great Hanging drew upon a tradition of violence not only in their everyday lives but also in their history as Americans.

4. Ross, in "At the Bar of Judge Lynch," emphasizes that the "impulse" for lynching originates in "fear and the desire for revenge" (p. 6). He classifies lynchings into seven categories, based upon the extent to which formalism obscures other impulses as well as the number of participants. The Great Hanging, which he briefly discusses, does not fit easily into any one of his categories, but his discussion of the degeneration of vigilante movements into less formal violence has strongly influenced this work.

The irony of the Great Hanging is that both the vigilantes and their victims shared a common concern for order and security. Imbued with a heightened sense of insecurity due to the frontier conditions in which they lived, a majority of Cooke County voters in 1861 rejected disunion, fearing the chaos and loss of military protection that might ensue. When the Confederate government of Texas organized units for frontier defense, many settlers along the Red River enlisted. However, after the removal of troops from the frontier, an influx of suspicious refugees, and the enactment of measures—especially conscription—to coerce support, a significant number of North Texans expressed their desire for the return of the order and security provided under Federal rule by joining the Peace party. This membership branded them as purveyors of disorder among those who remained loyal to the Confederacy—the manifest symbol of order through legal authority—and made them targets for the same tactics used against accused abolitionists before the war, albeit on a larger scale due to the intensifying effect of wartime experiences on intraregional tensions.

The Great Hanging does challenge some previous assertions about vigilantism. Richard M. Brown dissects southern society into three socioeconomic levels—upper, middle, and lower. He states that men of the upper level usually led vigilante movements because of their determination "to reestablish the community structure in which they were dominant." The "middle level inhabitants" supported these efforts because they were mainly directed against the lower class, who, because they had little property, were associated with the outlaws who preyed on unprotected settlers. Frontier society in antebellum Texas was too fluid to be so easily characterized. Although the instigators of the Great Hanging were certainly the region's economic and political elite, many of those whom they hanged were not propertyless. In the context of the antebellum Texas frontier, some of those hanged were doing well enough to be considered part of the middle class. The Great Hanging, then, instead of eliminating a marginal element, cut deeply into the settled populace, creating bloody divisions that would endure for generations to come.[5]

The circumstances surrounding the Great Hanging also suggest that family relationships had a greater influence on violence in North Texas than has been discussed in previous works on vigilantism such as Brown's studies. Families clustered in their sectional loyalties, following the lead of older or

5. Brown, *Strain of Violence*, 104–105; Brown, "Historical Patterns," in *Violence in America*, ed. Graham and Gurr, 68, 97.

more outspoken members. Many served together in the Confederate army, and some cooperated as members of various investigating committees or on the Citizens Court itself. At the same time, several victims may well have been condemned because they were related to a prominent Unionist. The vigilantes, in their zeal to crush dissent, shattered more than a few families, enhancing the bitter divisiveness within Cooke County.

Drawing upon the abundant material available to him, Brown also declares that "American opinion generally supported vigilantism," adding that any "extralegal activity by a provoked populace was deemed to be the rightful action of good citizens."[6] Reaction to the Great Hanging, however, split along regional lines. In the South, most newspaper editors and their correspondents, as well as public officials, applauded the lynchings as conducive to the eradication of disorder and the preservation of the Confederacy. The violence continued against those accused of dissent in North Texas through the end of the war. Many northerners, on the other hand, were appalled at the affair, and they prevailed upon the Federal government to try to assist the Unionists in North Texas.

But the Federal government, despite several attempts, proved unable to aid Unionists in the region during the war or to avenge them afterward. When the conflict ended, the people of Cooke and adjacent counties closed ranks once more, preferring the security of turning their backs on the past to the disruption of assessing blame and punishing the guilty. It has been asserted that those who supported the Confederacy lost the war but achieved their goals through violence and the courts during Reconstruction.[7] This was certainly true in North Texas, where attacks against those who brought turmoil by opposing the Confederacy continued after the war, while those brought to trial for their role in the Great Hanging and other atrocities were acquitted. Attempts by angry Unionists to obtain redress came to naught, and decisions by many grieving families to try to resume a normal life, coupled with a flood of newcomers, facilitated the imposition of a conspiracy of silence regarding wartime violence.

An inquiry into the circumstances surrounding the Great Hanging offers a unique perspective on disaffection in the Confederacy. Not only is it the most spectacular of many such events in Civil War Texas, it is also the

6. Brown, *Strain of Violence*, 130.

7. The effectiveness of "political terrorism" in the post–Civil War South is thoroughly discussed in George G. Rable, *But There Was No Peace: The Role of Violence in the Politics of Reconstruction* (Athens, Ga., 1984).

largest incident of its kind in United States history.[8] Every Confederate
state harbored dissenters, and the crippling effect of dissension upon the
Confederacy has been discussed previously in other studies.[9] The suppression of wartime dissent by southerners, though, has been less carefully ex-
plored.[10] For Texas, an exception to the rule is James Marten's *Texas Divided: Loyalty and Dissent in the Lone Star State, 1856–1874.* Marten capably
demonstrates that "dissension sprang from a multitude of seeds," and that
"'loyal' Texans had many ways of eliminating dissent and dissenters."[11] For
those involved in the Great Hanging—to which Marten devotes little attention—both wartime disaffection and its suppression originated in a common desire for order and security. The Great Hanging suggests that, in an

8. Brown, in *Strain of Violence*, provides a list of 323 vigilante movements. The most
lethal of these was a Montana vigilance committee that claimed thirty-five victims in 1884,
and so he concedes that the Great Hanging was "probably the greatest mass spectacle of lynch
law in American history" (241). If this study does little else, it should secure that macabre
distinction for Gainesville.

9. See, for example, Albert B. Moore, *Conscription and Conflict in the Confederacy* (New
York, 1924), and Ella Lonn, *Desertion During the Civil War* (New York, 1928). Georgia Lee
Tatum, in *Disloyalty in the Confederacy* (Chapel Hill, 1934), discusses dissent by region, but her
chapter about Texas provides little about the internecine conflict there. Carl N. Degler, in *The
Other South: Southern Dissenters in the Nineteenth Century* (Boston, 1982), analyzes opposition
to secession in the South but devotes little attention to disaffection during the war. Richard
Beringer *et al.*, in *Why the South Lost the Civil War* (Athens, Ga., 1986), include a summary of
the available literature on dissent in the Confederacy.

10. No recent study of disaffection and persecution in the Confederacy as a whole has appeared, but Philip S. Paludan, in *Victims: A True Story of the Civil War* (Knoxville, 1981), offers
a compelling insight into the execution of thirteen Unionists in the mountains of western
North Carolina. Bell I. Wiley, in *The Plain People of the Confederacy* (Baton Rouge, 1943), and
Charles W. Ramsdell, in *Behind the Lines in the Southern Confederacy* (Baton Rouge, 1944), discuss the war's impact on southerners but do not examine efforts to counter dissent. Harold M.
Hyman, in *To Try Men's Souls: Loyalty Tests in American History* (Berkeley, 1959), asserts that
"nowhere in Dixie were the deeds of the irregulars bloodier than in the Southwest" (220) but
does not elaborate because "few such accounts" (232) survive. Frank L. Klement, in *Dark
Lanterns: Secret Political Societies, Conspiracies, and Treason Trials in the Civil War* (Baton Rouge,
1984), focuses almost exclusively on the North.

11. James Marten, *Texas Divided: Loyalty and Dissent in the Lone Star State, 1856–1874*
(Lexington, Ky., 1990), 1, 2. Five of the eight chapters in Marten's work are devoted to an
explication of the theme of diversity in wartime dissent and its suppression. For more about
disaffection in Confederate Texas, see Robert L. Kerby, *Kirby Smith's Confederacy: The Trans-
Mississippi South, 1863–1865* (New York, 1972), 91–93; and Robert P. Felgar, "Texas in the
War for Southern Independence" (Ph.D. dissertation, UT, 1935), 358–67.

era wracked by varied dissent and reactions thereto, security through the maintenance of order was the paramount goal for at least one remote corner of the South, and perhaps other portions as well.

The enforced silence regarding the Great Hanging has restricted historical writing on the subject. A participant in the affair, Thomas Barrett, privately published an account, *The Great Hanging at Gainesville*, in 1885, but it was soon suppressed and remained a rare item of Texas ephemera until 1961, when it was reproduced by the Texas State Historical Association. That group also resurrected a narrative of the Great Hanging written by George W. Diamond, the younger brother of a participant. Begun about 1867 from the official transcripts of the Gainesville proceedings, which have since been lost, Diamond's work, for unknown reasons, was never completed.[12] It remained unpublished until 1963, when the Texas State Historical Association printed a version edited from the original by Sam Acheson and Julia Ann Hudson O'Connell.

The appearance of these primary accounts prompted two scholarly but disappointing articles. Philip Rutherford, in "The Great Gainesville Hanging," *Civil War Times Illustrated*, XVII (April 1978), 12–16, provided a colorful narrative that did not extend much beyond the material written by Barrett and Diamond. James Smallwood published a more substantial study, "Disaffection in Confederate Texas: The Great Hanging at Gainesville," two years earlier in *Civil War History*, XXII (1976), 351–60, but he incorporated few sources other than Barrett and Diamond. The most complete history of the Great Hanging appeared in Michael Collins' *Cooke County, Texas: Where the South Meets the West* (Gainesville, 1981). Collins corrected many inaccuracies in the previous two articles, as well as those of earlier local and county histories, but again left important questions unanswered. The answers offered by L. D. Clark—grandson of James Lemuel Clark, and great-grandson of Nathaniel M. Clark, who was hanged at Gainesville on October 13, 1862—in his introduction to *The Civil War Recollections of James Lemuel Clark* (College Station, Tex., 1984), complement the ac-

12. Rex Strickland, the secretary of the Red River Valley Historical Association and a noted scholar in his own right, wrote to local historian Lillian Gunter on September 21, 1925, that the records of the Citizens Court were in the possession of Adam Hornback, a resident of Grayson County. This is the last known location of these materials. A transcript of this letter appears in Pete A. Y. Gunter, ed., "Lillian Gunter Papers on Cooke County History" (Typescript in Morton Museum, Gainesville, Tex.), 232.

count given by Collins, but unfortunately reflect the strong biases of family tradition.[13]

This inquiry into the Great Hanging follows the advice of George H. Ragsdale, an amateur historian from Gainesville who began an investigation into the event while many participants were still living. In his "Texas War History Written in 1892," he declared that the "whole transaction should be studied from a thorough knowledge of the people connected with it."[14] He could not do so because he lived too close to his subject; many people involved in the Great Hanging refused to cooperate with him. A more distinguished and objective scholar, Barnes F. Lathrop, repeated the essence of Ragsdale's directive in the introduction to his pioneering study of the historical demography of Texas, *Migration into East Texas, 1835–1860* (Austin, 1949). He inspired numerous analyses of Texas based on the census and other public records, but these materials have not been systematically used for a study of dissent in the Confederate Southwest, until now.

All the battles and campaigns of the principal armies during the Civil War have been examined at length and will be again, but events such as the Great Hanging, which had a similarly profound and enduring effect on the people involved, have been overlooked. After 1867, as Reconstruction sputtered on to its disappointing close, the Great Hanging began to fade from the national memory. It endured primarily as a part of the increasingly distant past for the people of North Texas, to be hidden from public view and discussed infrequently, if at all, by adults after the children had gone to sleep. Because it suggests how the concerns for order and security among nineteenth-century southerners shaped the course of the Civil War, the Great Hanging deserves as large a modern audience as it reached during the war, when newspaper editors across the country printed reports of the vigilantes in North Texas.

13. L. D. Clark also wrote "The Great Hanging at Gainesville, October 1862," *American West* (November–December, 1984), 45–49. He compiled much of this article, as well as the introduction to the edited memoir of James Lemuel Clark, from materials still in the possession of his family. For another popular account by a Gainesville native, see Pete A. Y. Gunter, "The Great Gainesville Hanging, October, 1862," *Blue and Gray*, III (April–May 1986), 48–55.

14. A photocopy of George H. Ragsdale's manuscript, dated April 2, 1892, as well as a typescript from the original are in the George H. Ragsdale Papers, BHTC.

ONE

The Foundations of Dissent

Cooke County straddles the divide between the watersheds of the Trinity and Red rivers in North Texas, in the area historically referred to as "the Forks of the Trinity" or "the Forks." This region remained sparsely settled until after the mid–nineteenth century, when homesteaders followed a new stage road into North Texas. Although most of these settlers were nonslaveholders from the Upper South or Midwest, a small group of slaveholders from the Lower South dominated Cooke County economically and politically throughout the Civil War, as they did much of Texas. Living on the frontier, both groups shared a great concern for security and order, and slaveholders enhanced their authority by leading settlers in violent, sometimes illegal actions against those who threatened the best interests (as defined by the slaveholders) of the county. The two groups split, however, over secession, and though nearly three-fourths of the Texas electorate endorsed disunion, Cooke County delivered a solid majority in favor of the Union. When confronted with the most momentous decision of their lives, most of the settlers in Cooke County chose the security of maintaining the Union, a choice that would leave many of them in the dangerous position of challenging the established authority of their slaveholding neighbors.

Cooke County did not exist until shortly before the beginning of the Civil War. Spanish Texas sprawled from the Nueces River in the south to the Red River in the north, but the Forks remained distant from early colonization efforts. The settlement of that area began under an agreement between William S. Peters and the Republic of Texas in 1841. The trickle of colonists increased after United States Army Captain Randolph B. Marcy surveyed a trail in 1849 that crossed the Red River at Colbert's Ferry and meandered southwest through Cooke County, but most emigrants continued west looking for California gold, while many who had settled on the Forks went with them.[1]

On the whole, early settlement proved disappointing, and to make matters worse, Peters was plagued with legal problems that gave rise to vigilantism, replicating a pattern that was unfortunately common in the antebellum South, especially on the frontier. To attract settlers, Peters promised supplies and other support in exchange for half of the land that each homesteader would receive from the Republic, later state, of Texas. Peters did not deliver the supplies, but he did send Henry O. Hedgecoxe to press for his half of each homestead. Angry colonists allied with disappointed investors, and a vigilante committee forced Hedgecoxe to flee for his life in July, 1852. The settlers' hostile actions forced Governor Peter H. Bell to call a session of the legislature in January, 1853, during which representatives Samuel A. Bogart and James W. Throckmorton from the Forks region were instrumental in securing the passage of measures that forced Peters to repudiate Hedgecoxe and to settle all claims in favor of the homesteaders. It was the first of many times that settlers in North Texas, like those elsewhere in the South and on the frontier, found vigilantism to be the most efficient method of protecting their interests.[2]

The official seat of government for Cooke County was founded in a

1. Michael Collins, *Cooke County, Texas: Where the South and the West Meet* (Gainesville, Tex., 1981), 4–5; David W. Meinig, *Imperial Texas: An Interpretive Essay in Cultural Geography* (Austin, 1969), 23–24, 28; William C. Pool, *Historical Atlas of Texas* (Austin, 1975), 39; Rupert N. Richardson, *The Frontier of Northwest Texas, 1846–1876* (Glendale, Calif., 1963), 28–31, 38–39; A. Morton Smith, *The First 100 Years in Cooke County* (San Antonio, 1955), 2–6; Walter P. Webb, H. Bailey Carroll, and Eldon S. Branda, eds., *The Handbook of Texas* (3 vols.; Austin, 1952, 1976), I, 275, II, 141; Seymour V. Connor, *The Peters Colony of Texas* (Austin, 1959), 21–22, 53–56, 87; William R. Strong, *His Memoirs*, ed. Pete A. Y. Gunter and Robert A. Calvert (Denton, Tex., 1982), 1, 16; Averam B. Bender, *The March of Empire: Frontier Defense in the Southwest, 1848–1860* (Lawrence, Kans., 1952), 56–57; W. Eugene Hollon, *Beyond the Cross Timbers: The Travels of Randolph B. Marcy, 1812–1877* (Norman, Okla., 1955), 84; Charles N. Jones, *Early Days in Cooke County* (Gainesville, Tex., 1936), 36–37; Joseph C. McConnell, *The West Texas Frontier* (Jacksboro, Tex., 1933), 101. Strong settled in Cooke County before the Civil War.

2. Connor, *Peters Colony*, 67, 84–85, 90, 136, 142–44, 150–51; Claude Elliot, *Leathercoat: The Life History of a Texas Patriot* (San Antonio, 1938), 27, 29–32. For more about Samuel A. Bogart, see Webb, Carroll, and Branda, eds., *Handbook*, I, 181, as well as William De Ryee and R. E. Moore, *The Texas Album of the Eighth Legislature, 1860* (Austin, 1860), 19–20. *Leathercoat* is a biography of Throckmorton; Elliot also wrote an article on Throckmorton in Webb, Carroll, and Branda, *Handbook*, II, 778.

similarly peremptory manner. Cooke County was created in 1848. The county commissioners met for the first time in March of that year at Aaron Hill's home on the Elm Fork of the Trinity River; it was not until May, 1849, that they asked slaveholder Daniel Montague to survey a permanent seat. The United States Post Office rejected the name they chose for their planned community—Liberty—because there was already a town by that name in Texas, thus forcing them to postpone a final decision until August, 1850, when they decided to hold a referendum on a townsite. The election was never held; while a group of voters were inspecting a tract on Wheeler Creek, county court chief justice Robert Wheelock, tired of the debate, climbed on his horse with a demijohn of whiskey and invited all who wanted the county seat to be located on Elm Fork to follow him. Most did, and on August 19, 1850, the commissioners endorsed their selection. Several settlers had served under General Edmund P. Gaines, and so the prospective town was named Gainesville in his honor.[3]

The northern side of Gainesville's central square fronted on California Street, on which followers of Marcy's trail traveled, but the new town developed slowly. William Bean, who had earlier opened a trading post on the Red River, built three log cabins in Gainesville during the fall of 1852. One served as a store; his family and three slaves occupied the other two. The following year slaveholder James G. Bourland, a former Texas state senator, established a dry goods store, investing a settlement awarded him by a Federal court for an incident during which he, as an official of the Republic of Texas, had been bound and gagged by the crew of a United States ship. Alexander Boutwell, the first sheriff of Cooke County, opened the town's first saloon during the summer of 1854 in a log cabin that had been a school. With such auspicious beginnings, Gainesville was officially designated as the seat of Cooke County in a bill signed into law on January 26, 1854, though the town was not incorporated until 1873.[4]

3. H. P. N. Gammel, comp., *The Laws of Texas, 1822–1897* (10 vols.; Austin, 1898) II, 1,313–14, 1,332–33, 1,350–51, 1,363–64, III, 183–84, 452, IV, 183–85, 203–204, 480–82, 903–904, 905–906; Webb, Carroll, and Branda, eds., *Handbook*, I, 375, 406–407, 459–60, 492, 658–59, 726, 900, II, 196, 224, 337–38, 707–708, 926; Dallas *News*, March 23, 1924, January 1, 2, 1955; Gainesville (Tex.) *Register*, August 30, 1948; Collins, *Cooke County*, 6, 7; Smith, *First 100 Years*, 5, 7, 11–12; Strong, *Memoirs*, 23.

4. Lemuel D. Clark, ed., *The Civil War Recollections of James Lemuel Clark* (College Station, Tex., 1984), 102; Strong, *Memoirs*, 23–24, 29; Cooke County, County Clerk, Deed Record, 1850–present, II, 60, in Cooke County Courthouse, Gainesville, Tex.; Plat of Gainesville, Texas, in Map Collection, Archives Division, TSL; Gammel, comp., *Laws of Texas*, III, 1567,

The establishment through North Texas of the Butterfield Overland Mail route, which paralleled the trail blazed by Marcy, brought a dramatic increase in the population. The stages entered Texas across the Red River at Colbert's Ferry, then stopped in Sherman and Diamond's Station before arriving in Gainesville. From there they rolled west to Davidson's Station in western Cooke County, then angled southwest through a corner of neighboring Montague County. The first Butterfield stagecoach rattled west from St. Louis on September 15, 1858, and rolled into Gainesville five days later. Settlers followed in droves; David J. Eddleman, an earlier arrival, recalled, "In 1859 there came to Texas a flood of emegration [*sic*] from the north such as had never been known before." The population of Cooke County in 1850 was a sparse 220; by 1860, it swelled to a more substantial 3,760. The influx continued until the onset of the Civil War, when the Butterfield Overland Mail suspended its operations in Texas and shifted to a route farther north.[5]

In the few years that the Butterfield Overland operated in Texas, it brought the appearance of civility to many of the communities along its route, including Gainesville. When Marcy came through the region again in 1854, his adjutant recorded that Gainesville was only a "collection of five or six log cabins, dignified with the name of a town." Three years later, wagon master James B. Leach found a "flourishing village" that served as the "center of considerable trade." A visitor in 1859 reported that Gainesville had fifty or sixty houses, "most of them neat edifices and none shabby";

VII, 743–47; Gainesville *Register*, August 30, 1948; Connor, *Peters Colony*, 185; Smith, *First 100 Years*, 13–16, 19.

5. David J. Eddleman, "Autobiography of the [?]" (Typescript in UNT), 24; Sam Acheson and Julia Ann Hudson O'Connell, eds., *George Washington Diamond's Account of the Great Hanging at Gainesville, 1862* (Austin, 1963), 5; Roscoe P. Conkling and Margaret B. Conkling, *The Butterfield Overland Mail, 1857–1869* (3 vols.; Glendale, Calif., 1947), I, 105–18, 125, 290, 294, II, 325–26, III, Map 2, Section 1; W. Eugene Hollon, *The Southwest: Old and New* (Lincoln, Neb., 1961), 201–205; Gainesville *Register*, August 30, 1948; Jesse W. Williams, "The Butterfield Overland Mail Road Across Texas," *SWHQ*, LXI (1957), 1, 3, 4–6; *Ancestors and Descendants: Grayson County, Texas* (Dallas, 1980), 14, 58; Ida L. Huckaby, *Ninety-Four Years in Jack County, 1854–1848* (Austin, 1949), 30–31; Barnes F. Lathrop, *Migration into East Texas, 1835–1860* (Austin, 1949), 60, 62, 65; Jones, *Early Days*, 37–38; Smith, *First 100 Years*, 26; Webb, Carroll, and Branda, eds., *Handbook*, I, 258–59; William W. White, "Migration into West Texas, 1845–1860" (M.A. thesis, UT, 1948), 40–44. George W. Diamond was a brother of John R. Diamond, a proprietor of Diamond's Station, and of James J. Diamond, a principal in the Great Hanging. All can be found in Webb, Carroll, and Branda, eds., *Handbook*, III, 243–44.

the 1860 census revealed that 280 people lived in these homes. The town had four stores and two hotels, and boasted sidewalks paved with white gravel scooped from the bed of the nearby Elm Fork of the Trinity River. The *Texas Almanac* for 1861 asserted that Gainesville was "perhaps one of the most pleasant towns in North Texas."[6]

Gainesville by 1860 also had the amenities of an established seat of government. A rude log courthouse, built for a paltry sum by Boutwell and a partner, fell victim to an errant bull and was replaced by a more substantial frame structure that, like the first, also served as a meeting house and school. The press of legal affairs compelled the county commissioners to rent the upper story of a store on the square as well. A jail was built in 1857 of stout timbers; most of the time, it served as a holding tank for drunkards, but in 1860 it did house William Pitman, a convicted murderer who on June 8, 1860, earned the dubious distinction of being the first person to be legally executed in Cooke County. Gainesville also served as the only post office for Cooke County during the antebellum period: Jeremiah E. Hughes, a native of New Jersey who also served as county clerk, received and distributed mail at his home.[7]

Only a fraction of the newcomers who followed the stage road to Cooke County settled in Gainesville; most scattered wherever the land suited them. The Eastern Cross Timbers extended along the boundary between Cooke and Grayson counties, and blanketed a third of the former. West of the Eastern Cross Timbers lay the Grand Prairie , largest of the geographic divisions of Cooke County, and upon the western edge of this open land were the Western Cross Timbers. Although the climate could be hostile—annual rainfall varied from twelve to fifty inches with no discernible pattern, and Cooke County lay at the south end of "Tornado Alley"—there was plenty of surface water, and the land supported a variety of crops.[8]

6. William B. Parker, *Unexplored Texas: Notes Taken During the Expedition Commanded by Capt. R. B. Marcy, U.S.A.* (Philadelphia, 1856), 84, 86–87; Clarksville (Tex.) *Standard*, April 30, 1859; L. W. Williams, "Journey of the Leach Wagon Train Across Texas, 1857," *WTHA Yearbook*, XXIX (1953), 122; Collins, *Cooke County*, 8; Hollon, *Beyond the Cross Timbers*, 174; McConnell, *West Texas Frontier*, 275; *The Texas Almanac for 1861* (New Orleans, 1860), 188.

7. Strong, *Memoirs*, 23; Cooke County Commissioners' Court, "Minutes, 1857 to 1878," I, 40 (sheet 2), 59 (sheet 2), 62, typescript in Works Progress Administration Historical Records Survey, BTHC; *Register of the Officers and Agents, Civil, Military and Naval in the Service of the United States for the Year 1859* (Washington, D.C., 1859), 369; Gainesville *Register*, August 30, 1948; Jones, *Early Days*, 14–16, 80; Smith, *First 100 Years*, 12–13, 16, 18–19, 25.

8. Strong, *Memoirs*, 13; Clarksville *Standard*, April 30, 1859; Robert T. Hill, *Geography*

Most antebellum settlers in Cooke County homesteaded in one of three areas: in the Eastern Cross Timbers, on tributaries of the Elm Fork of the Trinity River south of Gainesville, or along the Red River and its tributaries north of the county seat. Gainesville thus found itself surrounded by a loose aggregation of isolated communities. Odd Steer Settlement lay on Indian Creek, south of the county seat, while Flat Head Nation and Tarrapin Valley were to the east, in the Eastern Cross Timbers. People who settled in the southeast corner of Cooke County, also in the Eastern Cross Timbers, were called Sandlappers; they constructed a schoolhouse that also served as a Christian church on land donated by Rama Dye. East of Dye's school was Smoke Springs; to the south was a settlement on Wolf Creek that was later known as Mountain Home, where the first school in Cooke County opened in 1847. Montague along with some other slaveholders settled along Fish Creek, a tributary of the Red River in the northern part of the county, while still others clustered their small plantations on the Red River at Sivell's Bend and Delaware Bend, where Bourland built a home and trading post.[9]

Geography was not the only cause for diversity within Cooke County on the eve of the Civil War. The flood of settlers into the county was representative of immigration into Texas as a whole during the late 1850s; of

---

and Geology of the Black and Grand Prairies, Texas (Washington, D.C., 1901), 61, 588–89; Terry G. Jordan, "Forest Folk, Prairie Folk: Rural Religious Cultures in North Texas," *SWHQ*, LXXX (1976), 137–38, 140; Terry G. Jordan, "The Imprint of the Upper and Lower South on Mid–Nineteenth Century Texas," *Annals of the Association of American Geographers*, LXXVII (1967), 679; Collins, *Cooke County*, 2, 5, 8; Connor, *Peters Colony*, 46–47, 95; Pool, *Atlas of Texas*, 7, 12; Webb, Carroll, and Branda, eds., *Handbook*, I, 537, II, 885; Clarksville *Standard*, April 30, 1859; Terry G. Jordan, John L. Bean, Jr., and William M. Holmes, *Texas: A Geography* (Boulder, 1984), 30–31, 38–40; A. W. Spaight, *Resources, Soil, and Climate of Texas* (Galveston, 1882), 72–73.

9. Bettie L. Gunter, "Recollections of an Early Cooke County Settler" (Typescript in Morton Museum, Gainesville, Tex.); Letitia McCormick, "Early Days in Cooke County Are Described," and Willie Russell, "Sivells Bend Community History," (Typescripts in Cooke Cty. Historical File, Cooke Cty. Library, Gainesville, Tx.); Clark, ed., *Recollections of James Clark*, 51–52; Strong, *Memoirs*, 9, 11–12, 30, 53; Cooke Cty. Deed Record, II, 593; Gainesville *Register*, August 30, 1948; Collins, *Cooke County*, 6; Jones, *Early Days*, 11–12; Smith, *First 100 Years*, 8, 15–16. Gunter moved to Sivells Bend on the Red River in 1861. McCormick settled in the Eastern Cross Timbers southeast of Gainesville in 1854. It is interesting to note that while Gainesville was the site of the only post office in Cooke County before and after the Civil War, during that conflict a number of post offices operated in other communities in Cooke County. See *The Texas Almanac for 1862* (Houston, 1862), 54–55; *The Texas Almanac for 1864* (Austin, 1864), 41–42; *The Texas Almanac for 1865* (Austin, 1865), 53, 55.

421,294 free residents in 1860, almost two-thirds had been born outside the state. The Upper and Lower South were the principal places of origin of immigrants, and the differences between the two regions accounted for those between the new settlers. Those from the Lower South had been raised within an economy dominated by slavery and cotton. Most of those from the Upper South were nonslaveholders who grew subsistence crops. Although most Texans in 1860 were upper southerners, economic and political power were concentrated among lower southerners. With the involuntary aid of black slaves—the number of which grew rapidly until 1860 when there were 182,566 in Texas—lower southerners were economically preeminent by the late 1850s, primarily through the production of cotton. The cotton harvest of the United States doubled between 1850 and 1860, but Texas crops increased more than sevenfold to 431,463 bales. This boon provided an economic base for political influence; the number of slaveholders from the Lower South in public office by 1860 was disproportionate to their actual share of the population.[10]

By 1860, then, slavery provided economic dominance for settlers from the Lower South in Texas, linking the state's leaders but not all of its residents to the heartland of what would be the Confederacy. Cooke County experienced a similar shift in the 1850s. Although nonslaveholding upper southerners remained a majority as they had been since the first settlements, a few slaveholders, primarily from the Lower South, established themselves in creek bottoms and along the Red River. These seventy-four families—10.9 percent of the free households in Cooke County—owned 369 slaves but produced little cotton because their access to markets was

10. United States Bureau of the Census, *The Seventh Census of the United States* (Washington, D.C., 1853), 504, *Population of the United States in 1860; Compiled from the Original Returns of the Eighth Census* (Washington, D.C., 1864), v, vi, xvi, xxxiii, 486, 490–91, and *Agriculture of the United States in 1860; Compiled from the Original Returns of the Eighth Census* (Washington, D.C., 1864), xxx, xciii, xciv; Lewis C. Gray, *History of Agriculture in the Southern United States to 1860* (2 vols.; Washington, D.C., 1933), II, 907; Randolph B. Campbell and Richard G. Lowe, *Wealth and Power in Antebellum Texas* (College Station, Tex., 1977), 14–15, 27; Jordan, "Imprint of the Upper and Lower South," 667, 669–72, 675, 677–78; Emory M. Thomas, *The Confederate Nation, 1861–1865* (New York, 1979), 5; Ralph A. Wooster, *The People in Power: Courthouse and Statehouse in the Lower South, 1850–1860* (Knoxville, 1969), 32–33, 38–39, 60, 79, 96–100, 111, 150–53, 163; Robert P. Felgar, "Texas in the War for Southern Independence" (Ph.D. dissertation, UT, 1935), 2; Abigail Curlee, "A Study of Texas Slave Plantations, 1822 to 1865" (Ph.D. dissertation, UT, 1932), 21–22; Samuel L. Evans, "Texas Agriculture 1865–1880" (M.A. thesis, UT, 1955), 2, 8, Map IIIa.

limited: the Red River was choked with debris, and railroads were nonexistent. Instead, slaveholders dominated the production of goods that could be sold to neighbors or the Federal garrisons posted along the frontier close by. Despite their small numbers, slaveholders in Cooke County by 1860 herded 40 percent of the milch cows, 50.8 percent of the sheep, and 59 percent of the cattle; they also raised 37 percent of the wheat and 47.8 percent of the oats. They thought in terms of markets and profits and relied on the continuation of slavery for prosperity, while the remaining nine-tenths of the families in Cooke County simply farmed for subsistence.[11]

As elsewhere, economic prominence became political dominance for slaveholders in Cooke County. In 1861 the chief justice, sheriff, and three of the four county commissioners owned slaves. These and other slaveholders enhanced their authority through community activism. The Gainesville Masonic lodge provided an important forum for their activities; among its members on the eve of the Civil War were slaveholders James G. Bourland, William R. Hudson, a county commissioner, James M. Peery, and James J. Diamond, a partner with his brother John R. Diamond in the Butterfield

11. B. D. Burch, "Statement," November 16, 1913 (MS in Lillian M. Gunter Papers, UNT); Sarah I. S. Rogers, "Memoirs" (Typescript in Morton Museum), 34–35; Acheson and O'Connell, eds., *Diamond's Account*, xli; Malissa C. Everett, "A Pioneer Woman," *WTHA Yearbook*, III (1927), 61; Strong, *Memoirs*, 13–15, 24; Census of 1860, Cooke Cty., Tex., Schedule 1 (Free Inhabitants), Schedule 2 (Slave Inhabitants), Schedule 4 (Productions of Agriculture) all in Genealogy Division, TSL; U.S. Bureau of the Census, *Agriculture, 1860,* 140–49; U.S. Bureau of the Census, *Population, 1860,* 484–86; *The Texas Almanac for 1859* (Galveston, 1858), 64–71; Bender, *The March of Empire*, 73–74, 77–78; Michael B. Dougan, *Confederate Arkansas: The People and Policies of a Frontier State in Wartime* (Tuscaloosa, Ala., 1976), 3; Gray, *Agriculture in the South*, II, 696, 816; Fred Tarpley, *Jefferson: Riverport to the Southwest* (Austin, 1983), 53–55, 59; Webb, Carroll, and Branda, eds., *Handbook*, II, 449–51, 714; Collins, *Cooke County*, 6; Mattie D. Lucas and Mita H. Hall, *A History of Grayson County, Texas* (Sherman, Tex., 1936), 90–91; Meinig, *Imperial Texas*, 43–44, 48–50, 59; Terry G. Jordan, "Population Origins in Texas, 1850," *Geographical Review*, LIX (1969), 90–92, 94; Jordan, "Imprint of the Upper and Lower South," 675–79, 685; Jordan, "Forest Folk, Prairie Folk," 138, 141; Charles W. Ramsdell, "The Frontier and Secession," in *Studies in Southern History and Politics, Inscribed to William Archibald Dunning,* (New York, 1914), 63–65; Connor, *Peters Colony,* 104–105, 107, 108, 110; Lathrop, *Migration into East Texas,* 37, 40–41, 60, 65; Allan C. Ashcraft, "Texas: 1860–1866—The Lone Star State in the Civil War" (Ph.D. dissertation, Columbia University, 1960), 9–10, 12–13, 22, 26–27; Walter L. Buenger, "Stilling the Voice of Reason: Secession and the Union in Texas" (Ph.D. dissertation, Rice University, 1979), 267, 292, 298, 299, 313, 327, 351, 360, 373, 388; Evans, "Texas Agriculture," 4–5, 10–11, 76, 80, Maps IVa, IVb, IXa, IXb, IXc, Xa, Xb, Xc; White, "Migration into West Texas," 16–23. Burch and Rogers migrated to Cooke County before the Civil War as did Everett, who settled in the Eastern Cross Timbers southeast of Gainesville.

Overland Mail depot at Diamond's Station. Masonic membership overlapped that of the International Order of Odd Fellows, which organized a lodge in Gainesville in 1859. Both fraternal groups worked with Southern Methodist Episcopal trustees Harvey Howeth, Montague, and Hill—two county commissioners and the district clerk, respectively—to construct a church and schools, while Hudson and Peery in 1862 financed the construction of a Cumberland Presbyterian church in Gainesville, enhancing the county seat as well as their status.[12]

While Gainesville by 1860 appeared settled and secure, it still lay upon the frontier. Farms and settlements in western Cooke County were easy prey for warlike nomads such as the Comanche and Kiowa, who have been labeled as "perhaps the most predatory and bloodthirsty of all prairie tribes." These horsemen attacked Cooke County settlers with alarming regularity in the nineteenth century and were often joined by newcomers from tribes relocated in the Indian Territory just north of the Red River. The Federal government built a series of forts along the Texas frontier to protect homesteaders—including Washita, Cobb, and Arbuckle north of Cooke County, and Belknap to the west—but these proved only partly successful. Most Texans believed that mounted volunteer companies were a necessary adjunct to the United States regulars, most of whom were infantry. Texas troops patrolled the frontier and established a line of outposts as early as 1847, with Fort Fitzhugh, near the site of Gainesville, as a northern anchor.[13]

12. Texas Secretary of State, Election Register, 1848–1900, in Archives Division, TSL; Acheson and O'Connell, eds., *Diamond's Account*, 37–38; Cooke Cty. Deed Record, II, 356, 489; United States Bureau of the Census, *Statistics of the United States in 1860; Compiled from the Original Returns and Being the Final Exhibit of the Eighth Census* (Washington, D.C., 1866), 471–73; Dallas *Herald*, January 5, 1859; Gainesville *Register*, August 30, 1948; Collins, *Cooke County*, 6; Macum Phelan, *A History of Early Methodism in Texas, 1817–1866* (Dallas, 1924), 381, 422; Smith, *First 100 Years*, 19, 23, 28, 33–34; Price M. Cheaney, "William R. Hudson" (Typescript in Price M. Cheaney Papers, Morton Museum); Pete A. Y. Gunter, ed., "Lillian Gunter Papers on Cooke County History" (Typescript in Morton Museum), 51; Lucas and Hall, *Grayson County*, 114; Mrs. Reavis Sappenfield, "The Story of Whitesboro" (Typescript in Grayson County Historical File, Sherman Municipal Library, Sherman, Tex.); Williams, "The Butterfield Overland Mail Road," 4; Tom Bomar, *Glimpses of Grayson County from the Early Days* (Sherman, Tex., 1894), 25; Conkling and Conkling, *Butterfield Overland Mail*, I, 291–92; Graham Landrum and Allen Smith, *An Illustrated History of Grayson County, Texas* (2d ed.; Fort Worth, 1967), 137; W. H. Walker, *Odd Fellowship in America and Texas* (Dallas, 1911), 195; Webb, Carroll, and Branda, eds., *Handbook*, II, 899.

13. W. W. Newcomb, *The Indians of Texas: From Prehistoric to Modern Times* (Austin, 1961), 157–58, 161, 249–50, 335–37, 355; Gainesville *Register*, August 30, 1948; Bender, *The March*

The state companies were supplemented by volunteer levies, which in Cooke County were led by slaveholders as emerging leaders of the community. In 1858 Indians attacked a house in northwestern Cooke County, killing everyone but a boy who, though wounded, escaped by hiding under the floorboards. Some settlers joined a company led by Bourland's brother, William, but they failed to find any hostile Indians. Governor Hardin R. Runnels authorized James G. Bourland to muster another company for an extended patrol. Bourland, in addition to his experience as a civil official, was a determined veteran of nearly two decades of Indian warfare. His troops, among whom was Boutwell, a lieutenant, remained in the field for six months, despite the fact that they officially failed to contact any enemy warriors. Those who knew the ruthless Bourland, however, agreed that his extended sortie had undermined other attacks.[14]

Bourland's actions during his patrol took place far from official scrutiny, but extralegal acts by groups led by other North Texas slaveholders were well documented. Many Cooke County settlers attributed raids to Indians living on two reservations located in West Texas: the Comanche Reserve

---

of Empire, 9–10, 27–28, 33–35, 37, 131–34, 138, 140–46; Connor, *Peters Colony*, 84; Huckaby, *Jack County*, 35–38, 60–64; Smith, *First 100 Years*, 6–7; Webb, Carroll, and Branda, eds., *Handbook*, II, 620, 634, 904–905, III, 296; J. W. Wilbarger, *Indian Depredations in Texas* (Austin, 1889), 379–418, 429–31, 436–39, 514–17, 521–22, 534–39; Annie H. Abel, *Indians as Slaveholders and Secessionists* (Cleveland, 1915), frontispiece, 52; Richardson, *The Frontier of Northwest Texas*, 56, 185; Robert M. Utley, *The Indian Frontier of the American West, 1845–1890* (Albuquerque, 1984), 37–38, 57; Gunter, ed., "Gunter Papers," 112; Dallas *News*, March 23, 1924, January 1, 2, 1955; Collins, *Cooke County*, 6.

14. Hiram R. Runnels to James G. Bourland, October 4, 1858, Bourland to Runnels, February 16, 1859, Muster Roll of James G. Bourland's Company, all in James G. Bourland Papers, LC; George L. Scott, "History of Early Days in Gainesville" (MS in Cooke Cty. Historical File); H. S. Woodward *et al.* to Runnels, September 18, 1858, and Manuel W. Estes *et al.* to Runnels, October 14, 1858, in Memorial and Petitions File, Archives Division, TSL; Gammel, comp., *Laws of Texas*, IV, 949–50, 1138, 1382–83, 1421; Dorman H. Winfrey and James M. Day, eds., *The Indian Papers of Texas and the Southwest* (5 vols.; Austin, 1960–1966), III, 302–303; Austin *Texas State Gazette*, October 9, 1858; Dallas *Herald*, October 20, 27, November 3, 1858; Edward F. Bates, *History and Reminiscences of Denton County* (Denton, Tex., 1918), 162–63; John H. Brown, *History of Texas From 1685 to 1892* (2 vols.; St. Louis, 1893), II, 375–76; Collin, *Cooke County*, 18; William J. Hughes, *Rebellious Ranger: Rip Ford and the Old Southwest* (Norman, Okla., 1964), 153; Jones, *Early Days*, 25; Wilbarger, *Indian Depredations*, 320–33; Guy R. Donnell, "The History of Montague County, Texas" (M.A. thesis, UT, 1940), 51–52. Scott served with James G. Bourland 1858–1859 and in the latter's Border Regiment during the Civil War.

on Salt Creek near Fort Belknap, and the Brazos Agency on the Clear Fork of the Brazos River. In 1859 John R. Baylor, a slaveholder from nearby Parker County, led over a hundred men from the counties along the Forks in an attack on the agencies. They were stymied by two companies of United States regulars, but the Texans' continued animosity led to the removal of the reservation Indians to the Indian Territory later that year. Removal, however, only increased Indian resentment by further restricting their food supply, and so raids and reprisals by both sides continued for many years, establishing a continuing legacy of extralegal violence.[15]

Extralegal enforcers also focused on elements among the settlers. Rumors persisted that white renegades rode with Indians in their raids, fostering suspicions among the newcomers who had poured down the Butterfield Overland Mail route that some among them were "men guilty of every species of crime." The settlers on the Forks would not tolerate a disruptive element within their own ranks, and acted swiftly to eradicate offenders. An 1858 raiding party in Jack County, which had been carved from Cooke County two years earlier, killed several settlers. The attackers included four white men, all of whom were acquitted by the state district court but were subsequently hanged by vigilantes.[16]

Vigilantes in Cooke County were just as violent in their actions against those accused of abolitionist sentiments. North Texas lay closer to the "bleeding ground" of Kansas than to the state capitol at Austin, and reports of violence from that beleaguered territory were all too familiar to settlers who had migrated through nearby states such as Missouri and Arkansas. Slave owners in Cooke County received strong support from nonslavehold-

15. John R. Baylor to "Captain," December 15, 1859, and James B. Barry to Sam Houston, August 14, 1860, in GOR; Dallas *Herald*, June 15, 1859; Birdville (Tex.) *Union Extra*, n.d., quoted in San Antonio *Herald*, May 21, 1859; John M. Elkins, *Life on the Texas Frontier* (Beaumont, 1908), 8–18; Bates, *Denton County*, 161–62; Bender, *The March of Empire*, 207–17; Brown, *History of Texas*, II, 377–79; Huckaby, *Jack County*, 48–51, 53–60; McConnell, *West Texas Frontier*, 275–334; Rupert N. Richardson, *The Comanche Barrier to South Plains Settlement* (Glendale, Calif., 1933), 211–59; Richardson, *The Frontier of Northwest Texas*, 195–212; Utley, *Indian Frontier*, 55–56; Arrie Barrett, "Federal Military Outposts in Texas, 1846–1861" (M.A. thesis, UT, 1927), 155. For more about John R. Baylor, see Webb, Carroll, and Branda, eds., *Handbook*, I, 124. Elkins participated in the 1859 raids on the reservations.

16. Acheson and O'Connell, eds., *Diamond's Account*, 5; Petition from Wise County, Tex., January 9, 1860, and William C. Dalrymple to Houston, February 15, 1861, in GOR; Austin *Texas State Gazette*, June 30, July 21, 1860; Dallas *Herald*, January 2, 1861; Huckaby, *Jack County*, 35–38; Richardson, *Comanche Barrier*, 259–66; Wilbarger, *Indian Depredations*, 334–39, 538–40.

ers in their efforts to quell abolitionism. Many members of both groups had come to Texas to avoid the disorder and instability to the north, and neither would permit people who might instigate an insurrection by speaking of abolition to stay in Cooke County.[17]

Reports of abolitionist activity began almost as soon as the new wave of immigration reached North Texas. On June 11, 1858, at the plantation of widow Ann D. Black along the Red River in Grayson County, several slaves protested against the punishment of one of their number. Black's overseer, together with James G. Bourland's son, William, reacted violently to the challenge, shooting two of the rebellious blacks. The editor of the Sherman *Patriot*, E. Junius Foster, blamed abolitionists for the incident that had claimed the lives of two slaves, and warned that anyone caught tampering with slaves "would require a super-natural imposition to save them from the lynch code."[18]

This attitude proved infectious. The district court of Grayson County in the spring of 1859 convicted George C. Humphreys, a New Yorker employed by the Butterfield Overland Mail, of "gaming with a negro" and exiled him. Mindful of the vigilante proclivities of his neighbors, Humphreys left in a hurry, abandoning some of his personal effects. Among these were found in the fall of 1859 a letter from E. C. Palmer—an itinerant surveyor who recently had moved from Marshall, Texas, to Gainesville—that allegedly implicated both Humphreys and Palmer in an abolitionist plot.[19]

An "indignation meeting" was held in Gainesville on October 14, 1859, to consider action against Palmer. Samuel C. Doss, a Cooke County rancher and slaveholder who was Bourland's son-in-law, chaired the assembly. The letter was read so that all could understand its belligerent tone: "These

---

17. Acheson and O'Connell, eds., *Diamond's Account*, xiii; Wendell G. Addington, "Slave Insurrection in Texas," *Journal of Negro History*, XXXV (1950), 414–18; Thomas, *The Confederate Nation*, 11.

18. Sherman (Tex.) *Patriot*, n.d., quoted in Austin *Southern Intelligencer*, July 15, 1858; Dallas *Herald*, December 15, 1858. E. Junius Foster, a North Carolina native born in 1814, purchased the Marshall *Patriot* in 1853, which at that time was the only Whig journal in East Texas. He subsequently bought out his partner and moved the press several times, finally settling in Sherman. He remained a Whig in his political ideals and, after the Civil War began, was condemned as a Republican, but he continued to publish the *Patriot* until his assassination in 1862. Landrum and Smith, *Illustrated History of Grayson County*, 24–25; Marilyn M. Sibley, *Lone Stars and State Gazettes* (College Station, Tex., 1983), 245, 368.

19. Clarksville *Standard*, December 3, 1859; Dallas *Herald*, October 26, 1859.

Southern people here are saying it is an old woman's fight, that [the North-erners] could not fight a Southern man, &c., &c., because they do not know how to use pistols, bowie knives, &c. . . . The Northern people had [better] begin . . . to practice killing the *dam Southern sons of bitches*, for . . . they are the descendants of the old tory stock, and we will have to kill them off before we can have a peaceful government." Palmer could offer no satisfac-tory explanation. A committee of five penned a resolution, adopted by the rest of the vigilantes, declaring that Palmer had "forfeited all claims to the protection of this community," and that he had six hours to leave town or "be rode upon a rail." [20]

Palmer fled to Marshall, but the news of his exile was printed in several newspapers at the request of the Gainesville vigilantes. Robert W. Lough-ery, editor of the Marshall *Texas Republican* and a Calhoun Democrat who later endorsed secession, published Palmer's letter with a conspiratorial postscript that appeared in no other printed version: "You must let our friends read this letter, for what I fail to write to one, I will write to an-other—you must keep in with one another." Loughery also published a statement from Palmer in the same issue. He wrote that he had made a few enemies as a surveyor, though he had never intended to swindle anyone, and it was these men who had altered his original letter to Humphreys or forged a new one. Palmer pointed out that he had lived in the South for fourteen years, had spoken in favor of slavery, and had relatives in the South. In another letter printed in radical Democrat Charles R. Pryor's Dallas *Herald*, Palmer added that he favored reopening the African slave trade and insisted the evidence against him was forged. Palmer denied re-ports that he had confessed, but he admitted that he did not remember all he said to the Gainesville vigilantes.[21]

A call went forth for a town meeting in Marshall to consider the evidence against Palmer. The assembly on November 26, 1859, made no decision, but several diatribes were delivered against Palmer, who was ordered to produce evidence of his innocence or face the consequences. Too, a vigi-lance committee organized and sent a petition to the legislature asking that the state code be amended to require the death penalty for those convicted

20. Clarksville *Standard*, December 3, 1859; Dallas *Herald*, October 26, 1859; Marshall *Texas Republican*, October 17, November 12, 19, 1859.

21. Marshall *Texas Republican*, November 12, 1859; Dallas *Herald*, November 23, 1859. For more about Robert W. Loughery, see Sibley, *Lone Stars*, 260–62, 269, 274, 285, 290, 351, and Webb, Carroll, and Branda, eds., *Handbook*, II, 84–85.

of inciting an insurrection or "uttering or publishing sentiments calculated to create discontent and insubordination among the slaves." Over fifty people attended a second meeting in Marshall on December 10 to hear Palmer defend himself. Unfortunately for the accused, a messenger from Gainesville won the crowd with his own copy of the damning letter, which was accepted as proof of Palmer's guilt. A third meeting was held on December 12, but the crowd had to be content with adopting more antiabolitionist resolutions because Palmer had fled the state. During the Civil War, Palmer was declared an alien enemy and his property was sequestered.[22]

Unfortunately for many who sought peace, there were abolitionists among the arrivals during the late 1850s, including some "fanatic preachers, preaching the antislavery question." These were ministers of the Northern Methodist Episcopal church who refused to recognize the 1844 schism in the Methodist church over slavery and continued to preach in areas claimed by the southern branch of the church. Because of the common fear of insurrection, the ministers, some of whom did openly speak of abolition, kept North Texas in turmoil. In Dallas in August, 1858, Northern Methodist ministers Solomon McKinney and William Blount were whipped and ordered not to preach again in the area. They fled north and petitioned the Iowa and Wisconsin legislatures to demand redress from Texas, prompting Pryor of the *Herald* to write, "If they will return in *propia persona* and behave as they did before, they will be re-dressed and no mistake."[23]

John Brown's raid on Harper's Ferry in October, 1859, increased the tension along the Forks, and then tempers flared when a series of fires

22. Marshall, *Texas Republican*, November 19, December 3, 17, 1859; United States Dept. of Justice, District Court, Western District of Texas, Austin, Confederate Court Case Files, 1862–1865, No. 2280: *Confederate States of America* v. *John W. Hale*, in Record Group 21, Federal Records Center, Fort Worth; Dallas *Herald*, December 14, 1859.

23. Eddleman, "Autobiography," 24; Dallas *Herald*, August 17, 31, 1859, March 14, 1860; Frederick W. Sumner, "Written by F. W. Sumner During the Civil War, 1860–1865" (Typescript in Sherman Historical Museum, Sherman, Tex.); Austin *Texas State Gazette*, August 27, 1859; Floyd F. Ewing, "Unionist Sentiment on the Northwest Texas Frontier," *WTHA Yearbook*, XXXIII (1957), 59; Wesley Norton, "The Methodist Episcopal Church and the Civil Disturbances in North Texas in 1859 and 1860," *SWHQ*, LXVIII (1965), 323–29; Charles Elliott, *Southwestern Methodism: A History of the M. E. Church in the Southwest from 1844 to 1864* (Cincinnati, 1868), 127–31, 137; Phelan, *Early Methodism*, 442–52; James G. Randall and David H. Donald, *The Civil War and Reconstruction* (2d ed.; Lexington, Mass., 1969), 25–26; Sibley, *Lone Stars*, 281, 319–20; Anne Stark, "A History of Dallas County" (M.A. thesis, UT, 1935), 63–64. Sumner, a jeweler, lived in Sherman. More about Charles R. Pryor can be found in Webb, Carroll, and Branda, eds., *Handbook*, II, 418.

struck North Texas in the summer of 1860, destroying large portions of several towns. On July 8 a fire in Dallas consumed every store, both hotels, and the offices of the *Herald*. To the north a fire in the seat of Denton County, which lay just south of Cooke County, began an hour and a half later. Twenty-five kegs of powder exploded in a store, leveling all but one of the buildings on the west side of the square and igniting others across town. Flames destroyed a store in Pilot Point, in northern Denton County, and fires later erupted in Gainesville. The destruction spread south and east into more populated areas of the state, with fires in Waxahachie, Austin, and Jefferson.[24]

Some tried to avert the impending storm of reaction by offering rational explanations for the series of fires. A store owner in Waxahachie who had lost everything insisted that he had seen the fire start in his shelves; he believed the intense heat of the day—the noon temperature at Dallas on the day of the big fire was 105 degrees—had ignited phosphorous matches that were being offered for the first time that summer. On July 14, 1860, editor Charles DeMorse of the Clarksville *Standard* published a letter from John W. Swindells, proprietor of the Dallas *Herald*, reporting the fires at Dallas and the destruction of his office. Swindells offered no explanation, but DeMorse, ever a voice of reason in the hysteria that attended the secession movement in Texas, asserted that the culprit was overheated matches.[25]

Many people were convinced that the fires were part of a plot by abolitionists to spark an insurrection, and demonstrations were staged to persuade others. Phosphorous matches were placed in direct sunlight for several hours to test the theory that they had spontaneously ignited. When the matches failed to burst into flame, that settled the question in favor of conspiracy for many people. On July 28, 1860, John Marshall—editor of the Austin *Texas State Gazette* and a firebrand secessionist—printed a note from

24. George Fisher, *The Yankee Conscript* (Philadelphia, 1864), 33–34; William E. White, "The Texas Slave Insurrection of 1860," *SWHQ*, LII (1949), 259–61; Bates, *Denton County*, 346–49; C. A. Bridges, *History of Denton, Texas: From Its Beginning to 1960* (Waco, 1960), 92–93; Donald E. Reynolds, *Editors Make War* (Nashville, 1966), 101; Frank M. Cockrell, "History of Early Dallas" (Typescript in BTHC), 70–76, 77–78. Fisher was a schoolteacher from Ohio who settled in Collin County in 1858.

25. Fisher, *The Yankee Conscript*, 35; Clarksville *Standard*, July 14, 1860; H. Smythe, *Historical Sketch of Parker County and Weatherford, Texas* (St. Louis, 1877), 145; Cockrell, "History of Early Dallas," 71. For more about Charles Demorse, see Sibley, *Lone Stars*, 142–43, 282, 292–93; Webb, Carroll, and Branda, eds., *Handbook*, II, 489; Ernest Wallace, *Charles DeMorse, Pioneer Editor and Statesman* (Lubbock, 1943).

Pryor of the Dallas *Herald,* who asserted that the fires were obvious evidence of a "deep laid scheme of villainy to devastate the whole of Northern Texas" among abolitionist ministers. Pryor added that some slaves who had been arrested for burning a house on July 12 had confessed that the arson was just a prelude to an insurrection on election day in August to be led by agents from the northern states, including McKinney and Blount. Pryor added that every North Texas county had white supervisors waiting for the signal to lead a slave uprising, and he concluded, "I write in haste; we sleep upon our arms, and the whole country is most deeply excited."[26]

Many people fled North Texas during the hysteria that followed the fires, fearing the wrath of vigilantes, but others were not so fortunate. William H. Crawford was found lynched near Fort Worth on July 17, 1860, the day after a town meeting had warned all abolitionists to leave at once. He was posthumously accused of being an agent of the underground railroad, of trying to hire a slave to kill another white man, and of distributing revolvers to slaves to be used during an insurrection, all of which his widow hotly denied in a letter printed in the New York *Tribune.* Nearly a hundred slaves were arrested in Dallas; three—Pat Jennings, allegedly the one who started the fires in Dallas, Sam Smith, a "preacher" and "hardened old scoundrel" who had been associated with McKinney and Blount, and "Cato," who it was claimed had "always borne a bad character in this country"—were hanged on July 24, 1860, after being tried by a makeshift trial commission of fifty-two men. The remainder of the slaves were released, but were ordered to be whipped for good measure.[27]

26. Austin *Texas State Gazette,* July 28, 1860; Eddleman, "Autobiography," 25; White, "Texas Slave Insurrection," 261–52; Reynolds, *Editors Make War,* 98; Sibley, *Lone Stars,* 319–20. For more about John Marshall see Larry J. Gage, "The Texas Road to Secession and War: John Marshall and the *Texas State Gazette,* 1860–1861," *SWHQ,* LXII (1958), 192, 195–97; Sibley, *Lone Stars,* 264–71, 306; Webb, Carroll, and Branda, eds., *Handbook,* II, 148, 662–63. Fisher recalled that the new "prairie matches" would burst into flame if set near a fire or a window, and blamed them for the fires. See Fisher, *The Yankee Conscript,* 35.

27. Austin *Texas State Gazette,* August 11, 1860; Eddleman, "Autobiography," 25; San Antonio *Ledger and Texan,* August 18, 1860; Dallas *Herald,* May 15, 1861; White, "Texas Slave Insurrection," 262–64; Cockrell, "History of Early Dallas," 76–77; Frank H. Smyrl, "Abolitionism, Unionism, and Vigilantism in Texas, 1856–1865" (M.A. thesis, UT, 1961), 54, 55–56; Stark, "A History of Dallas County," 62–63. Frederick W. Sumner later wrote that in Dallas, after the fires of 1860, a suspected abolitionist was caught and accused of setting fire to a church. His captors tied him to a piece of sheet iron laid across a smoldering fire; then, after he confessed that he was involved in a widespread conspiracy, they allowed him to roast to death. This has not been corroborated by any other source, but it may provide some insight into Crawford's fate. See Sumner, "Written During the Civil War."

Rumors of abolitionist plans for arson and murder spread quickly, and vigilance committees formed to combat the threat. Many men were killed or exiled; the total was never known because some were hanged secretly on the Forks and elsewhere. Although most reports proved to be false and no definite proof of a conspiracy emerged, many newspapers published stories of abolitionist or insurrectionist activities no matter how spurious. Allegations increased with each retelling; Pryor's list of intended crimes included poisoning, assassination, kidnapping, and rape as well as arson. Amid the hysteria, even the *Texas Christian Advocate*, the organ of the Southern Methodist church, endorsed vigilante acts, asserting that "self-protection" was an "inalienable right" and those who did not take action "deserve to be enslaved."[28]

Enough scraps of evidence surfaced to keep the rumors current. A few documents of uncertain origin were published as being the private correspondence of the conspirators. According to these letters, an organization sponsored by New Englanders had been created in Kansas to populate North Texas with free-soilers through both the emigrant aid societies that had won that territory and new paramilitary legions to be commanded by free-state warriors James H. Lane and Charles Montgomery. Indian attacks would be encouraged, towns and mills burned, proslavery sympathizers exiled, and free-soil settlers imported. Marshall on September 22, 1860, published a letter allegedly written from Lowell, Massachusetts, which reported that abolitionist leaders in New England knew that fires were to be set in North Texas several weeks before they occurred. Furthermore, the "Anti-Slavery Emigration Society" had enlisted a hundred men to colonize North Texas in the fall of 1860. If they could not settle together, these agents were to scatter and find employment as teachers, ministers, and laborers, and to prepare the way for a peaceful abolitionist coup.[29]

In the wake of such revelations, many committees for "public safety" formed to censor the mails and to watch for abolitionists. Although Gov-

28. *Texas Christian Advocate*, August 30, 1860, quoted in John R. Ross, "At the Bar of Judge Lynch: Lynching and Lynch Mobs in America" (Ph.D. dissertation, Texas Tech University, 1983), 101–102; Fisher, *The Yankee Conscript*, 34–38; John Townsend, *The Doom of Slavery in the Union: Its Safety out of It* (Charleston, S.C., 1860), 35–36; Houston *Telegraph*, July 21, 1860; Austin *Texas State Gazette*, July 14, 1860; Paul D. Lack, "Slavery and Vigilantism in Austin, Texas, 1840–1860," *SWHQ*, LXXXV (1981), 17–18; White, "Texas Slave Insurrection," 277–85; Reynolds, *Editors Make War*, 99–100, 105–106, 108–109; Sibley, *Lone Stars*, 276–78, 281–86; Smyrl, "Unionism, Abolitionism, and Vigilantism," 30–35, 50–74.

29. Austin *Texas State Gazette*, September 22, 1860; Ramsdell, "The Frontier and Secession," 75–76.

ernor Sam Houston minimized the importance of the fires, meetings were chaired by secessionists who insisted the blazes were a first step toward a planned insurrection fomented by abolitionists. The legislature had passed acts in 1846 and 1850 authorizing county patrols, but few had been established. Now almost every settlement, including Gainesville, organized a company under the nearly dormant law. These committees proved ruthlessly efficient, and in early August, 1860, Marshall printed a letter from "Quidnunc," a correspondent in Grayson County, who reported that the "nigger excitement" had "somewhat abated" in North Texas.[30]

The violence came full circle when presiding elder Anthony Bewley of the Northern Methodist Episcopal church became a target for the vigilantes. A letter dated July 3, 1860, was produced that implicated Bewley in an organization, referred to as the "mystic red," dedicated to abolishing slavery in Texas by introducing free-soil settlers and distributing abolitionist literature. The document was a clumsy forgery but it circulated widely in Texas, where it was accepted as genuine, and appeared in newspapers in places as remote as St. Louis and New Orleans, although acceptance of its validity dwindled with distance.[31]

After hearing of Crawford's lynching, Bewley and his family fled Dallas on July 17, 1860. They were overtaken in Missouri by a posse eager to collect the reward of a thousand dollars offered by vigilance committees in Fort Worth and Sherman. The riders took Bewley to Fort Worth, where he was lynched on the night of his arrival, September 13, 1860, from the same tree from which Crawford had been hanged. One vigilante allegedly declared the time had come when ninety-nine innocent men should suffer rather than let one guilty man escape, but editor Marshall insisted that a trial had been held and Bewley confessed that the letter was his. Bewley's

30. Austin *Texas State Gazette*, August 11, 18, 1860; Fisher, *The Yankee Conscript*, 29–30, 38–40; Townsend, *Doom of Slavery*, 35–36; Bill Ledbetter, "The Impact of Black Republicanism in Ante-Bellum Texas," *Texana*, X (1972), 339, 345–46; White, "Texas Slave Insurrection," 264–65; Bates, *Denton County*, 346–49; Walter L. Buenger, *Secession and the Union in Texas* (Austin, 1984), 107–109; Bridges, *History of Denton*, 92–93; Lucas and Hall, *Grayson County*, 98–99; Reynolds, *Editors Make War*, 101–103, 111–12; Clarence R. Wharton, *Texas Under Many Flags* (2 vols.; Chicago, 1930), II, 77–80.

31. Addington, "Slave Insurrection in Texas," 428–29; Norton, "The Methodist Episcopal Church and Civil Disturbances," 333–36; White, "Texas Slave Insurrection," 265–67; Elliott, *Southwestern Methodism*, 150–52, 154–61, 181–86; Phelan, *Early Methodism*, 452–56. For more on Anthony M. Bewley, see *Dictionary of American Biography*, II, 233; Elliott, *Southwestern Methodism*, 21–25, 28–31, 34, 45, 79, 91, 109, 154; Phelan, *Early Methodism*, 440–41.

body was cut down and dumped in a shallow grave. Because the burial was done in haste, the hole was not large or deep enough, and his knees protruded from the ground. A local physician had him exhumed after about three weeks, stripped the remaining flesh from the bones, and laid the skeleton out to dry on the roof of a nearby storehouse. While it lay there, local ruffians made sport of Bewley's remains.[32]

Editors throughout Texas praised Bewley's executioners. H. A. Hamner, vitriolic editor of the *White Man*, published in Parker County, declared: "By some means [Bewley] got on the Abe-Lincoln-Sam-Houston platform, and somehow, or somehow else, got a string entangled about his neck, and just as he stept on the Squatter Sovereignty plank of that platform, some of the screws gave way, and down came this 'Viceregent,' and broke his pious neck. . . . May these worthy 'Viceregents' all stand on the same platform sooner or later, and share the same fate." Bewley's death did not go unnoticed outside Texas. The New York *Christian Advocate* condemned the lynching, but the staid Richmond *Examiner* defended it. The debate foreshadowed the conflict in the media over events in North Texas during the Civil War, when vigilantism reached a grisly crescendo.[33]

Such virulence was symptomatic of the growing radicalism in Texas politics as the Democratic party became militant in its defense of slavery and embraced secession during the late 1850s. Despite efforts to forge a consensus on slavery, however, the voters of Cooke County consistently cast a higher percentage of their votes than the rest of the state against the increasingly disunionist Democrats. Their concern for order and security, together with a lack of any compelling economic reason for supporting slavery, led them to reject the call for disunion. If Federal authority was repudiated, with it would go the small but welcome measure of protection provided by Federal garrisons. Too, they realized that separation might mean civil war, which could mean that many men from Cooke County would serve in the military on a distant front, leaving their families alone in an

32. Austin *Texas State Gazette*, September 28, October 6, 1860; Dallas *Herald*, December 26, 1860; Norton, "Methodist Episcopal Church," 333–36; White, "Texas Slave Insurrection," 265–67; Elliott, *Southwestern Methodism*, 150–52, 154–73, 181–86; Phelan, *Early Methodism*, 452–58.

33. Weatherford (Tex.) *White Man*, September 28, 1860, quoted in Austin *Texas State Gazette*, September 29, 1860; Austin *Texas State Gazette*, October 6, 1860; Buenger, *Secession in Texas*, 116; Sibley, *Lone Stars*, 278–79, 288–89; Smythe, *Historical Sketch of Parker County*, 141.

isolated and hostile environment. Finally, few Cooke County residents participated significantly in the slave economy, so they refused to accept the idea that sacrificing all to protect that institution was in their best interest. When former Whigs such as Throckmorton and others who opposed the Democrats spoke out against disunion, then, they found a receptive audience in Cooke County.[34]

The first clear referendum on disunion in Texas was the election of a governor in 1859. Incumbent Runnels, a Democrat, endorsed reopening the African slave trade, a measure regarded by many as an open invitation to sectional combat, and threatened to secede if the Lecompton constitution of Kansas was not ratified. Runnels' opponent was Houston, whom he had defeated in 1857 for the governor's seat and whose opposition to secession was unequivocal. In 1859, Houston portrayed himself as a moderate alternative to the radicalism infecting the Democratic party in Texas and exemplified in Runnels. Houston won 56.2 percent of the state gubernatorial vote in August, but 73 percent of Cooke County's voters endorsed him. To be sure, much of his margin can be attributed to his attack on Runnels' frontier defense policy, which was generally regarded as a failure, but just as important was the antipathy of many Texans on the frontier toward Runnels' risking sectional disruption by stressing the slave trade issue. Votes for Houston, then, were not only for protection against Indians, but also against the chaos of disunion.[35]

Cooke County voters were not alone in opposing disunion in 1859; a conservative backlash against secession swept the entire South that summer. They were quickly left behind, though, as John Brown's raid in October, 1859, and the abolitionist alarms in the summer of 1860 radicalized most

34. James A. Baggett, "The Constitutional Union Party in Texas," *SWHQ*, LXXXII (1979), 250, 252; Frank H. Smyrl, "Unionism in Texas, 1856–1861," *SWHQ*, LXVIII (1964), 194–95; Buenger, *Secession in Texas*, 23, 24, 28, 32, 96, 99–101, 106; Campbell and Lowe, *Wealth and Power*, 115, 119; Buenger, "Stilling the Voice of Reason," 267, 292, 298, 299, 313, 327, 351, 360, 373, 388.

35. Baggett, "Constitutional Union Party," 250, 252; Ramsdell, "The Frontier and Secession," 67; Oran M. Roberts, "The Political, Legislative, and Judicial History of Texas for Its First Fifty Years of Statehood, 1845–1895," in *A Comprehensive History of Texas 1685 to 1897*, ed. Dudley G. Wooten (2 vols.; Dallas, 1898), II, 55–56; Anna I. Sandbo, "Beginnings of the Secession Movement in Texas," *SWHQ*, XVIII (1914), 61; Ralph A. Wooster, *The Secession Conventions of the South* (Princeton, 1962), 121–22; Buenger, *Secession in Texas*, 35, 36, 38, 112, 184–86; Wharton, *Texas Under Many Flags*, II, 71, 73; Buenger, "Stilling the Voice of Reason," 267, 292, 298, 299, 313, 327, 351, 360, 373, 388; Smyrl, "Unionism, Abolitionism, and Vigilantism," 5.

southerners. North Texas leaders who campaigned for the compromise-minded John Bell of the Constitutional Union party, such as Benjamin H. Epperson and Robert H. Taylor, were harassed at speaking engagements in Sherman and Dallas by Democrats who told the crowds that Constitutional Unionists were proponents of secession and insurrection. These tactics worked well—John Bell did not win a single Texas county—but Cooke did cast 33.9 percent of its votes for Bell. It was becoming clear that a significant number of men there "were willing to accept a hybrid as strange as the Union electoral ticket rather than risk the disruption of their nation."[36]

The election of Abraham Lincoln as president of the United States sent "something of a shock" throughout the South. Slaveholders along the Forks, as in many other regions of Texas, organized to take their state out of the Union rather than risk an uncertain future under the Lincoln administration. John R. Diamond chaired a secessionist rally at Diamond's Station on November 23, 1860. His brother James had attended the Democratic convention as a member of the Texas delegation, which bolted after Stephen F. Douglas was nominated, and had served as chair of a steering committee. Most of those who attended owned slaves; only four refused to endorse a resolution declaring that Lincoln's election on a "platform of principles in violent opposition to Southern interests and Southern institutions" demonstrated that the states could no longer coexist peacefully. They raised the Lone Star flag of Texan independence and petitioned Governor Houston for a convention, declaring the time had come for Texas to consider severing its ties to the Union. At the same time, they recruited a company in Grayson and Cooke counties to defend "Southern interests and Southern equality in the Union, or out of it."[37]

36. Buenger, *Secession in Texas*, 77; Texas Secretary of State, Election Register; Clarksville *Standard*, September 29, October 27, November 3, 1860; McKinney (Tex.) *Messenger*, September 14, 1860; Baggett, "Constitutional Union Party," 240, 245, 257, 258; Stephen B. Oates, "Texas Under the Secessionists," *SWHQ*, LXVII (1963), 167; Smyrl, "Unionism, Abolitionism, and Vigilantism in Texas," 177, 180; Ralph A. Wooster, "An Analysis of the Texas Know Nothings," *SWHQ*, LXX (1967), 420; Avery O. Craven, *The Growth of Southern Nationalism, 1848–1861* (Baton Rouge, 1953), 313; Smyrl, "Unionism, Abolitionism, and Vigilantism," 5. For more about Benjamin H. Epperson, see Webb, Carroll, and Branda, eds., *Handbook*, I, 568–69; Ralph A. Wooster, "Ben H. Epperson: East Texas Lawyer, Legislator, and Civic Leader," *East Texas Historical Journal*, V (1967), 29–42; De Ryee and Moore, *Album of the Eighth Legislature*, 73–74. For more about Robert H. Taylor, see Webb, Carroll, and Branda, eds., *Handbook*, II, 716, and De Ryee and Moore, *Album of the Eighth Legislature*, 178–79.

37. Craven, *Southern Nationalism*, 352–54; Lucas and Hall, *Grayson County*, 99–101; Austin *Texas State Gazette*, December 1, 15, 29, 1860, January 12, 1861; Clarksville *Standard*,

James J. Diamond also served on the steering committee for a town meeting chaired by James G. Bourland in Gainesville on December 15, 1860. Prominent slaveholders again dominated the debate on secession, but this time the result was less harmonious. Diamond and Bourland pressed hard for secession, but were opposed by a faction led by William C. Young, a United States marshal who owned more slaves than anyone else in Cooke County. Ironically, Young had fought alongside Bourland against the Indians for many years and had commanded a volunteer regiment in which Bourland served as lieutenant colonel in the Mexican War. Young was supported by slaveholder and former Tennessee legislator John E. Wheeler, district attorney William T. G. Weaver, and chief justice Ralph G. Piper. When a resolution that endorsed secession and called for a convention was introduced, Young and his allies angrily opposed it. They argued in vain: Diamond and Bourland prevailed, and a majority voted in favor of a convention to consider disunion.[38]

These meetings along the Forks and elsewhere in Texas had little effect on Governor Houston, who steadfastly opposed secession despite a deluge of petitions, letters, and newspaper editorials. The radicals circumvented him by posting dates for the election of delegates in many prominent newspapers in the state. These arrangements were of doubtful legality, but so was vigilantism, and radicals justified both by arguing that the circumstances required extraordinary action. Their strategy proved effective;

December 22, 1860; Dallas *Herald*, December 5, 1860, January 2, 30, 1861; Ernest W. Winkler, ed., *Journal of the Secession Convention of Texas, 1861* (Austin, 1912), 405, 407; Philip Lindsley, *A History of Greater Dallas and Vicinity* (2 vols.; Chicago, 1909), II, 66; *Ancestors and Descendants*, 58; Buenger, *Secession in Texas*, 116, 143; Bridges, *History of Denton*, 94–95; Sibley, *Lone Stars*, 290–2; Collins, *Cooke County*, 10; Landrum and Smith, *Illustrated History of Grayson County*, 63; Smith, *First 100 Years*, 29–30; George W. Sergeant, "Early History of Tarrant County" (M.A. thesis, UT, 1953), 143; Stark, "A History of Dallas County," 139.

38. John E. Wheeler Diary, 1850–1880 (MS in Morton Museum); Clarksville *Standard*, June 1, 1861; Dallas *Herald*, January 9, 1861. Weaver was elected district attorney in 1860. In February, 1862, he joined the 16th Texas Cavalry and became a captain before he was captured at Pleasant Hill in April, 1864, and paroled eleven days later. See Census of 1860, Cooke Cty. Schedule 1, Family Number [hereafter cited as F.N.] 54, in TSL; Texas Secretary of State, Election Register; CSR, 16th Texas Cavalry; Sam H. Dixon, *The Poets and Poetry of Texas* (Austin, 1885), 325–27; David F. Eagleton, comp., *Writers and Writings of Texas* (New York, 1913), 70–79. Both of Wheeler's sons served in the Confederate army. See John E. Wheeler to Andrew Johnson, January 17, 1868, in Andrew Johnson Papers, LC; Robert M. McBride, ed., *Biographical Directory of the Tennessee General Assembly, Volume I: 1796–1861* (Nashville, 1974), 774; Census of 1860, Cooke Cty. Schedule 1 and Schedule 2, F.N. 378, in TSL; Smith,

three-fourths of the counties in Texas sent delegates to the 1860 convention, and a majority of the delegates, including most of those from the Forks, endorsed secession. William W. Diamond, a brother of John and James, was one of three delegates elected on January 12, 1861, to represent Grayson County, and nine days later James allegedly won in Cooke County, though the returns were "misplaced." [39]

The slaveholders' precipitous actions did generate some protests. Foster, editor of the Sherman *Patriot*, disseminated a proposal to separate many counties on the Red River from Texas. They would ally with some of the peaceful nations in the Indian Territory and ask for admission as a new state into the Union. This scheme attracted a number of settlers, who signed a petition endorsing it as an alternative if secession was not submitted to a popular vote, as Governor Houston had proposed. The petition was forwarded to Anthony B. Norton, the staunchly Unionist editor of the Austin *Southern Intelligencer*, who published it, without the accompanying list of signatures, on January 31, 1861. [40]

Predictably, the reaction to the proposed dismemberment of Texas was hostile. It was common knowledge that the Chickasaw and Choctaw nations just north of the Red River were deeply divided over secession, and that many there might support such a radical effort to sustain the Union. Austin *Texas State Gazette* editor Marshall wrote in response to the separatist proposal published by Norton, "Every honest man should trample under foot this mischievous development of Helperism, and treat its authors as public

---

First 100 Years, 2, 35; Walter N. Vernon, *Methodism Moves Across North Texas* (Dallas, 1967), 130–31.

39. Wheeler Diary; Joseph C. Terrell, "Reminiscences of Early Days of Fort Worth" (Typescript in Texas Writer's Project: Fort Worth History Notes, Vol. 1, Pt. 2, BTHC), 123, 295–96; Austin *Texas State Gazette*, February 2, 1861; Dallas *Herald*, December 18, 1860, January 2, 9, 16, 1861; Winkler, *Journal of the Secession Convention of Texas*, 1, 21, 26, 405–407, 425, 432–34; Ralph A. Wooster, "An Analysis of the Membership of the Texas Secession Convention," *SWHQ*, LXII (1959), 333; J. Evetts Haley, *Charles Goodnight, Cowman and Plainsman* (New York, 1936), 69–70; Cliff D. Cates, *Pioneer History of Wise County* (Decatur, Tex., 1907), 114, 120; Marcus J. Wright, *Texas in the War*, ed. Harold B. Simpson (Hillsboro, Tex., 1965), 26; Buenger, *Secession in Texas*, 2, 125; Sibley, *Lone Stars*, 278–79, 288–89; Smythe, *Historical Sketch of Parker County*, 141; 166–68; Wooster, *Secession Conventions*, 123, 330; Felgar, "Texas in the War for Southern Independence," 24–28; Sergeant, "Early History of Tarrant County," 135.

40. Acheson and O'Connell, eds., *Diamond's Account*, 8–9; Claude Elliot, "Union Sentiment in Texas, 1861–1865," *SWHQ*, L (1947), 449; Jacob L. Stambaugh and Lillian J. Stambaugh, *A History of Collin County, Texas* (Austin, 1958), 62.

enemies." Because it allegedly involved Unionists in Austin, Norton was warned to print no more on the subject by radical secessionists, and he complied.[41]

Hoping the legislature would refuse to recognize the secession convention, Governor Houston called a special session in January, 1861. In spite of determined opposition by several legislators from the Forks—including Epperson and Taylor in the House and Throckmorton, now a prominent Collin County Unionist, in the Senate—the legislature endorsed the caucus by a two-thirds vote on January 28, 1861, the day that the secession convention met. Taylor was especially passionate in denouncing secession, asking, "In this new *Cotton Confederacy what will become of my section, the wheat growers and stock raisers?*" He answered his own query by railing against those who urged disunion: "I fear they will hang, burn, confiscate property and exile any one who may be in the way of their designs." Other legislators, ignoring Taylor, required only that secession be approved in a general election.[42]

Taylor's outburst exposed the dark side of the secession movement in Texas. Even as he spoke, Oran M. Roberts, John S. Ford, and other secessionists were breaking up Unionist meetings in Austin. Marshall expressed the sentiments of many such radicals when he declared, "We cannot tolerate in our midst the presence of an internal hostile element, who are treacherously remaining here, to sow the seeds of servile war, and to give aid and comfort to blockading fleets and invading squadrons." His solution to the problem was simple: "Helperism, its aiders and abettors, should be strangled by the hangman's knot, and crowned with an infamous martyrdom." Secessionists organized a huge parade on Congress Avenue, the central thoroughfare of the city, to demonstrate their strength, and most of the arriving delegates joined their ranks. On the opening day of the secession convention, Roberts was elected president amid cheers.[43]

41. Austin *Texas State Gazette*, February 2, 1861; Acheson and O'Connell, eds., *Diamond's Account*, 8; Marshall *Texas Republican*, February 23, 1861; Abel, *Indians as Slaveholders and Secessionists*, 67–72, 75–79.
42. Broadside, in Robert H. Taylor Papers, BTHC; Winkler, *Journal of the Secession Convention of Texas*, 14; Buenger, *Secession in Texas*, 3; Felgar, "Texas in the War for Southern Independence," 31. Robert H. Taylor's speech was also published in the McKinney *Messenger*, March 1, 1861.
43. Austin *Texas State Gazette*, January 26, 1861; Oates, "Texas Under the Secessionists," 167–68. For more on John S. Ford and Oran M. Roberts, see Webb, Carroll, and Branda, eds., *Handbook*, II, 617–18, II, 484–85.

Throckmorton became the vocal leader of the convention delegates who opposed secession. When the final vote was taken on the ordinance of secession on February 1, he disregarded the rules requiring that he say only yes or no and said, "Mr. President, in view of the responsibility, in the presence of God and my country, and unawed by the wild spirit of revolution around me, I vote no." Refusing to be intimidated by a hiss from the gallery, he added, "Mr. President, when the rabble hiss, well may patriots tremble." Only seven other delegates followed his example and voted against secession. The overwhelming majority, including most of those from the Forks counties, approved the ordinance.[44]

Throckmorton and the Unionists attempted to rally Texas voters against secession. Eighteen legislators—including Throckmorton, Taylor, Epperson, and representative William A. Ellet of Cooke County—signed a petition against disunion and presented it at an antisecession rally in Austin on February 9, 1861. Their words, however, had little impact on most voters or a majority of the delegates. Confident of victory, the convention appointed seven representatives to the provisional Confederate government at Montgomery, Alabama, and adjourned February 21 to reconvene in March after the election.[45]

Both secessionists and Unionists stumped the state after the convention adjourned. Along the upper Forks, James J. Diamond and Bourland campaigned in favor of disunion. Throckmorton was the only prominent Unionist active in the region, so most of the Union crusade was conducted by more common folk such as farmer Abraham McNeese and blacksmith John M. Crisp in Cooke County, both of whom earned a dangerous notoriety for their efforts. The referendum itself was marred by violence from

44. LaGrange (Tex.) *True Issue*, February 7, 1861; Winkler, *Journal of the Secession Convention of Texas*, 48–49, 55–56; Noah Smithwick, *The Evolution of a State* (Austin, 1900), 334; Buenger, *Secession in Texas*, 148; Elliot, *Leathercoat*, 54–56; T. R. Fehrenbach, *Lone Star: A History of Texas and the Texans* (New York, 1968), 345; Wharton, *Texas Under Many Flags*, II, 84; Felgar, "Texas in the War for Southern Independence," 35–36. Throckmorton was one member of the antisecession "triumvirate"; the others were Taylor and Bogart, of Collin County, who died on March 11, 1861. Rallying around Bogart and Throckmorton, Collin County residents were especially outspoken against disunion. See Dallas *Herald*, January 9, 23, 1861. Throckmorton's defiant outburst has been reprinted many times.

45. Broadside, in Taylor Papers; Winkler, *Journal of the Secession Convention of Texas*, 14, 21, 85n; Austin *Southern Intelligencer*, February 13, 1861; De Ryee and Moore, *Album of the Eighth Legislature*, 75–76, 87–88; *Members of the Texas Legislature, 1846–1980* (Austin, 1981), 31–34; Elliot, *Leathercoat*, 57–58; Felgar, "Texas in the War," 37–38.

those on the Forks who advocated disunion; secessionists armed with shot-guns guarded polling places in Grayson County.[46]

The secession vote clearly revealed a breakdown in the political domi-nance of slaveholders in Cooke County, where a majority of the voters re-jected the imperative for disunion in favor of the measure of order and security provided by the federal government. Texas as a whole returned a majority of more than three to one in favor of secession; only 18 of its 122 counties voted against disunion. Among the latter was Cooke, which cast 61 percent of its votes against secession. The true extent of Cooke County's opposition to secession was obscured because 11 percent fewer voters took part in the 1861 referendum than in the election of 1860, but a message was sent to those who advocated disunion.[47] Most of Cooke Coun-ty's voters were not interested in risking chaos by repudiating the govern-ment under which they had lived all their lives, and the opposition of Throckmorton and others to the Texas Democrats encouraged them in their stand. Tragically what they did not realize was that as Texas rushed toward disunion, those who remained faithful to the Union would them-selves become a threat to the interests of the established leaders in Cooke County: the slaveholders and their allies who supported the Confederacy.

46. Sylvester Olinger to Johnson, March 15, 1861, in Johnson Papers; John M. Crisp, Jr., to George M. Crisp, October 20, 1921 (Typescript in Great Hanging File, Morton Museum); Sumner, "Written by Sumner During the Civil War"; Clark, ed., *Recollections of James Clark*, 95; Fisher *The Yankee Conscript*, 41–42; Grayson *Monitor*, n.d., quoted in Austin *Texas State Gazette*, February 23, 1861; Austin *Texas State Gazette*, March 9, 1861; Dallas *Herald*, January 23, February 20, 27, 1861; McKinney *Messenger*, March 1, 1861; C. A. Bridges, "The Knights of the Golden Circle: A Filibustering Fantasy," *SWHQ*, XLIV (1941), 292, 300; Roy S. Dunn, "The KGC in Texas, 1860–1861," *SWHQ*, LXX (1967), 550, 556, 560–61, 566; Anna I. Sandbo, "The First Session of the Secession Convention of Texas," *SWHQ*, XVIII (1914), 175; Joe T. Timmons, "The Referendum in Texas on the Ordinance of Secession," *East Texas Historical Journal*, XI (1973), 14, 16, 20–22; Bridges, *History of Denton*, 94–95; Thomas Wilson, *Sufferings Endured for a Free Government* (Washington, D.C., 1864), 259; Elliot, *Leathercoat*, 58; Felgar, "Texas in the War for Southern Independence," 39–40.

47. Clark, ed., *Recollections of James Clark*, 101; Floyd F. Ewing, "Origins of Unionist Sentiment on the West Texas Frontier," *WTHA Yearbook*, XXXII (1956), 21–26; Buenger, *Secession in Texas*, 66, 68, 95, 109. The decline in voter participation between 1860 and 1861 has been attributed to the "studied indifference" of many of those who did not support secession, but may also have been due to an attempt by some in North Texas to follow the example of the free-soilers in Kansas and undermine secession with a boycott. See Buenger, *Secession in Texas*, 116, 143; Dallas *Herald*, January 30, 1861.

TWO

Dissent Becomes Treason

As many settlers along the Forks had feared, the establishment of a new regime in Texas brought disruption in the form of a national civil war. A substantial number of homesteaders left North Texas after the state joined the Confederacy, only to be replaced by hundreds of white and black refugees from areas that became battlefields. Tensions were exacerbated by the imposition of sequestration, war taxes, impressment, and, especially, conscription. Seeking to win the loyalty of people on the northwestern frontier, Confederate officials in Texas authorized military units to remain in that region to combat a growing sense of insecurity. However, when these troops were sent elsewhere to combat the North, many who had enlisted to protect the frontier deserted and returned home, adding to the increasing populace along the Forks who were alienated from the Confederacy. Alarmed at the chaos, many residents resorted once more to vigilantism in an attempt to maintain order and security, undertaking vendettas that were encouraged by the appointment of vindictive military officials, in particular James G. Bourland as provost marshal.

The secession convention formally withdrew Texas from the Union on March 4, 1861, then allied the state with the Confederacy, to which the delegates required all state officers to take an oath of allegiance. When Governor Sam Houston refused, he was removed from office on March 16. He chose not to resist the new regime in spite of pledges of support from North Texas leaders, such as James W. Throckmorton and Benjamin H. Epperson, and an offer of military assistance from Abraham Lincoln. Deprived of effective leadership, organized opposition to secession in Texas collapsed, and Lieutenant Governor Edward Clark replaced Houston for the balance of his term.[1]

1. N. R. McFarland to Elisha M. Pease, February 14, 1861, Thomas Lewellin to Pease,

Tainted Breeze

Many settlers in North Texas, dismayed by the dissolution of the Union, chose to flee. A Northern Methodist minister in May, 1861, found the road from Texas and Arkansas to Kansas clogged with refugees. James G. Bourland observed during a trip to the Indian Territory that more than 120 wagons filled with settlers from the Forks area were en route to Kansas. Without identifying himself, he talked to them and learned that "they had proposed by the ballot box to abolitionize at least that portion of the State." Having failed, an estimated 500 were returning "whence they came." A train of wagons carrying 268 people, 125 of whom were men of military age, was organized in Jack County in May, 1861, and left for California along the Butterfield Overland route. An observer commented that the travelers after passing beyond the line of settlement "all turn[ed] to Black Republicans." Sherman *Patriot* editor E. Junius Foster informed his readers of the exodus, commenting, "We think there are more who would do well to take the same track."[2]

The collapse of organized resistance to secession and the exodus of numerous Unionists from the Forks region prompted many supporters of the Confederacy to believe, mistakenly, that disaffection with the new regime had been eliminated. One optimistic Confederate declared Unionism at an "end" in North Texas in a letter printed in the New Orleans *Picayune* on May 30, 1861, while another wrote to Governor Clark that Unionism had

---

April 20, 1861, Benjamin H. Epperson to Pease, May 22, 1861, all in Elisha M. Pease Papers, Austin History Center; Ernest W. Winkler, ed., *Journal of the Secession Convention of Texas, 1861* (Austin, 1912), 233, 235; Amelia Williams and Eugene C. Barker, eds., *The Writings of Sam Houston*, (8 vols.; Austin, 1943), VIII, 271–93; *OR*, Ser. I, Vol. I, 551, 598–99, 609–10; New York *Herald*, April 11, 1861; Howard C. Westwood, "President Lincoln's Overture to Sam Houston," *SWHQ*, LXXXVIII (1984), 129, 133–36, 139–44; Ralph A. Wooster, "Texas," in *The Confederate Governors*, ed. W. Buck Yearns (Athens, Ga., 1985), 195–96, 199; Walter L. Buenger, *Secession and the Union in Texas* (Austin, 1984), 1, 3; Claude Elliot, *Leathercoat: The Life History of a Texas Patriot* (San Antonio, 1938), 59–60; Walter P. Webb, H. Bailey Carroll, and Eldon S. Branda, eds., *The Handbook of Texas* (3 vols.; Austin, 1952, 1976), I, 354, III, 173; Robert P. Felgar, "Texas in the War for Southern Independence" (Ph.D. dissertation, UT, 1935), 50.

2. Sherman (Tex.) *Patriot*, n.d., quoted in Austin *Texas State Gazette*, November 2, 1861; *OR*, Ser. IV, Vol. I, 323–25, Vol. XIII, 659; Clarksville *Standard*, July 20, 1861; Mark W. Delahy to Andrew Johnson, June 25, 1861, in Andrew Johnson Papers, LC; George Fisher, *The Yankee Conscript* (Philadelphia, 1864), 43–45, 53–54; Sam Acheson and Julia Ann Hudson O'Connell, eds., *George Washington Diamond's Account of the Great Hanging at Gainesville, 1862* (Austin, 1963), 5–6. See also Austin *Texas State Gazette*, May 4, 1861; Charles Elliott, *Southwestern Methodism: A History of the M. E. Church in the Southwest from 1844 to 1864* (Cincinnati, 1868), 275; James Farber, *Fort Worth in the Civil War* (Belton, Tex., 1960), 20.

"vanished" in Grayson County. Just a few weeks later, however, Unionist J. P. Whitaker resumed publishing his outspoken Sherman *Journal.* A writer from Denton about that time reassured Oran M. Roberts that Denton, Wise, and Cooke counties were "all right," but confessed that Grayson was "almost hopeless" because quite a few residents believed there was "nothing objectionable in Mr. Lincoln and his doctrine." [3]

The unease of those settlers who were willing to accept the new Confederacy as the extant source of legal authority increased with the arrival of a flood of often troublesome refugees from areas that had become battlefields. Dallas *Herald* editor Charles R. Pryor initially welcomed an influx of men who claimed to be loyal Confederates from Missouri in the fall of 1861, but he soon began to suspect that something was amiss. On November 6, 1861, he complained that while "everybody who comes down from the Red River country now, claims to be a Missourian, fleeing from the wrath of Lincoln," many newcomers were obviously trying to avoid Confederate military service. Their presence added to an atmosphere of suspicion settling over North Texas. [4]

Apprehension increased when it became apparent that the flood of refugees was significantly changing the racial composition of the Forks. Two-thirds of the newcomers were not slave owners, but the rest brought slaves as well as "every other species of property they could escape with." The number of slaves in North Texas increased rapidly in proportion to the prewar total. In 1860, slaveholders in Cooke County paid taxes on 340 slaves; by 1862, after a year of war, the assessment had swelled to 500, which it remained for the duration of the conflict. Although the actual number of slaves remained small, a perception of invasion became implanted in the minds of many settlers. [5]

3. Otis Welch to Oran M. Roberts, March 24, 1861, W. E. Saunders to Edward Clark, May 7, 1861, in GOR; Acheson and O'Connell, eds., *Diamond's Account,* xv; John M. Elkins, *Life on the Texas Frontier* (Beaumont, 1908), 25; Dallas *Herald,* March 13, December 25, 1861; Houston *Telegraph,* August 14, 1861; McKinney (Tex.) *Messenger,* March 1, 1861; Marilyn M. Sibley, *Lone Stars and State Gazettes* (College Station, Tex., 1983), 293; Frank H. Smyrl, "Unionism, Abolitionism, and Vigilantism in Texas, 1856–1865" (M.A. thesis, UT, 1961), 91; Felgar, "Texas in the War for Southern Independence," 75.

4. Dallas *Herald,* October 16, 30, November 6, 27, 1861; Fisher, *The Yankee Conscript,* 80–81.

5. Clarksville *Standard,* November 23, 1861; extract from Sherman (Tex.) *Patriot,* n.d., in Austin *Texas State Gazette,* November 2, 1861. The information on the slave population in North Texas was provided by Randolph B. Campbell, of the University of North Texas, from the published reports of the comptroller in *The Texas Almanac,* 1861–1865. The increase may

Attempts by the Confederate government to sustain its war effort further augmented the tension on the Forks. President Jefferson Davis in August, 1861, signed a controversial bill providing for the confiscation of property from "alien enemies" and those who offered them material aid. Proceeds from all forced sales were supposed to be deposited in the national treasury, but most of the funds and property were retained by local authorities for their own use, a practice that encouraged them to act more promptly than might otherwise have been the case. Of 2,774 cases heard by the Confederate Western District Court of Texas—whose jurisdiction included the counties immediately west of Cooke—only 28 were not concerned with sequestration. At the same time, the caseload of the Eastern District Court, which reviewed the cases from Cooke, reflected a similar preoccupation.[6]

To those who refused to support the Confederacy in Cooke County, sequestration was not the most alarming economic policy. War taxes and impressment were of more immediate concern for most of them. The latter began almost as soon as the war erupted as the South mounted a major military effort, although the Confederate Congress did not officially authorize it until March, 1863. It was commonly practiced along the Forks, especially by officials who took arms from suspected Unionists and gave them to Confederate recruits. County commissioners imposed the first taxes in the summer of 1862, and these increased as the war continued. Tax collectors such as Jeremiah E. Hughes, who accepted the task after being defeated for reelection as clerk for Cooke County in 1862, became as hated among many dissenters as the impressment details and court-appointed receivers of sequestered property.[7]

The war turned sour for the Confederacy in the spring of 1862 with the

be higher, because slave counts by tax assessors were generally conservative for the simple reason that a slaveholder would try to have his property taxed as little as possible.

6. T. R. Havins, "Administration of the Sequestration Act in the Confederate District Court for the Western District of Texas, 1862–1865," *SWHQ*, XLIII (1940), 295–322; E. Merton Coulter, *The Confederate States of America* (Baton Rouge, 1950), 93; William M. Robinson, Jr., *Justice in Grey: A History of the Judicial System of the Confederate States of America* (Cambridge, Mass., 1941), map following page 146, 493–96.

7. Cooke County Commissioners' Court, "Minutes, 1857 to 1878," I, 98, typescript in Works Progress Administration Historical Records Survey, BTHC; *The Texas Almanac for 1862* (Houston, 1862), 44; Fisher, *The Yankee Conscript*, 47–51; *The Texas Almanac for 1864* (Austin, 1864), 44; Jonnie M. Megee, "The Confederate Impressment Acts in the Trans-Mississippi States" (M.A. thesis, UT, 1915), 6–33, 38–46, 135–59; Felgar, "Texas in the War for Southern Independence," 228–31.

loss of Forts Henry and Donelson and the port of New Orleans. Too, volatile John R. Baylor from Parker County had been appointed governor of the Territory of Arizona, but his dream of empire collapsed after the defeat of the Confederate forces in New Mexico at Glorieta Pass. Many Texans were lost at Shiloh and Pea Ridge, neither of which could be claimed as a victory for the South. Union General James G. Blunt led an expedition into the Indian Territory after Pea Ridge. Albert G. Pike had taken command of the southern forces in the region, but demoralized by the fighting at Pea Ridge, he refused to advance to meet Blunt, initiating a heated controversy that cost him his commission. In Cooke County, the county commissioners organized a committee to provide assistance to the families of soldiers, a humanitarian gesture that confirmed doomsayers' predictions that it would be a long war.[8]

The Confederacy responded to these crises with a conscription act, the first imposed in the United States. Signed by Davis on April 16, 1862, it authorized the drafting of able-bodied white males from eighteen to thirty-five years of age. A list of exemptions endorsed days later released few from their obligation. Led by Clark's successor as governor, Francis R. Lubbock, who asked only that settlers on the frontier be exempted to defend against Indians, Texas officials supported the draft. Because the Confederate Congress never organized a national supreme court, the rulings of state courts on constitutionality were paramount, and the Texas Supreme Court was the first of several to endorse conscription. When an expansion of age limits was considered by the Confederate House of Representatives, Texan Claiborne C. Herbert threatened that his state would abandon the Confederacy rather than comply, but he was repudiated in the Texas press and the measure passed.[9]

8. Cooke Cty. Commissioners' Court, "Minutes," I, 95, 101 (sheet 2); Mark M. Boatner III, *The Civil War Dictionary* (New York, 1959), 590–91; Larry C. Rampp and Donald L. Rampp, *The Civil War in the Indian Territory* (Austin, 1975), 11–17; James G. Randall and David H. Donald, *The Civil War and Reconstruction* (2d ed.; Lexington, Mass., 1969), 235; Emory M. Thomas, *The Confederate Nation, 1861–1865* (New York, 1979), 123–28, 136, 138, 146–47; Charles N. Jones, *Early Days in Cooke County* (Gainesville, 1936), 18.

9. Mary S. Estill, ed., "Diary of a Confederate Congressman," *SWHQ*, XXXVIII (1935), 277–78; Francis R. Lubbock, *Six Decades in Texas*, ed. C. W. Raines (Austin, 1900), 379; *OR*, Ser. I, Vol. LIII, 828–30; *Reports of Cases Argued and Decided in the Supreme Court of the State of Texas* (65 vols.; St. Louis, 1848–1886), XXVI, 386–435; *The Supreme Court of Texas on the Constitutionality of the Conscript Laws* (Houston, 1863), 527; Austin *Texas State Gazette*, October 1, 1862; Houston *Telegraph*, October 6, 1862; Washington *National Intelligencer*, Octo-

The draft threatened to eliminate the small measure of security furnished by the Texas state government for those on the Forks. Beginning early in the war, Confederate officials in Texas had struggled to have state units permanently assigned to defend the northwestern frontier. These efforts had been greatly limited by the increasing need of the government in Richmond for troops to combat the North on distant fronts that were of more immediate concern to the Davis administration. Not only did conscription laws increase disaffection among those on the Forks who were liable to be drafted and sent far from their homes, but they also prompted a significant number of refugees and other suspect persons to seek exemption by joining state units posted in North Texas, thereby undermining the effectiveness of these organizations.

The secession convention had first provided for the defense of the Texas frontier by creating a "Committee of Public Safety"—among whose members was James J. Diamond—before Texas seceded. The committee divided the Texas frontier into three districts, then ordered the muster of a regiment for each of these. Henry E. McCulloch, a slave owner and former federal marshal, commanded the regiment assigned to the northwest district, which included Cooke County. Like the other commanders, he was to confiscate all United States property; nothing was to be wasted, destroyed, or recaptured by "Federal troops, Indians or Abolition marauders." The legislature earlier had mandated the enlistment of companies in each frontier county for defense, and McCulloch mustered these units along with other volunteers. On February 20, 1861, before the secession vote, McCulloch led his troops out of San Antonio to occupy Federal posts in North Texas. Companies raised on the Forks forced the Federal garrison at Camp Cooper to surrender, then turned that facility over to McCulloch along with abandoned Fort Belknap, which had been used by the troopers from the Forks as a rendezvous.[10]

---

ber 5, 1832; J. G. de Roulhac Hamilton, "The State Courts and the Confederate Constitution," *Journal of Southern History*, IV (1938), 425–31, 435; Robinson, *Justice in Grey*, 420–36, 448–55, 458–91; Albert B. Moore, *Conscription and Conflict in the Confederacy* (New York, 1924), 13, 163–67; Marcus J. Wright, *Texas in the War*, ed. Harold B. Simpson (Hillsboro, Tex., 1965), 202; Felgar, "Texas in the War for Southern Independence," 202, 209–10.

10. Winkler, *Journal of the Secession Convention*, 271, 318, 367, 404; William C. Dalrymple to Sam Houston, February 15, 23, 1861, Dalrymple to S. D. Carpenter, February 18, 19, 1861, W. O. Fuller to Houston, February 19, 1861, Dalrymple to Clark, April 7, 1861, H. A. Hamner to Clark, April 18, 1861, all in GOR; Carpenter to Dalrymple, February 18, 20, 1861, Dal-

McCulloch formally organized his troops with the expectation of remaining in North Texas. His brother, Ben McCulloch, received authorization to raise a regiment for Confederate service, but he passed it on to Henry, who filled out the companies already under his command with new recruits for muster as the 1st Texas Mounted Rifles. Most of this regiment remained with McCulloch in San Antonio while he served as commander of Texas until Earl Van Dorn arrived, but the troopers returned to the northwestern frontier at McCulloch's request during early June, 1861. They were posted along a line from the Red River on the north to the Concho River on the south; four companies and a battery of four pieces of artillery were stationed near the Forks.[11]

McCulloch's regiment secured the frontier west of Cooke County, but the Red River border with the suspect Chickasaw and Choctaw nations was undefended after the withdrawal of Federal troops. Several other regiments were mustered along the Forks to protect this boundary. The first was commanded by William C. Young, who, though he owned more slaves and grew more cotton than anyone else in Cooke County, was at best a lukewarm Confederate. Age and prosperity had made him quite conservative, and he had been vocal in his opposition to secession during the Gainesville caucus in December, 1860. Although Texas congressman John H. Reagan, his friend, had decided further efforts at compromise were useless and wrote

rymple to Houston, February 25, 1861, E. W. Rogers to Dalrymple, March 9, 1861, all in AGR; H. P. N. Gammel, comp., *The Laws of Texas, 1822–1897* (10 vols.; Austin, 1898), V, 346–47; Dorman H. Winfrey and James M. Day, eds., *The Indian Papers of Texas and the Southwest* (5 vols.; Austin, 1960–1966), IV, 118–20; *OR*, Ser. I, Vol. I, 523, 540–41, 543–44; Dallas *Herald*, February 27, March 20, April 3, 1861; Clarksville *Standard*, March 23, 1861; J. J. Bowden, *The Exodus of Federal Forces from Texas, 1861* (Austin, 1986), 70–73; Stephen B. Oates, *Confederate Cavalry West of the River* (Austin, 1961), 5; David P. Smith, *Frontier Defense in the Civil War: Texas' Rangers and Rebels* (College Station, Tex., 1992), 17–18, 21, 23–28; Caroline S. Ruckman, "The Frontier of Texas During the Civil War" (M.A. thesis, UT, 1926), 9–10; Felgar, "Texas in the War for Southern Independence," 2, 4, 66–68. For more on Henry E. McCulloch, see Webb, Carroll, and Branda, eds., *Handbook*, II, 106–107.

11. Henry E. McCulloch to Charles C. Jones, January 22, 1889, in McCulloch Family Papers, BTHC; James B. Barry, *A Texas Ranger and Frontiersman: The Days of Buck Barry in Texas, 1845–1906*, ed. James K. Greer (Dallas, 1932), 125–30; *OR*, Ser. I, Vol. I, 573–76, 609–10, 617–18, 623, 627; *Dictionary of American Biography*, X, 185–86; Oates, *Confederate Cavalry West of the River*, 5; Smith, *Frontier Defense in the Civil War*, 28–33; Webb, Carroll, and Branda, eds., *Handbook*, II, 106; Felgar, "Texas in the War," 70–71; Ruckman, "Frontier of Texas," 31–32, 34–36, 37–39.

him in January, 1861, urging him to embrace disunion, Young still had doubts. He accompanied prosecession delegates Hardin R. Runnels—the former governor of Texas—and James J. Diamond to Dallas for a conference with editor Pryor before they traveled to Austin, but these prominent Democrats still could not persuade Young to endorse disunion.[12]

Although Young opposed secession, he shared the concern of many in North Texas for order and security. Governor Clark offered him the command of a regiment to defend the northwest frontier on April 24, 1861, and he accepted at once. Young used the company raised following the secession meeting at Diamond's Station as a nucleus, and then published calls in several North Texas newspapers for volunteers to invade the Indian Territory. He mustered a few infantry and cavalry companies in Grayson County on May 3, 1861, then conducted elections in which he was confirmed as colonel of the new regiment, Throckmorton as lieutenant colonel, and Hugh F. Young—a slaveholder and former chief justice of Grayson County—as major. Three-fourths of those under their command had voted against secession, but they had a common goal of securing their homes as they had done before the war, and so they obeyed.[13]

Soon after William C. Young organized his regiment, he committed them to action. Late in the afternoon on May 3, 1861, he sent a detachment across the Red River to seize Fort Washita, having heard that it was abandoned. The next day he led the rest of his regiment—which amounted to only 530 troopers armed with rifles, shotguns, hatchets, and knives—

12. Acheson and O'Connell, eds., *Diamond's Account*, xvi; Sherman (Tex.) *Monitor*, n.d., quoted in Dallas *Herald*, February 6, 1861. See also Dallas *Herald*, January 30, 1861; Ben H. Proctor, *Not Without Honor: The Life of John H. Reagan* (Austin, 1962), 120–21.

13. Muster Roll of the Staff Officers Appointed and Elected of the 3d Regiment of Mounted Volunteers, Commanded by Colonel William C. Young, October 2, 1861, in AGR; Saunders and Simon B. Allen to John M. Crockett, May 3, 1861, William C. Young to Clark, April 27, May 2, 1861, all in GOR; Clarksville *Standard*, May 11, 18, 1861; Dallas *Herald*, May 27, 1861; Wooster, "Texas," in *The Confederate Governors*, ed. Yearns, 196–97; Oran M. Roberts, "Texas," in *Confederate Military History*, ed. Clement A. Evans (12 vols.; Atlanta, 1899), XI, 47; John H. Brown, *History of Texas from 1685 to 1892* (2 vols.; St. Louis, 1893), II, 411–14; Graham Landrum and Allen Smith, *An Illustrated History of Grayson County, Texas* (2d ed.; Fort Worth, 1967), 46; A. Morton Smith, *The First 100 Years in Cooke County* (San Antonio, 1955), 30; Oates, *Confederate Cavalry West of the River*, 10–11; Rampp and Rampp, *Indian Territory*, 3–8. For more about Hugh F. Young, see Webb, Carroll, and Branda, eds., *Handbook*, II, 947; Stephen B. Oates, "Hugh F. Young's Account of the Snively Expedition as Told to John S. Ford," *SWHQ*, LXX (1966), 73–74.

through Washita to Fort Arbuckle, which he also found empty as expected. By the second week of May he held the third Federal post in the southern Indian Territory, Fort Cobb. He deliberately avoided a clash with the retreating regulars, knowing well the divided sentiments of those under his command. As a participant recalled, Young easily could have been defeated by any show of force, and in fact his advance companies were repulsed by a small contingent of Union soldiers.[14]

Young's entry into the Indian Territory was facilitated by the diplomatic efforts of another Cooke County slaveholder, James G. Bourland. He and two other commissioners were appointed by the Texas secession convention to negotiate with the five Civilized Tribes—Choctaw, Chickasaw, Creek, Seminole and Cherokee—and they entered the Chickasaw Nation on February 27, 1861. The governor of the Indian Territory, C. Harris, proved anxious to cooperate, and on March 12 they joined a council of Chickasaws and Choctaws, who welcomed them. Cherokee chief John Ross did not encourage their advances, but at another council on April 8, 1861, with the Cherokees, Creeks, Seminoles, and others, the commissioners were assured that all of those present would support the Confederacy. Bourland accompanied Young on his march into the Indian Territory, and after the Federal posts were secured, the pair signed more treaties. The Chickasaws managed their agency at Fort Arbuckle themselves, while James J. Diamond supervised the Wichita and Caddo reservations. By the fall of 1861 most of the tribes, including the Comanches, had signed treaties, reassuring many North Texas settlers.[15]

14. L. H. Graves, "Diary, 1861–1864" (Typescript in BTHC), 1–3; James M. Lindsay, "Statement," 1917 (MS in Lillian M. Gunter Papers, UNT); Mrs. W. H. Lucas, "Interview with Mrs. John Young," 1928 (Typescript in Mattie D. Lucas Papers, Sherman Municipal Library, Sherman, Tex.); William C. Young to Clark, May 2, 1861, in GOR; Lemuel D. Clark, ed., *The Civil War Recollections of James Lemuel Clark* (College Station, Tex., 1984), 52–56; *OR*, Ser. I, Vol. I, 648–49, 652; Austin *Texas State Gazette*, July 20, 1861; Clarksville *Standard*, May 18, 1861; Dallas *Herald*, May 27, 1861; Annie H. Abel, *Indians as Slaveholders and Secessionists* (Cleveland, 1915), 79–80, 99–102; Rampp and Rampp, *Indian Territory*, 3–5. Graves and Lindsay served in William C. Young's regiment during the march into the Indian Territory; John [D.] Young was the colonel's son.

15. Lindsay, "Statement"; James J. Diamond to Clark, July 3, 1861, William C. Young to Clark, August 2, 1861, in GOR; Gammel, comp., *Laws of Texas*, IV, 1521; *OR*, Ser. I, Vol. I, 653, and Ser. IV, Vol. I, 323–25; Winkler, *Journal of the Secession Convention of Texas*, 221; Austin *Texas State Gazette*, June 8, 1861; Clarksville *Standard*, June 22, 1861; Abel, *Indians as*

William C. Young returned to Sherman about the first of June and established his headquarters as the self-styled "Major General of the Northern Division of Texas." On June 10 he was appointed the commander of Texas' 8th Military District, with broad authority to recruit in Cooke and the surrounding counties, and he soon had more than 800 troopers in the Indian Territory. Nowhere was he more successful than in Cooke County. The county commissioners there authorized the refurbishing of eighty guns and distributed them to five local companies: one each in the communities of Gainesville, Clear Creek, and Fish Creek, and two in the Eastern Cross Timbers. Cavalry companies organized in Cooke and Grayson counties marched north under the command of James J. Diamond and William C. Twitty, Daniel Montague's son-in-law. As elsewhere, they departed amid frantic flag-waving and a torrent of rhetoric. They settled at Fort Cobb with a company led by Throckmorton, while three others occupied Arbuckle and four garrisoned Washita. Discipline was lax; they trained by holding shooting matches and riding tournaments, and drank freely. The atmosphere was more like a picnic than a combat expedition, and Young did little to correct that.[16]

Ever mindful of the antisecession sentiment of most of his men, Young sought assurances that although they were to be part of Ben McCulloch's forces in Arkansas, they would not be sent far from their homes in Texas. He traveled to Richmond, then to Arkansas to speak with McCulloch, and

Slaveholders and Secessionists, 96–102; Rampp and Rampp, *Indian Territory*, 1–2; Ruckman, "The Frontier of Texas During the Civil War," 50, 51, 55, 60–61, 64–65, 66, 68–69. James G. Bourland, in a letter to President Andrew Johnson asking for pardon, denied having been with Young on his march into the Indian Territory in May, 1861, but other sources indicate that he was. See James G. Bourland to Johnson, September 18, 1865, in Amnesty Files.

16. Jesse Marshall to McCulloch, July 20, 1861, in Ed Burleson, Jr., Papers, BTHC; Graves, "Diary," 9, 12; Cooke Cty. Commissioners' Court, "Minutes," I, 81 (sheet 2), 83 (sheet 2); John E. Wheeler Diary, 1850–1880 (MS in Morton Museum, Gainesville, Tex.); Muster Rolls of James J. Diamond's Company, May 15, 1861, of William C. Twitty's Company, July 1, 1861, and of Staff Officers, 3d Regt. Mtd. Vols., October 2, 1861, all in AGR; Young to Clark, April 27, 1861, in GOR; Clarksville *Standard*, May 18, June 1, 20, 29, July 20, 1861; Austin *Texas State Gazette*, June 15, 1861; Dallas *Herald*, June 5, 12, August 14, 1861; Stephen B. Oates, "Recruiting Confederate Cavalry in Texas," *SWHQ*, LXIV (1961), 477; Stephen B. Oates, "Texas Under the Secessionists," *SWHQ*, LXVII (1963), 183; Smith, *First 100 Years*, 31; *Biographical Souvenir of the State of Texas* (Chicago, 1889), 836; Bill Winsor, *Texas in the Confederacy: Military Installations, Economy, and People* (Hillsboro, Tex., 1978), 18, 38.

finally to Austin for a meeting with Clark. The governor designated Young's regiment as one of five—later reduced to four—detailed to protect North Texas. Young, who was retained as colonel, was assured that they might range as far north as Kansas or Missouri, but they would not be sent east of the Mississippi River. Clark officially mustered Young's troops as the 1st Texas Regiment on July 25, 1861, and authorized them to be mounted as cavalry in order to support McCulloch more effectively.[17]

A reorganization of the command structure ensued soon after the formal muster of Young's regiment. James J. Diamond was elected in place of Throckmorton as lieutenant colonel, so Diamond's second lieutenant, James D. Young, the colonel's son, succeeded him as captain of the company mustered in Cooke and Grayson counties. Hugh F. Young relinquished his rank of major and went home, but Throckmorton mustered a company and joined another regiment, the 6th Texas Cavalry, that was assigned to frontier duty as well. On August 28, 1861, Governor Clark tendered the services of the 1st Texas Division, which included Young's regiment, to the Department of War, with the request that it be assigned to the frontier of Texas.[18]

Anticipating that the regiment would remain on the Red River, the Cooke County commissioners provided money to refurbish Twitty's and James D. Young's companies. A change in commanders for the Department of Texas quashed these plans. General Paul O. Hebert arrived three weeks after Governor Clark's request. A West Point graduate who had spent much of his career in Europe, Hebert proved to be "arrogant, arbitrary, and cavalier." He had little sympathy for the concerns of the settlers along the Forks, and ordered that William C. Young's regiment be transferred to regular Confederate service with no guaranteed station. Young's foot dragging had attracted notice, and ugly rumors circulated that he was an abolitionist at heart. The muster of his regiment as the 11th Texas Cavalry in

17. Marshall to McCulloch, July 20, 1861, in Burleson Papers; James W. Throckmorton to Clark, July 9, 1861, in GOR; Young to Clark, April 26, 1861, in CSR, 11th Texas Cavalry; *OR*, Ser. I, Vol. IV, 95–96; Clarksville *Standard*, August 3, 10, 1861; Dallas *Herald*, July 31, August 21, 1861.

18. Graves, "Diary," 20, 25–26; Throckmorton to Hamilton P. Bee, September 4, 1866, in James W. Throckmorton Papers, BTHC; Muster Roll, Staff Officers, 3d Regt., Mtd. Vols., October 2, 1861, in AGR; CSR, 6th Texas Cavalry; Census of 1860, Cooke Cty., Tex., Schedule 1 (Free Inhabitants), Family Number [hereinafter cited as F.N.] 636, in Genealogy Division, TSL; *OR*, Ser. I, Vol. IV, 98–100; Tom Bomar, *Glimpses of Grayson County from the Early Days* (Sherman, Tex., 1894), 25; Elliot, *Leathercoat*, 67–69; Landrum and Smith, *Illustrated History of Grayson County*, 61.

Grayson County on October 2, 1861, pleased many suspicious observers because the unit could now be assigned to any theater of the war. Many of the troopers in the regiment reacted quite differently; one in five hired substitutes and returned to their homes, the defense of which had originally prompted their enlistment.[19]

William C. Young tried a few last gambits. Clark wrote to Hebert on October 3, 1861, acknowledging the transfer of Young's troops into Confederate service and stating that he presumed they would be posted on Texas' northern frontier. Hebert curtly told him to forward the regiment to Ben McCulloch with no further delay. The protests of the "old Union party" on the Forks impelled Young to address a barely veiled plea for an assignment on the Red River to the new Secretary of War, Judah P. Benjamin. Young demanded that some unit be assigned to Forts Arbuckle, Washita, and Cobb to guard against the Reserve Indians, whose loyalty could not be trusted, as well as many renegade Creeks and Cherokees and the volatile Comanches and Kiowas. He insisted that at least two hundred runaway slaves lived among the Cherokees and about five hundred jayhawkers were in camp with disaffected Creeks, all of whom posed a great danger to settlers in North Texas. He concluded, "There is a very considerable dread amongst our people on Red River on this account." Benjamin also gave no satisfactory answer.[20]

James J. Diamond had already led the 11th Texas Cavalry north when Young wrote to Benjamin. They were supposed to join the army commanded by Ben McCulloch for a march into Missouri, but unrest in the Indian Territory forced a temporary reassignment. The Kiowas and Comanches repeatedly violated the treaties they had signed, and factions of other tribes repudiated any alliances with the South. A large party of dissident Creeks and Seminoles marched for Kansas, and seven companies of

19. Clark to Diamond, September 19, 1861, in James G. Bourland Papers, LC; Cooke County Commissioners' Court, "Minutes," I, 87 (sheet 2), 88; Muster Rolls of Twitty's Company, October 2, 1862, and of Staff Officers, 3d Regt., Mtd. Vols., October 2, 1861, in AGR; *OR*, Ser. I, Vol. IV, 98, 105–106; Clarksville *Standard*, October 5, 1861; T. R. Fehrenbach, *Lone Star: A History of Texas and the Texans* (New York, 1968), 359; Landrum and Smith, *Illustrated History of Grayson County*, 46; *DAB*, IV, 492–93. Some members of the 11th Texas Cavalry did not bother with the formality of hiring a substitute; when John H. Young, apparently no relation to the colonel, was asked to take an oath of allegiance, he deserted. (CSR, 11th Texas Cavalry.)

20. *OR*, Ser. I, Vol. IV, 113–14; Clark to Diamond, September 19, 1861, in Bourland Papers; Young to Clark, October 8, 1861, Paul O. Hebert to Clark, October 16, 1861, in GOR; *DAB*, VII, 593–95.

the 11th Texas Cavalry joined the pursuing Confederate troopers. The campaign reunited William C. Young, who joined his regiment, with Bourland, who had served briefly as an aide-de-camp for the 11th Texas Cavalry but now rode with another unit in the chase.[21]

Under Young, the 11th Texas Cavalry fought its first engagement on December 26, 1861, at Chustenahlah against Indian dissidents, whom they routed. Young's troopers anchored the left side of the Confederate line, and they acquitted themselves well. The Cooke County companies commanded by Twitty and James D. Young were in the thick of the fight, and the latter was wounded. William C. Young, in addition to receiving the distressing news about his son, had his fears confirmed. Others had reported that in earlier clashes many of the dead found on the field were white and black jayhawkers; among the prisoners taken at Chustenahlah were thirty escaped slaves.[22]

The 11th Texas Cavalry joined Ben McCulloch in time to fight at Pea Ridge in March, 1862. Now battle-tested veterans, they were sent east of the Mississippi River the next month; after 1863, their transfer became permanent. Having secured North Texas by occupying the Indian Territory, though, many members of Young's regiment saw no need to serve so far from the frontier they had enlisted to defend. The 11th Texas Cavalry mustered 796 troopers on January 1, 1862; three months later, when enlistments approached expiration, only 252 remained on the rolls. Officers as well as enlisted men went home. Young resigned in April, 1862, because of poor health and fears of "bad men" in North Texas who threatened him and others with economic ruin and violence. His son, James, quit in May, 1862. James J. Diamond followed after failing to be elected colonel of the 11th Texas Cavalry; with him came his brother John, who had been the regimental quartermaster. James J. Diamond toured North Texas offering amnesty to those who would rejoin their units, but soon returned to Cooke County. Twitty's resignation in April, 1862, antedated that of his lieutenant, Alexander Boutwell, by only three months.[23]

21. Bourland to M. A. Elliott, September 7, 1861, in Bourland Papers; Bourland to Johnson, September 18, 1865, in Amnesty Files; *OR*, Ser. I, Vol. IV, 113–14, Vol. VIII, 11–12, 23–25, 26–27, 713, 718–19; Dallas *Herald*, August 14, 28, 1861; Rampp and Rampp, *Indian Territory*, 6–8.

22. *OR*, Ser. I, Vol. VIII, 23–25, 26–27; Dallas *Herald*, December 11, 1861, January 15, 29, 1862; Rampp and Rampp, *Indian Territory*, 6–8; Landrum and Smith, *Illustrated History of Grayson County*, 46.

23. CSR, 11th Tex. Cav.; William C. Young to Clark, May 2, 1861, in GOR; Graves,

The transfer of the 11th Texas Cavalry left North Texas without a permanent garrison to defend it. State officials resorted to a familiar expedient to provide security: the muster of volunteer units to combat Indians and disruptive elements among white and black settlers. Because the enlistees were supposed to be exempt from regular service, many who otherwise refused to support the Confederacy joined. The creation of state regiments to protect the Texas frontier drained regular Confederate units of manpower and munitions, but the practice was continued throughout the war to provide some security for areas such as Cooke County.[24]

The first of these state units were militia, which were revived during the summer of 1861 in response to frequent rumors of a Federal invasion from Kansas and Missouri. Governor Clark called for the muster of home defense companies, and settlers along the Forks responded warmly when it became known that such units would not be transferred to Confederate service. In a Montague County settlement known as Head of Elm, a "minuteman" company was organized on June 22, 1861, "for the defence of our homes and our rights." A company in Grayson County had already been drilling for two weeks, and the "Cooke County Home Guard Cavalry" had just elected its officers. Clark assured Davis that such measures would secure Texas against not only Indians but also "a spirit of dissatisfaction and dissension with the Confederate States."[25]

"Diary," 4; Wheeler Diary; Noah Smithwick, *The Evolution of a State* (Austin, 1900), 336, 341; *OR*, Ser. I, Vol. VIII, 293–94, 297–98, 728, 776; Clarksville *Standard*, May 5, June 7, 21, 22, July 5, 26, 1862; Oates, "Recruiting Confederate Cavalry," 477; Oates, "Texas Under the Secessionists," 183; Landrum and Smith, *Illustrated History of Grayson County*, 47–48; Wright, *Texas in the War*, 25, 114–15; Felgar, "Texas in the War," 339; Brown, *History of Texas*, II, 411–14; Francis W. Johnson, *A History of Texas and Texans*, ed. Eugene C. Barker (5 vols.; Chicago, 1914), IV, 1688; Dudley G. Wooten, ed., *A Comprehensive History of Texas 1685 to 1897* (2 vols.; Dallas, 1898), II, 630; Webb, Carroll, and Branda, eds., *Handbook*, III, 99. Among the enlisted men who departed was James G. Bourland's son, William, who had been a private in James J. Diamond's company. He was discharged for chronic rheumatism and dyspepsia, but later joined the quartermaster corps in Texas. Sadly, James J. Diamond's successor as lieutenant colonel, Joseph M. Bounds, a farmer from Collin County who joined the 11th Texas Cavalry in May, 1861, was assassinated on October 27, 1863.

24. Lubbock, *Six Decades in Texas*, 347; Frank L. Owsley, *States Rights in the Confederacy* (Chicago, 1925), 14, 41; Felgar, "Texas in the War," 339.

25. Clarksville *Standard*, June 29, July 13, 20, 1861; Weatherford (Tex.) *News*, n.d., quoted in Dallas *Herald*, August 21, 1861; Certificate of Election of Officers of Cooke County Home Guard Cavalry by Chief Justice Robert D. Stone, June 29, 1861, in AGR; Ben McCulloch to

The militia system was formalized by Clark's successor, Lubbock, a secessionist who had joined James J. Diamond and the other Texas delegates when they boycotted the 1860 Democratic convention. On Christmas Day, 1861, Lubbock signed a bill that reorganized the state into thirty-three districts, each to be commanded by a brigadier general of militia. In June, 1861, Bourland had been appointed to command the 21st District—which included Cooke, Jack, Denton, Montague and Wise counties—and he was William C. Young's choice to continue in that position. He declined the honor, however, due to "circumstances of business transactions and sickness in my family," and upon his recommendation William R. Hudson was chosen in his place. To the east, Hugh F. Young was assigned to command the 15th District, which encompassed Grayson and Collin counties.[26]

Because his district took in a large portion of the Forks region, Hudson inherited a tremendous responsibility. Unfortunately for him, the counties west of Cooke remained sparsely populated, and he was never able to assemble a full complement. Hugh F. Young recruited more than 2,000 men by March, 1862, but Hudson had to be content with about half that number. Hudson organized his troops into three battalions: one commanded by Twitty—following his resignation from the 11th Texas Cavalry in April, 1862—in Cooke and Montague counties; another in Denton County under Samuel P. C. Patton; and a third in Wise County led by former sheriff and county surveyor John W. Hale, who served as Hudson's adjutant as well. Hale established a subpost in Decatur, which he stocked with firearms, ammunition, and other supplies.[27]

"Pa," July 24, 1861, in McCulloch Family Papers; Wooster, "Texas," in *The Confederate Governors*, ed. Yearns, 197. Head of Elm became Saint Jo in 1872.

26. Texas Secretary of State, Election Register, 1848–1900, in Archives Division, TSL; Jeremiah Y. Dashiell to Bourland, December 30, 1861, in Bourland Papers; Lubbock, *Six Decades in Texas*, 359; List of Brigadier Generals of Texas State Troops, Hugh F. Young to Dashiell, January 13, 1862, Bourland to Dashiell, January 28, 1862, Dashiell to William R. Hudson, February 14, 1862, Hudson to Dashiell, March 4, 1862, Dashiell to Hugh F. Young, May 26, 1862, all in AGR; William C. Young to Clark, October 28, 1861, in GOR; Gammel, comp., *Laws of Texas*, V, 455–56; Wooster, "Texas," in *The Confederate Governors*, ed. Yearns, 198, 199–200; Edward F. Bates, *History and Reminiscences of Denton County* (Denton, Tex., 1918), 109; Clarence R. Wharton, *Texas Under Many Flags* (2 vols.; Chicago, 1930), II, 91. For more about Francis R. Lubbock, see Webb, Carroll, and Branda, eds., *Handbook*, II, 89.

27. CSR, 11th Tex. Cav.; Dashiell to Hudson, March 29, September 16, 1862, Hudson to Dashiell, March 22, 1863, Muster Rolls of Charles L. Roff's Company, Border Battalion, January 7 and April 23, 1863, in AGR; Hugh F. Young to Francis R. Lubbock, March 2, 1862,

On December 21, 1861, Lubbock also signed legislation creating a new Frontier Regiment to replace Henry E. McCulloch's 1st Texas Mounted Rifles, whose enlistments expired. Its members would remain in state service and be stationed in small detachments of 25 men on the frontier both to protect against Indians and to chase deserters. The regiment was organized in February, 1862; though the response along the Forks was overwhelming, only nine companies, a total of 1,089 men, were enlisted to garrison eighteen posts.[28]

Conscription had a great impact on these state units, undermining efforts to provide security in isolated areas such as the Forks. Those who previously had been neutral were now opponents of the Confederacy; some stayed at home or hid in the brush, but quite a few joined the Frontier Regiment or militia to take advantage of their exemption from the draft. Confederate enrolling officers' periodic combing of the state musters for shirkers had little effect. Hudson earlier had complained that he could not enlist enough men. Now he found this task easier, but another problem arose; as Hugh F. Young wrote, "Our families, our property, our all is now comparatively in the care and keeping of strangers." Violence enhanced suspicion and undermined effectiveness. Former Texas state senator Alfred T. Obenchain commanded the Frontier Regiment detachments upon the northwest frontier—most of which were from Cooke County—until he was killed in August, 1862, by two privates who resented Obenchain's officious manner. By early 1863, the command of Red River Station in Mon-

Hudson to Lubbock, March 13, 1862, in GOR; Mary C. Moore, *Centennial History of Wise County, 1853–1953* (Dallas, 1953), 38; Cliff D. Cates, *Pioneer History of Wise County* (Decatur, Tex., 1907), 117–18. John Hale immigrated with his family to Texas during the period of the Republic, and finally settled in Wise County in 1854. A staunch Southern Methodist, he was elected the county's first sheriff in 1856 and county surveyor in 1858 and 1860. The census taker in 1860 recorded him as a thirty-six-year-old farmer, born in Tennessee, with $400 in property. See Texas Secretary of State, Election Register; Census of 1860, Grayson Cty., Tex., Schedule 1, F.N. 838, in TSL; Cates, *Pioneer History of Wise County*, 35, 38, 57, 64, 66, 301–303, 310; Moore, *Centennial History of Wise County*, 15, 23.

28. Dashiell to Alfred T. Obenchain, April 25, 1862, in AGR; Lubbock, *Six Decades in Texas*, 357; Gammel, comp., *Laws of Texas*, V, 452–54; Austin *Texas State Gazette*, March 29, 1862; Oates, "Texas Under the Secessionists," 184; Smith, *Frontier Defense in the Civil War*, 42–43; Harry M. Henderson, *Texas in the Confederacy* (San Antonio, 1955), 142; Webb, Carroll, and Branda, eds., *Handbook*, I, 651–52, II, 685; Wright, *Texas in the War*, 30; Felgar, "Texas in the War," 150–52; Allan R. Purcell, "The History of the Texas Militia, 1835–1903" (Ph.D. dissertation, UT, 1981), 132–33, 135–38.

tague County—the northern anchor of the Frontier Regiment's defensive line—had fallen to John T. Rowland, who was promoted to captain after his predecessor suddenly resigned.[29]

Sequestration, impressment, taxation, and conscription pushed additional Texans into the ranks of those who opposed the Confederacy, thus convincing many settlers on the Forks that peacefully maintaining order and security was impossible. Suspicions had grown between the antebellum populace and the newcomers until "mutual distrust and dislike, criminations and recriminations characterized the intercourse between the two parties." Threatened with apparent chaos, many turned once more to proven leaders—especially the slaveholders whose authority had been enhanced by their efforts to defend North Texas—and proven methods, such as vigilantism. Now, however, the victims were not Indians and abolitionists but accused Unionists. By opposing the Confederacy, or simply by trying to be neutral, many North Texans, both old and new, had unwittingly moved beyond the pale of law.[30]

This shift toward vigilantism against those who did not support the Confederacy began on the Forks at the outset of the war. In Grayson County, Frederick W. Sumner, a jeweler from Vermont, raised a homemade

29. Hugh F. Young to Dashiell, March 10, 1862, Dashiell to Obenchain, January 29, 1862, Dashiell to Allen Brunson, March 15, 1862, Obenchain to James M. Norris, June 25, 1862, Dashiell to "A. H. Page & Others," July 14, 1862, Norris to Dashiell, August 24, 1862, Dashiell to Norris, August 29, October 2, 14, 19, 1862, Dashiell to James E. McCord, September 22, 1862, Dashiell to James B. Barry, September 22, 1862, List of Captains in the Frontier Regiment, Texas State Troops, April 21, 1862, all in AGR; Barry, *A Texas Ranger and Frontiersman*, 144–46, 166–71; William R. Strong, *His Memoirs*, ed. Pete A. Y. Gunter and Robert A. Calvert (Denton, Tex., 1982), 55; Clark, ed., *Recollections of James Clark*, 83; Richmond (Va.) *Enquirer*, October 28, 1863; Glen D. Wilson, "Old Red River Station," *SWHQ*, LXI (1958), 352; *Members of the Texas Legislature, 1846–1980* (Austin, 1981), 37, 38; Jeff S. Henderson, ed., *100 Years in Montague County, Texas* (Saint Jo, Tex., 1957); Smith, *First 100 Years*, 43; Fehrenbach, *Lone Star*, 362–63; Thomas, *The Confederate Nation*, 152–55; Webb, Carroll, and Branda, eds., *Handbook*, I, 115–16, II, 103–104, 452; Guy R. Donnell, "The History of Montague County, Texas" (M.A. thesis, UT, 1940), 191; Purcell, "History of the Texas Militia," 142–43, 145–48. For more on John T. Rowland, for whom a town in Montague County is named, see Strong, *Memoirs*, 10; Census of 1860, Collin Cty., Tex., Schedule 1, F.N. 773, in TSL; *Biographical Souvenir of Texas*, 734; Webb, Carroll, and Branda, eds., *Handbook*, II, 510–11; Sue Wood and Ronnie Howser, eds., *Fairview Cemetery, Gainesville, Cooke County, Texas* (Gainesville, 1985), 47.

30. Acheson and O'Connell, eds., *Diamond's Account*, 6; Hugh F. Young to Lubbock, March 2, 1862, in GOR.

United States flag over the courthouse in Sherman on New Year's Day, 1861. When secessionists protested, a Lone Star banner was flown as well until after secession, when Sumner's flag was removed. During May, 1861, to silence Unionist editor Foster, vandals ruined his press. When someone retaliated by cutting down the Confederate banner over the courthouse, over a hundred armed men occupied the town. The inevitable occurred on May 25, 1861, when two Unionists were attacked by two vengeful Confederates. One of the former pair was killed, the other seriously wounded. Both Confederates, one of whom had a finger shot off, were acquitted by a justice of the peace. Another Confederate flag was raised and an ardent secessionist sat with a rifle by the flagpole, daring anyone to cut it down again.[31]

Vigilantism in nearby Parker County proved even more bloody. A grand jury during May, 1861, reacting to reports that Anthony B. Norton, the Unionist editor of the Austin *Southern Intelligencer*, had fled into North Texas, condemned him as an associate of the unfortunate Anthony M. Bewley and a "dangerous man to society and the institutions of Texas." They also denounced W. Frank Carter of Weatherford as a "man unfavorable to the institutions of the South." Both of their intended victims escaped, but four slaves accused of fomenting an insurrection did not. Without a trial, they were hanged from the wooden frame over the well in the town square of Weatherford, the county seat.[32]

Efforts to maintain order and security on the Forks by assailing those who opposed the Confederacy became more systematic as the war escalated. A hostile meeting in Grayson County on June 8, 1861, resulted in the denouncement of all those who refused to support secession, and the reestablishment of a vigilance committee, which had been allowed to lapse during the relatively peaceful interlude after the fires of 1860. Cooke County's commissioners were a step ahead of their neighbors; they appointed a board of patrollers for Gainesville on May 21, 1861. Among the board members

31. Mattie D. Lucas, "Interview with William Walsh, November 1928" (Typescript), and Fragment of MS, n.d., in Lucas Papers; Frederick W. Sumner, "Written by F. W. Sumner During the Civil War 1860–1865" (Typescript in Sherman Historical Museum, Sherman, Tex.); Dallas *Herald*, May 27, 1861; Mattie D. Lucas and Mita H. Hall, *A History of Grayson County, Texas* (Sherman, Tex., 1936), 112; Thomas Wilson, *Sufferings Endured for a Free Government* (Washington, D.C., 1864), 258–59; Landrum and Smith, *Illustrated History of Grayson County*, 63; Smyrl, "Unionism, Abolitionism, and Vigilantism in Texas," 91–92.

32. Dallas *Herald*, May 27, 1861; G. A. Holland, *History of Parker County and the Double Log Cabin* (Weatherford, Tex., 1937), 89; H. Smythe, *Historical Sketch of Parker County and Weatherford, Texas* (St. Louis, 1877), 159–60; Sibley, *Lone Stars*, 298.

were Boutwell, who departed to serve as second lieutenant of Twitty's company but returned, Hudson, slaveholder James M. Peery, and deputy sheriff James B. Davenport, Jr., the son of a prominent slaveholder and later a captain in the 22d Texas Cavalry. To the west, eight men were elected to a Montague County vigilance committee. These organizations were quite active; Pryor reported on November 13, 1861, "The Sherman and Paris papers mention the hanging of several men in Northern Texas, for unsoundness on the Southern question." Ever the fiery partisan, he added, "We suppose they were all served about right."[33]

Vigilantism in Cooke County became more frequent as tension grew due to wartime conditions. The shooting death of Joe Means at Jim McCall's saloon in Gainesville occasioned some excitement, but it was quickly eclipsed by the grisly end of McCall himself. He made the mistake of taunting a father and his son who had come on January 9, 1862, to enlist with Hudson's militia. The pair had new pocketknives and boasted of how they would kill Yankees with these. When McCall scoffed at them, asking if they thought that was all they would need, they rushed him and stabbed him to death. That night, McCall's friends took the impetuous pair from the Gainesville jail and hanged them from the horse rack in front of the victim's saloon. A young girl who came to town with her father the next day noticed the bodies hanging from the rack; she later wrote, "Just why they were hanged, no one seemed to know or care."[34]

A rash of cotton gin fires erupted in North Texas in early 1862. Clarksville *Standard* editor Charles DeMorse opined that Unionist agents, whom he scorned as "Lincoln's myrmidons," were to blame, and he added that "some several persons" were "probably deserving of a hempen necklace." After several more months of unrest, DeMorse asserted again that a "speedy hanging" should be given "vile miscreants" who supported the Union. Downstate, the editors of two even more reactionary newspapers, the Aus-

33. Dallas *Herald*, June 12, November 13, 1861; Cooke Cty. Commissioners' Court, "Minutes," I, 35, 82 (sheet 2); Muster Roll of Twitty's Company, October 2, 1861, in AGR; CSR, 22d Texas Cavalry; Clarksville *Standard*, June 29, July 13, 1861; Smith, *First 100 Years*, 32.

34. Sarah I. S. Rogers, "Memoirs" (Typescript in Morton Museum, Gainesville, Tex.), 53–54, 55–56; "Interview with Thant Gorham," March 27, 1925 (MS in Gunter Papers); Sherman (Tex.) *Journal*, n.d., quoted in Austin *Texas State Gazette*, February 1, 1862; Cooke Cty. Commissioners' Court, "Minutes," I, 5; Census of 1850, Cooke Cty., Schedule 1, F.N. 373, in TSL; Frances T. Ingmire, comp., "Cooke County, Texas, Marriage Records 1849–1879," p. 2, typescript in BTHC.

tin *Texas Almanac Extra* and the San Antonio *Herald*, reported the rash of arsons and, recalling the fires of 1860, demanded that General Hebert take steps against the arsonists who had surfaced once more.[35]

To quell unrest, and to enforce conscription more effectively, Hebert imposed martial law in Texas on May 30, 1862. Military officers were given greatly expanded powers of legal authority, a measure Lubbock and others supported. Hugh F. Young, concerned with the turmoil in his area, inquired whether he could "try an individual by Court martial for uttering treasonable sentiments," and both he and Hudson organized "Police Guards" for counties in their districts. Partisan ranger units, theoretically composed of men who were not subject to the draft, were mustered in the late summer of 1862 and assigned to chase shirkers. Along the Forks, Leonidas M. Martin and John S. Randolph commanded two such units created at the request of Pike. Both quickly expanded their commands to battalion strength; among Randolph's additions was a company enlisted at Gainesville under the command of James D. Young, who welcomed the chance to attack those who threatened the security of Cooke County.[36]

Perhaps the most effective foes of those who did not support the Confederacy were the provost marshals who directed local military law enforcement. Although they principally served as enrolling officers, with whom males over the age of sixteen had to register and to take an oath of loyalty to the Confederacy, they also issued passports for travel and could arrest anyone whom they considered "injurious to the interests of the country." Their authority was supposed to be analogous to that of a grand jury: if sufficient evidence of guilt was found, then the prisoner was to be sent to a military commission for trial. However, while provost courts were to be conducted "as far as practical" in accordance with procedures for civil courts, "no unnecessary delays" for "strict and technical compliance" were allowed. Provost marshals, then, could select rules they considered to be "conducive to the ends of justice," and ignore those they deemed unnecessary.[37]

35. Clarksville *Standard*, April 3, July 7, 1862; Austin *Texas Almanac Extra*, October 23, 1862; San Antonio *Herald*, October 23, 1862.

36. Hugh F. Young to Dashiell, March 31, 1862, Dashiell to Hugh F. Young, April 8, 1862, Dashiell to Hudson, June 10, 1862, all in AGR; Hugh F. Young to Lubbock, March 2, 1862, in GOR; CSR, 5th Texas Partisan Rangers; Lubbock, *Six Decades in Texas*, 382; *OR*, Ser. I, Vol. IX, 713, 717, 732; Wooster, "Texas," in *The Confederate Governors*, ed. Yearns, 203; Florence E. Holladay, "The Powers of the Commander of the Confederate Trans-Mississippi Department, 1863–1865," *SWHQ*, XXI (1918), 280; Fehrenbach, *Lone Star*, 362–63; Wright, *Texas in the War*, 201.

37. *OR*, Ser. I, Vol. IX, 715–16, 717; Clarksville *Standard*, September 13, 1862.

The instructions for provost marshals did make it clear that "no arbitrary or tyrannical acts" would be tolerated and that they could be dismissed and arraigned before a civil court, but those in remote regions had little to fear. After Hudson was appointed to command the 21st District upon Bourland's recommendation, he returned the favor by selecting Bourland as provost marshal for the area. Bourland proved to be a formidable foe for dissenters in Cooke County. He had an uncompromising nature and a violent temper. Many knew him as a "warm friend," but his victims found him to be "arbitrary" and "deadly," a "good fighter and a good hater." Bourland sought to maintain order and security with the same intensity he had displayed earlier against Indians. For that, he was despised by many in North Texas for being "as great a tyrant as ever reigned since Nero."[38]

Bourland soon became aware that the draft had become an "entering wedge" for a secret organization along the Forks devoted to avoiding conscription. Two captains who returned to Denton County in May, 1862, reported that loaded cannons had been trained on three Confederate regiments that mutinied at Corinth, Mississippi, when their initial enlistment expired, forcing them back to the lines. Such accounts enraged many North Texans, who staged protests and swore to resist the draft. Among the organizations that arose from this impulse for resistance was the Peace party, most of whose members lived in the Eastern Cross Timbers of Cooke County. A majority of those who joined were nonslaveholding farmers with little affinity for the Confederacy who wanted to remain at home to provide for their families, but a few were "unscrupulous men who deserved no quarter bent on ruin and plunder." It was the latter who fomented violent plots, alarming their neighbors and, by attracting the attention of Bourland, initiating events that would lead to tragedy.[39]

38. *OR*, Ser. I, Vol. IX, 715–16; Pete A. Y. Gunter, "The Great Gainesville Hanging, October, 1862," *Blue and Gray*, III (April–May, 1986), 50; Rogers, "Memoirs," 68; Dashiell to Bourland, December 30, 1861, in Bourland Papers; Bourland to Dashiell, January 28, 1862, and General Orders No. 15, Texas Adjutant and Inspector General's Office, June 12, 1862, in AGR; Michael Collins, *Cooke County, Texas: Where the South and the West Meet* (Gainesville, 1981), 11; Robinson, *Justice in Grey*, 395.

39. Thomas Barrett, *The Great Hanging at Gainesville* (Austin, 1961), 3; Acheson and O'Connell, eds., *Diamond's Account*, 6; Fisher, *The Yankee Conscript*, 61, 68–70; Joe T. Roff, *A Brief History of Early Days in North Texas and the Indian Territory* (Roff, Okla., 1930), 5–6; Claude Elliot, "Union Sentiment in Texas, 1861–1865," *SWHQ*, L (1947), 454. Barrett was a member of the Citizens Court during the Great Hanging. Roff moved into the Eastern Cross Timbers of Cooke County in 1861 with his family; his father was Charles L. Roff, who later served in James G. Bourland's Border Regiment.

Samuel McNutt, a carpenter from New York who had resided in Cooke County for eight years, led the first significant protest against conscription, and thus became one of Bourland's initial victims. At a meeting held at the home of Clement C. Wood—a mechanic from Tennessee—in Grayson County northeast of Gainesville, McNutt promulgated a petition against the draft even though at forty-nine years of age he was too old to be eligible (as was Wood, who was ten years younger). More than thirty people signed the declaration and allegedly sent it to the Confederate Congress. Newton J. Chance—a former resident of Kansas who had clashed often with Unionists during the secession campaign but was discharged from Confederate service twice due to disabilities—attended and gave a copy of McNutt's missive to Bourland, telling him that the meeting was clearly seditious. A contemporary later wrote that "Chance got the rong impresion as to what those mens intensions were," but moderation did not prevail. Bourland exiled McNutt from Cooke County.[40]

Bourland's actions drove organized resistance to the Confederacy underground, but Obediah B. Atkinson sustained it. Atkinson was a Mason who had been elected as second lieutenant of the Cooke County Home Guard Cavalry in June, 1861, and had retained that rank when the company was incorporated into Hudson's militia in March, 1862. Using McNutt's petition as a guide, he combed the region with the aid of several companions, initiating as many as two hundred men into the Peace party. Thomas Barrett, a Disciples of Christ minister, found a group of men discussing conscription at a grist mill. He noticed that when someone mentioned the draft, "its effect was like a spark lighting on powder"; everyone there, ex-

40. Clark, ed., *Recollections of James Clark*, 22, 95, 96, 103; James Smallwood, "Disaffection in Confederate Texas: The Great Hanging at Gainesville," *Civil War History*, XXII (1976), 351–52; Collins, *Cooke County*, 11. Samuel McNutt's wife was born in Ohio; both of their children were Texas natives. For more about him, see Texas Comptroller of Public Accounts, Ad Valorem Tax Division, County Real and Personal Property Tax Rolls, 1846–present, Cooke Cty. [hereinafter cited by county only, to wit: Cooke Cty. Tax Rolls], in Genealogy Division, TSL; Cooke County, County Clerk, Deed Record, 1850–present, II, 198, 356, 596, III, 137, 264, V, 267, in Cooke Cty. Courthouse, Gainesville, Tex.; Census of 1860, Cooke Cty. Schedule 1, F.N. 357, in TSL. Clement C. Wood's wife was from Virginia, and both their children were born in Indiana. He paid taxes in Grayson County for the first time in 1858—a year after his father died and he assumed his duties as a road overseer. In 1862 he was assessed for 221.5 acres plus 9 horses and 30 cattle. See Grayson Cty. Tax Rolls; Cooke County Commissioners' Court, "Minutes," I, 17; Census of 1860, Grayson Cty. Schedule 1, F.N. 672, in TSL.

cept him, expressed opposition. After much strong talk a man, perhaps Atkinson, declared he would organize a company to resist the draft. When Barrett confronted him, pointing out that such actions were dangerous, the man—probably realizing that his outburst in front of a possible informant was foolhardy—agreed, saying that upon reflection he had decided to drop the idea.[41]

In fact, Atkinson had not given up on the Peace party, and his efforts began to attract notice. The communities of Cooke County were isolated, but in places where people came together, such as Gainesville, information was shared and disturbing conclusions were drawn. Accurate reports of engagements and troop movements often circulated before they appeared in North Texas newspapers. Rumors flew that local members of a numerous and secret "clan" communicated regularly with Unionist conspirators in Kansas who planned to invade North Texas. Because "there were strong and mysterious things said which were not understood by the great mass of people," many settlers became fearful and demanded that Confederate authorities such as Bourland do something to restore order and provide security against this apparent threat.[42]

Bourland acted ruthlessly to restore order and security, trying to eradicate any semblance of disaffection. He arrested a "Mr. Hillier" in Cooke County for disloyalty, arraigned him before his provost court, and released him when he agreed to join the army. During the trial, Hillier's wife expressed her desire that the Federals would overrun Texas so her husband could stay at home and provide for his family. Six women—some said men dressed as women—came to her house after her husband departed and lynched her while their three young children watched. Bourland's role in this grisly affair was unclear, but suspicions mounted when he did not have the vigilantes arrested.[43]

Such brutality hardened many settlers against Bourland and led to an alarming confrontation. When the Butterfield Overland route was estab-

41. Barrett, *The Great Hanging*, 3; Clark, ed., *Recollections of James Clark*, 96; Certificate of Election of Officers of Cooke Cty. Home Guard Cavalry, June 29, 1861, and Hudson to Dashiell, May 5, 20, 1862, in AGR; Noel Parsons to author, April 25, 1989; Smallwood, "Disaffection in Confederate Texas," 351–52, 354.

42. Barrett, *The Great Hanging*, 3, 10.

43. Sumner, "Written by Sumner During the Civil War"; *Frank Leslie's Illustrated Weekly*, February 20, 1864; Wilson, *Sufferings*, 260. No official records concerning a "Mr. Hillier" survive.

lished in 1858, one of its employees, Elias J. Hawley, a young farmer from New York, settled in Gainesville with his wife, Lucretia, and her daughters. The women, being quite comely and gracious, attracted attention in the social circles of Cooke County. Soon after the war commenced, Hawley fled, leaving Lucretia "with no consolation but her wit, and no dowry but her beauty." Some of her neighbors suspected that she was a Union spy who would join her husband in Missouri when the opportunity came. In June, 1862, she, John M. Cottrell, her daughters, and A. N. Johnson—whom one of the girls had married that day—tried to leave for Missouri. Bourland refused to issue them a passport and arrested Johnson and Cottrell. A heavily armed crowd surrounded the prison in Gainesville, threatening the militia that stood guard. Bourland allowed both men to join James D. Young's partisan ranger company rather than be punished as shirkers, averting an open clash.[44]

Many in Cooke County attributed the lenient treatment of Cottrell and Johnson to the mob's demonstration, and Union sympathizers became bolder in their defiance of Bourland and other officials. During August, 1862, an advance by Indians and Federal soldiers forced the Confederates to retreat from Fort Cobb in the Indian Territory. Hudson mustered his militia and prepared for a march, but it was canceled when the enemy retreated. A significant number of settlers, however, had failed to respond to the muster, and it was rumored that others had done so with the intention of either deserting or staging a mutiny once they were near Federal lines. Their apparent success in undermining Hudson's campaign encouraged others; some openly refused to work for anyone who supported the Confederacy.[45]

Less than eighteen months after Texas seceded, Cooke County had been thrown into turmoil as dissent against secession had become defiance of the Confederacy by many settlers. Never more than nominally loyal to the nascent regime, they resented the lack of frontier defense and rebelled against sequestration, impressment, taxation, and conscription. Efforts by Bourland

44. Acheson and O'Connell, eds., *Diamond's Account*, 32, 87. For more about Elias J. Hawley and his family, see Census of 1860, Cooke Cty., Schedule 1, F.N. 333 in TSL. A. N. Johnson and John M. Cottrell may have been among the suspicious refugees who came into North Texas after the war began. The former does not appear in the census record nor the tax rolls for Cooke County, while the latter paid taxes in Cooke County for the first time in 1862 on 3 horses and 12 cattle, according to Cooke County Tax Rolls.
45. Acheson and O'Connell, eds., *Diamond's Account*, 15–16, 32, 87.

to enforce the last measure increased the vexation of disaffected settlers and facilitated the creation of the Peace party, whose members viewed Bourland and Confederate authority as the gravest threat to order and security in Cooke County. At the same time, though, a majority of the people in the county supported Bourland as both a proven leader and a representative of the Confederacy, the extant source of established legal authority. They distrusted Unionists and other dissenters and did not oppose brutal efforts by Bourland and others to combat them. Ironically, those who hoped for a return to order and security through restoration of the Union would become the targets of the bloodiest effort in American history to restore order and security through extralegal means.

THREE

The Great Hanging Begins

B y September, 1862, Confederate officials in Cooke County believed themselves to be under siege. A Union army advanced again within the Indian Territory, taking Fort Washita on September 16 and forcing the outnumbered Confederate army to retreat to Fort Arbuckle.[1] Rumors abounded of a Unionist uprising to facilitate an invasion of Texas itself. When evidence of a conspiracy to seize militia arsenals in North Texas was discovered in Gainesville, appeals for help were sent to state authorities, who could provide few troops but did authorize local leaders such as James G. Bourland to adopt drastic measures for combatting the threat of dissent. A committee chaired by Bourland ordered the arrest of numerous members of the Peace party, which was believed to be the source of the conspiracy, but the Citizens Court hanged only seven men. Angry at the tribunal's insistence on legal propriety, vigilantes lynched fourteen more prisoners in a gruesome attempt to reimpose order and security in Cooke County, bringing the initial phase of the Great Hanging to a close.

The investigation that would culminate in the Great Hanging began with a chance encounter in a Gainesville hotel. Private Jonas B. McCurley of the Denton County Rangers, a militia unit that had been incorporated into William R. Hudson's command, worked as a mail carrier along a route from Denton to Gainesville and back again. He routinely stayed overnight in the latter town before returning home. During the first week of September, 1862, he checked into a Gainesville hotel and settled down at the bar. There he talked with Ephraim Chiles, a young farmer who after several drinks asked McCurley if he was a Union man. McCurley said that he had been, and Chiles allegedly replied, "It may be that you are one still." Chiles

1. Clarksville *Standard*, September 20, 1862.

took McCurley to his room and gave him several secret signals, which of course the puzzled courier could not answer. They walked out onto the porch, where Chiles assured him that his brother, Henry, was one of the leaders of a secret party and would initiate McCurley.[2]

Ephraim Chiles revealed almost nothing about his organization to McCurley, but the latter had learned "enough . . . to excite his curiosity and his suspicion." McCurley was particularly alarmed at an allusion by Chiles to an impending attack on the militia arsenals located in Gainesville and Sherman. The next morning he started south on his route, but by the time he reached Denton County he had convinced himself that danger was afoot. He sought out a Confederate officer, who conveyed a warning back to Gainesville.[3]

Alarmed at McCurley's report, Bourland as provost marshal called several of his fellow Masons together as a vigilance committee to investigate matters. These included slaveholders James M. Peery, James J. Diamond, William C. Twitty, and Hudson. The sixth member was slaveholder Charles L. Roff, a recent arrival in Cooke County who commanded a company under Hudson and whose son was serving in the 11th Texas Cavalry. They elected to have McCurley meet with Henry Chiles to learn more about his activities.[4]

About two weeks later, McCurley returned to Gainesville on his rounds and met with the committee. He agreed to approach Chiles, a middle-aged physician who had recently emigrated from Missouri, about being initiated, and Bourland loaned him a horse to ride to the Unionist's home. McCurley told Chiles that he was looking for stray livestock, and then after more idle conversation, revealed that he had spoken to his brother earlier and that he wished to learn more about the "Union party." Chiles relaxed when McCurley mentioned his brother, and after swearing him to secrecy, told him

2. Sam Acheson and Julia Ann Hudson O'Connell, eds., *George Washington Diamond's Account of the Great Hanging at Gainesville, 1862* (Austin, 1963), 20; Thomas Barrett, *The Great Hanging at Gainesville* (Austin, 1961), 4; Card Index to Confederate Muster Rolls, in Archives Division, TSL.

3. Barrett, *The Great Hanging*, 4; Acheson and O'Connell, eds., *Diamond's Account*, 20–22.

4. Acheson and O'Connell, eds., *Diamond's Account*, 17–18, 20; CSR, 11th Texas Cavalry. Richard M. Brown, in *Strain of Violence: Historical Studies of American Violence and Vigilantism* (New York, 1975), notes that the "relationship between Freemasonry and vigilantism was frequently an intimate one" (106). Because the Masons usually recruited their members from among established community leaders, they provided leadership and a framework for organization during vigilante movements.

about a Unionist plot. He maintained that they had planned an uprising, but it had been postponed until the "Order" recruited more members. Chiles boasted that thousands in the northern and southern armies had joined, adding that he had enlisted more than fifty members himself during the last eight days. Federal authorities in Kansas kept in touch with him, he said, and when the time came, his organization would take part in an invasion of Texas from the north, to be coordinated with a landing at Galveston. The two armies would converge on Austin, where they would install a new governor. Some advocated James H. Lane, the abolitionist senator from Kansas, but Chiles said Sam Houston would probably be the most acceptable candidate.[5]

Chiles startled McCurley by declaring that all the secessionist "tories" who did not submit would be killed. The spy had readily taken an oath of secrecy, but balked when Chiles offered to give him the second degree of initiation, which involved learning the secret signs and more details regarding the nefarious schemes of the Peace party in exchange for more sanguinary vows of loyalty. McCurley tried one last feeble subterfuge to learn more without further implicating himself, asking Chiles for the names of some of the members, but Chiles suddenly became reticent, insisting that they communicated only in code and showing him a notebook filled with cryptic characters. He did translate the obligations of the members for McCurley, who noted in particular the ominous pledge "to protect and defend each other at all times and under all circumstances, even unto death."[6]

McCurley reported to Bourland and his committee that there was "nothing in this first degree to make a fuss about," but they wanted to know more about the mysterious second degree and the plans for an invasion of Texas. They had anticipated McCurley's failure of nerve and, while he was talking with Chiles, had contacted Newton J. Chance, the would-be Confederate who had betrayed Samuel McNutt to Bourland earlier in the year. Chance knew several of the men whom Bourland's committee suspected had joined the Peace party, and had already proven himself a bolder informant than McCurley. A contemporary later recalled Chance as a "man full of bone and muscle, courage and intelligence"; Thomas Barrett, who served

5. Acheson and O'Connell, eds., *Diamond's Account*, 20–22, 53; Barrett, *The Great Hanging*, 4.
6. Acheson and O'Connell, eds., *Diamond's Account*, 21; Barrett, *The Great Hanging*, 4.

as a juror on the Citizens Court, concluded after hearing his testimony that a "better man for this business would be hard to find."[7]

Chance met with Chiles along an isolated road on September 26, 1862. They rode some distance talking about the condition of the Confederate army, from which Chance had recently returned. He convinced the Unionist that although he had been a Confederate soldier, he was "not sound in the faith." When Chiles asked him if he was "pleased with the condition of things," Chance replied that he was not and added, "If you had been where I have been and seen and heard what I have, you would not be pleased yourself." Chance later testified that Chiles was "thrown completely off of his guard" by his defeatist attitude, and "bit heavy, swallowing the hook, bait and all." Chance then said he had heard rumors of a Peace party in the area, and that Chiles was the man to see about joining it. Without further ado, the two men dismounted and Chance took the oaths for both degrees of membership, which Chiles read from a scrap of paper.[8]

The secret signals revealed to Chance slavishly imitated that of more established secretive organizations, such as the Masons and the Odd Fellows, but the objectives proved to be quite different. In order to recognize a fellow member of the Peace party, one passed the fingers of the right hand slowly over the right ear, the correct response being to pass the fingers of the left hand slowly over the left ear. To confirm recognition, the group had a password, *Arizona*, and a handshake, which was a common grip with the forefinger extended and pressed on the inside of the other man's wrist. Of more interest to Chance were the pledges of each initiate "to do all he could for the north and to do all he could against the south," to reinstate the Constitution by any means necessary, to go to the aid of any member

7. Acheson and O'Connell, eds., *Diamond's Account*, 26, 45; Barrett, *The Great Hanging*, 4; Lemuel D. Clark, ed., *The Civil War Recollections of James Lemuel Clark* (College Station, Tex., 1984), 95, 101; James Smallwood, "Disaffection in Confederate Texas: The Great Hanging at Gainesville," *Civil War History*, XXII (1976), 353.

8. Barrett, *The Great Hanging*, 4; Acheson and O'Connell, eds., *Diamond's Account*, 45; Joe T. Roff, *A Brief History of Early Days in North Texas and the Indian Territory* (Roff, Okla., 1930), 7. It does seem incredible that Chance could be accepted so easily by the Peace Party. Its members, however, like many people of their period, placed a great emphasis on oaths and the inviolability of a freeman's word, and this may in part explain their trust. Unfortunately for them, Chance proved to be less concerned with the sanctity of an oath than they, or he may have justified his deception by weighing his pledge as a Confederate soldier against that given to traitors.

who was arrested, to support their families if they were lost, and to kill anyone who betrayed the Peace party.[9]

Chiles spoke freely after initiating Chance fully into the Peace party. Seeking corroboration for the charges he anticipated bringing against Chiles and his allies—a conviction for treason required two witnesses' testimony—Chance asked if he could bring his brother, Joseph, a private in Roff's company, to be initiated the next day. Chiles initially refused, then agreed after Chance convinced him that Joseph was no longer a "rabbid" secessionist. The following day Joseph took both degrees, then discussed the Peace party with his brother and Chiles. The Chances recalled that the Unionist "kept some of the most objectionable things back," but revealed enough to alarm them. He said the order had organized to resist conscription and all Confederate laws, and to protect those who still supported the Union. He repeated all that he had told McCurley but said an alternate plan might have to be implemented. The members would wait until a Federal army approached, join the state troops as they mustered, then mutiny at a prearranged signal. Success would be certain because two-thirds of the men at home on the Forks had joined, including a majority of those in Collin and Grayson counties, and they had at least six hundred allies in Austin and more in the regular Confederate army.[10]

The Chance brothers hurried to report to Bourland, traveling for safety's sake by separate routes to Gainesville. The committee that reviewed their statements differed markedly from that which had begun the investigation. Hudson was absent, a critical shift as he opposed any impetuous action by Bourland, and Diamond also was not present. But these vacancies were more than filled with the addition of slaveholders Daniel Montague, Samuel C. Doss, Bourland's son-in-law who had chaired the vigilance committee that had chased E. C. Palmer from Gainesville and who had served along with Peery in the town patrol, and Peery's father, William. These replacements for the moderate vote of Hudson created a new assembly dominated by slaveholders who strongly supported the Confederacy. Although the son of one of the men lynched at Gainesville later asserted that

9. Barrett, *The Great Hanging*, 4, 10; Acheson and O'Connell, eds., *Diamond's Account*, 22, 47–48.

10. Acheson and O'Connell, eds., *Diamond's Account*, 47–48; Barrett, *The Great Hanging*, 4; Roff, *A Brief History of Early Days*, 7; Muster and Pay Rolls for Charles L. Roff's Minute Company, Frontier Battalion, Texas State Troops, Commanded by Colonel William C. Twitty, January 7, 1863, in AGR.

"the massacre . . . was all the bloodier for Bourland's exercise of pure self-interest," the provost marshal acted with the endorsement of community leaders who shared his concerns.[11]

The committee members attacked the Peace party only after failing to obtain the intervention of state authorities. Hudson and Hugh F. Young wrote Governor Francis R. Lubbock that a plot was afoot and asked for troops to thwart the "Kansas connection." Lubbock forwarded their plea to General Paul O. Hebert, adding his observation that "marauding parties composed of Yankee Guerrillas aided by treacherous citizens" could do "much harm" on the Forks and proposing that a detachment of cavalry be posted there. Subsequent reports from Hudson convinced Lubbock that a raid by "Jay Hawkers, Indians, and others" was imminent, but despite a second request from the governor and another from John S. Ford, who forwarded a missive signed by William C. Young and Bourland, Hebert would not send troops. He needed all he had to defend the coast against Federal forces that would eventually capture Galveston during the first week of October.[12]

At Lubbock's request, Hebert did accept Hudson's brigade of state troops into Confederate service temporarily, implicitly endorsing their actions. Lubbock also assured Hudson in September that any measures taken would be fully supported by his administration. With permission from Lubbock and Hebert in hand, the vigilance committee acted quickly to suppress the expected Union uprising—which the Chances had insisted would take place soon—before it could get underway. Hudson on September 13, 1862, ordered his troops to muster under the command of Twitty to counter the

11. Clark, ed., *Recollections of James Clark*, 102; Price M. Cheaney, "William R. Hudson" (Typescript in Price M. Cheaney Papers, Morton Museum, Gainesville, Tex.); Acheson and O'Connell, eds., *Diamond's Account*, 27–28; Barrett, *The Great Hanging*, 4–7; Cooke County Commissioners' Court, "Minutes, 1857 to 1878," I, 102, typescript in Works Progress Administration Historical Records Survey, BTHC; H. A. Trexler, "Episode in Border History," *Southwest Review*, XVI (1931), 249n.

12. Francis R. Lubbock to Paul O. Hebert, September 13, 25, 1862, Lubbock to Hudson, September 25, 1862, James Paul to Dashiell, September 30, 1862, all in GOR; William C. Young and James G. Bourland to John S. Ford, September 3, 1862, and Ford to C. M. Mason, n.d., in CSR, 11th Tex. Cav.; Jeremiah Y. Dashiell to William R. Hudson, September 22, 30, 1862, in AGR; *OR*, Ser. I, Vol. LIII, 827–28; San Antonio *Herald*, October 23, 1862; Walter P. Webb, H. Bailey Carroll, and Eldon S. Branda, eds., *The Handbook of Texas* (3 vols.; Austin, 1952, 1976), I, 662–63; Marcus J. Wright, *Texas in the War*, ed. Harold B. Simpson (Hillsboro, Tex., 1965), 202.

threat of Federal invasion. Many Cooke County men, as expected, did not respond, and when the threat from the north had abated, troopers were sent to surround their homes during the night of September 30. Orders were given to arrest all those implicated by the Chances as soon it was light, as well as others who failed to answer Hudson's muster, their absence being accepted as evidence of complicity in a Unionist plot. Believing he could do nothing to avert a tragedy, Hudson absented himself and refused to carry out the arrests in person, though they were ordered in his name. Allegedly he "never got over grieving for this," but he also did not intervene.[13]

At daybreak on October 1, 1862, "every one so far as known" was arrested "in the name and by the authority of the people of the County of Cooke, State of Texas." The arrests were carried out in a pouring rain as the "heavens darkened with a raging storm cloud" from which descended, according to Barrett, "the heaviest rains I ever saw fall." Quantities of gunpowder, lead to mold bullets, and prepared cartridges were found concealed in "beds, ladies' wearing apparel & in every conceivable secret place," and were of course confiscated. Most of the men who were arrested, however, apparently did not have stores of munitions, and were puzzled by the assault from their neighbors.[14]

The militia arrested twenty in the "first grab," and by noon had about seventy prisoners corralled in a vacant store on the square in Gainesville. A few suspects escaped the dragnet, warned by loyal friends or by "Doc Edmonson" (Jonathan Edmiston), who rode his horse to death spreading the alarm. Some allegedly escaped by sheer bravado. Obediah B. Atkinson, the primary organizer of the Peace party, and a friend, John Davidson, were awakened by the sound of troops surrounding the cabin where they lay sleeping with their wives. Someone outside ordered a light to be raised in the home, but they refused. The squad was afraid to rush the house, and the inhabitants would not come out and surrender. The impasse was broken when the two men rushed out the back door of the cabin, each with a

13. Cheaney, "Hudson"; Lubbock to Hudson, September 25, 1862, in GOR; Dashiell to Hudson, September 30, 1862, in AGR; Acheson and O'Connell, eds., *Diamond's Account*, 15; Barrett, *The Great Hanging*, 7, 12; Roff, *A Brief History of Early Days*, 8; *OR*, Ser. I, Vol. XV, 818, Vol. LIII, 827–28; Trexler, "Episode in Border History," 249n. Nora Hudson Rose, daughter of William R. Hudson, and Price M. Cheaney, Hudson's granddaughter, told Trexler that Hudson was not in Gainesville at the time of the Great Hanging.

14. Acheson and O'Connell, eds., *Diamond's Account*, 29, 31; Barrett, *The Great Hanging*, 11; John E. Wheeler Diary, 1850–1880 (MS in Morton Museum).

feather mattress on his back, and escaped to Arkansas, leaving their wives behind. Others were not as fortunate: the militia shot and killed Hiram Kilborn, a Baptist lay minister, as he tried to run. A slave later recalled having helped bury him in the backwoods, but could not locate the site for the grieving family.[15]

A "most intense excitement" prevailed on the day of the arrests as "guards, prisoners, citizens, screaming women and children" streamed from every point of the compass into Gainesville. When Thomas Barrett arrived in response to a second muster order—intended to bring in every man regardless of age or condition—about eleven o'clock on the morning of October 1, he saw "crowds in sight in every direction, armed, pressing forward prisoners under guard." He estimated there were at least three or four hundred armed men in sight, and almost everyone "seemd [sic] to be unhinged." A man of some education, he later reflected poetically that "Reason had left its throne," an opinion echoed in the much less poetic reaction of Galveston *News* correspondent H. C. Stone, who arrived the next day amid "the wildest state of excitement."[16]

The prisoners remained remarkably calm despite the hysteria about them. Some were confident that their friends would rescue them, as they had pledged, and talked openly of this to the guards and bystanders. Others believed that because they were innocent of any crime, they would soon be

15. Barrett, *The Great Hanging*, 7; Acheson and O'Connell, eds., *Diamond's Account*, 30–31; Clark, ed., *Recollections of James Clark*, 75, 107–108, 109–10; Roff, *A Brief History of Early Days*, 8; William R. Hudson, "To the Hon the Legislature of the State of Texas," n.d., in Memorial and Petitions File, Archives Division, TSL; L. D. Clark, "The Great Hanging at Gainesville, October 1862," *American West* (November–December, 1984), 46; Michael Collins, *Cooke County, Texas: Where the South and the West Meet* (Gainesville, 1981), 12. Edmiston, Atkinson, and Davidson returned to Cooke County after the war ended. See Cooke County, County Clerk, List of Registered Voters, 1867–1869, in Cooke Cty. Courthouse, Gainesville, Tex. Hiram W. Kilborn, a native of Canada, was fifty-seven years of age in 1860, when the census taker reported that his property was worth $1,438. His wife was from Vermont, but three of their children, the youngest of which was eight years old, were born in Illinois. A fourth, age four, was born in Texas. Kilborn became a school trustee and a road overseer for Cooke County in September, 1858, a supervisor for the polling station at Henry Cockrum's mill in the fall of 1859 and the spring of 1860, and again for the polling station at John Ware's house in the fall of 1860 and in August, 1862. See Census of 1860, Cooke Cty., Tex., Schedule 1 (Free Inhabitants), Family Number [hereinafter cited as F.N.] 101; Cooke Cty. Commissioners' Court, "Minutes," I, 23, 28 (sheet 2), 33 (sheet 2), 52 (sheet 2), 58, and 96 (sheet 2).

16. Acheson and O'Connell, eds., *Diamond's Account*, 31; Barrett, *The Great Hanging*, 7; San Antonio *Herald*, October 25, 1862.

released; a fortunate few of them did soon regain their freedom. Reason Jones, who served as a member of the jury for the Citizens Court in Gainesville, secured the release of his brother-in-law, William C. West, who had signed Samuel McNutt's petition against conscription and had been arrested after answering a summons to come to Gainesville for the muster on October 1. West rejoined Roff's company, where he remained for the next three months until Hudson's militia was dismissed from Confederate service.[17]

Roff's company was one of three present in Gainesville on October 1, 1862. Hudson had reorganized the troopers of the 21st Brigade into three independent battalions headquartered in Cooke, Denton, and Wise counties. The "Frontier Battalion" of Cooke County, led by Twitty, had a little more than a hundred men enlisted into two companies led by Roff and A. G. Birdwell. Samuel P. C. Patton commanded the battalion from Denton County, which actually was a single company of about sixty men under the command of Captain William H. Jasper. Jasper's company arrived in Gainesville on the morning of October 1, then three days later were mustered into Confederate service by James J. Diamond, who acted as adjutant for the 21st Brigade. Together with Birdwell's and Roff's companies, they served under Twitty, who assumed the title of colonel for the "First Regiment." Twitty's troopers mingled with a flood of unattached volunteers. Because few wore uniforms, it was almost impossible to tell who belonged to a unit and who did not, but they all responded readily to the directives of provost marshal Bourland.[18]

Newton J. Chance and Alexander Boutwell, the former sheriff and saloonkeeper, held a rally on the town square during the morning of October 1, mustering support for Bourland before an official town meeting scheduled for noon. They spoke forcefully in favor of hanging all the prisoners. Barrett and others argued against violence but soon realized that a

17. Acheson and O'Connell, eds., *Diamond's Account*, 31; Clark, ed., *Recollections of James Clark*, 107–108; Muster and Pay Rolls for Charles L. Roff's Minute Company, Frontier Battalion, Texas State Troops, Commanded by Colonel William C. Twitty, January 7, 1863, in AGR.

18. David J. Eddleman, "Autobiography of the [?]" (Typescript in UNT), 41; Acheson and O'Connell, eds., *Diamond's Account*, 32–33; Muster Roll of Roff's Company, January 7, 1863, Muster Roll of William H. Jasper's Mounted Company C, October 15, 1862, January 7, 1863, Muster Roll of A. M. Birdwell's Company, January 7, 1863, Special Orders No. 1, Headquarters, 21st Brigade, Texas State Troops, October 4, 1862, Dashiell to Hudson, September 16, October 21, 1862, Hudson to Dashiell, November 4, 1862, all in AGR.

majority of the crowd of onlookers "seemed to be settling down on beginning to hang." In fact, they had already selected a large elm tree on nearby Pecan Creek, about a quarter mile east of town, to serve as a makeshift gallows. Both sides refused to yield, but the informal debate ended when a church bell rang to call the people to assemble for the town meeting.[19]

Like Barrett, many people of the public assembly opposed hanging, but supporters of Bourland, who was determined to eradicate the threat of dissent in Cooke County, dominated. Although James M. Peery served as secretary, the moderates won a small victory by electing William C. Young to chair the meeting. Young was a longtime friend of Bourland, and it was known that he was the only man to whom Bourland would listen. Young congratulated the militia on the arrests and agreed that some action must be taken, but added that he understood the object of the meeting was "to advance by proper and legitimate means the work already begun." While he expressed his wish that no man would falter in "this hour of trial," Young also said that he hoped that "wisdom & moderation" might characterize their proceedings.[20]

Anxious to keep the impending violence within reasonable bounds and to honor the proprieties of democracy and law, Young presided over the creation of a makeshift court. On a motion he appointed a council of five "good and true men, citizens of Cooke County." They were to select a dozen "good true and lawful men citizens of the county" to serve as jurors to "investigate, examine, and decide upon all cases that should be brought before them." The first appointee to the council was chief justice Ralph G. Piper, who, like Young, had opposed secession. Piper was joined by slave owners William Peery and James B. Stone, James B. Davenport, Jr.—just recently elected sheriff—and Aaron Hill. After "careful and mature deliberation," they chose jurors "not for their strong southern or secessionist predilections, or enmity toward Union men," but for "moderation, intelligence, and virtue as men and citizens." Their selections were endorsed by a general referendum, giving the sanction of democracy to the new Citizens Court.[21]

19. Barrett, *The Great Hanging*, 8; Smallwood, "Disaffection in Confederate Texas," 355.

20. Acheson and O'Connell, eds., *Diamond's Account*, 36–37; Barrett, *The Great Hanging*, 8; Pete A. Y. Gunter, "The Great Gainesville Hanging, October, 1862," *Blue and Gray*, III (April–May 1986), 50.

21. Acheson and O'Connell, eds., *Diamond's Account*, 37–38, 40; Texas Secretary of State, Election Register, 1848–1900, in Archives Division, TSL.

The twelve members of the jury—Barrett, Doss, John W. Hamill, Jeremiah E. Hughes, James Jones, Reason Jones, Wiley Jones, J. Pope Long, Montague, Benjamin Scanland, William J. Simpson, and Thomas Wright—were prosperous men well known for their community activism. Among the seven who owned slaves, Montague and Wiley Jones were county commissioners and both would be elected to the legislature in 1863, and Hughes had been a postmaster, county clerk, justice of the peace, and tax assessor and collector before the war, and was appointed to collect Confederate taxes in 1862. Barrett, another slave owner, was a minister of the Disciples of Christ church—the only denomination not to divide over slavery—while Hamill, a nonslaveholder, was a Southern Methodist minister who staunchly supported his church's stand against abolitionism. They were all too old for the draft and none had been in the Confederate army. However, Doss, the youngest at thirty-six, had equipped some of his employees for their enlistment and allegedly hired a substitute, and Simpson was a member of a company in Hugh F. Young's 15th Brigade of Texas State Troops.[22]

Resolutions were passed at the town meeting authorizing the Citizens Court to convict and sentence defendants, to set its own meeting time and place, to keep its proceedings secret, and to appoint a bailiff and a constable. Chief justice Piper would swear in all who testified, as well as the members of the court. Prisoners had the right to employ counsel (although there is no record that any of them did so) and to subpoena and cross-examine witnesses. Piper administered an oath to the jurors immediately after the town meeting adjourned, and they organized by appointing him and James M. Peery as clerks and William W. Bourland, the provost marshal's son and a veteran of Young's 11th Texas Cavalry, as constable. Piper also served along with Hill, militia captain Cincinnatus Potter, and James E. Sheegog, a planter and former county commissioner who had two sons serving in the 11th Texas Cavalry, as a committee of inquiry to examine all witnesses and record their testimony. Completing its preparations by electing Montague as foreman and choosing to meet in the upper floor of the store rented by the county court, the jury adjourned until the next day.[23]

22. Acheson and O'Connell, *Diamond's Account*, 38–42; Barrett, *The Great Hanging*, 8; Texas Secretary of State, Election Register; Card Index to Confederate Muster Rolls; Carter E. Boren, *Religion on the Texas Frontier* (San Antonio, 1968), 3–5, 32–33, 45, 50; Buckley B. Paddock, ed., *A Twentieth Century History and Biographical Record of North and West Texas* (2 vols.; Chicago, 1906), I, 669–70; Walter N. Vernon, *Methodism Moves Across North Texas* (Dallas, 1967), 91.
23. Acheson and O'Connell, eds., *Diamond's Account*, 39, 43; Barrett, *The Great Hanging*,

Consciously or not, the vigilantes in Gainesville had followed the tradition of American vigilantism closely. The democratic and legalistic formalities observed by the mob in the initial organization of the Citizens Court reflect the conservatism of vigilantism, both there and elsewhere. Concerned for order and security, the vigilantes in Cooke County argued, then and later, that the overwhelming magnitude of the threat posed by the Peace party required immediate action, which the legal authorities of Texas and the Confederacy had authorized them to take. Having made the decision to support extralegal efforts to restore order and security, the vigilantes in Cooke County sought to uphold at least the spirit of American law by confirming each step through popular sovereignty, by involving many prominent members of the community, and by allowing the accused to have the same rights as a prisoner arraigned before a regular court.[24]

The members of the Citizens Court and many others who gathered in Gainesville feared that Unionists still at large would attempt to rescue their comrades. A double line of sentinels was posted around the county seat on the night of October 1, and squads were sent to comb the countryside for suspicious groups. Hudson J. Esman, a member of the Peace party, had passed unchallenged into the town in the excitement of the day and observed preparations for defense. He knew a Unionist attack would be planned, and realized it would be folly with the number of armed men present. When night fell he requested a pass to go through the lines, but was refused. Undaunted, he removed his hat, boots, and coat, and crawled a half mile across the prairie that night to where his horse was pastured.[25]

As he expected, Esman found a nighttime meeting of settlers in the Eastern Cross Timbers who were "noisy to be led on to the assistance of their friends." They had convened at the request of Rama Dye, a former Peters Colonist who ironically had spent the day guarding prisoners in Gainesville. Dye was distraught about the arrest of M. D. Harper—a "resolute and

8; Texas Secretary of State, Election Register. Cincinnatus Potter had been elected captain of a company from the seventh precinct in William R. Hudson's 21st Brigade, Texas State Troops. See Hudson to Dashiell, May 5, 1862, in AGR.

24. Brown, *Strain of Violence*, 4, 45–49, 56, 59–61, 93, 109; Michael Feldberg, *The Turbulent Era: Riot and Disorder in Jacksonian America* (New York, 1980), 74, 90–91; Dickson D. Bruce, Jr., *Violence and Culture in the Antebellum South* (Austin, 1979), 87; John R. Ross, "At the Bar of Judge Lynch: Lynching and Lynch Mobs in America" (Ph.D. dissertation, Texas Tech University, 1983), 16–21, 76–78.

25. Acheson and O'Connell, eds., *Diamond's Account*, 78, 81; Barrett, *The Great Hanging*, 8–9, 11.

uncompromising" organizer of the Peace party—and had called the meeting that night to discuss a rescue. At least two dozen other men came and decided, at the suggestion of physician James T. Foster, to send Dye and John W. Morris to try a stealthy release of Harper and the other prisoners. After Esman convinced them that it would be "madness" to approach the town, some wanted to surrender. Others advocated flight, while a few argued in favor of a "bushwhacking" campaign. A determined minority elected Dye as their captain and planned to convene again the next night. Isham W. Welch was sent to confirm the number of militia in town, while Henry Cockrum was dispatched toward the Red River to make contact with allies in that direction. The decision not to flee proved tragic; only three returned the following night, and fifteen of those present at the first meeting were hanged in Gainesville within a few weeks.[26]

The early arrest of Harper and other prominent Unionists left any potential rescuers without effective leaders. The sole exception was a company of state troops from the 21st Brigade commanded by the "Rev. Captain" Hydeman P. Garrison, a reputed Northern Methodist minister whose residence in Cooke County "had inspired his neighbors with more fear of his villainies than respect for his Christianity," according to a Confederate sympathizer. He led about seventy men toward Gainesville on the night of October 1. A militia squad led by a lieutenant who knew him approached when they were no more than eight miles east of the town. The lieutenant tried to speak with Garrison, but beat a hasty retreat when he was met with an order to "hush" and the clicking of gun hammers. Garrison continued to advance until a courier brought Esman's report to him. The doughty Unionist reluctantly withdrew into the brush along the Red River and dis-

26. Acheson and O'Connell, eds., *Diamond's Account*, 62, 77–79, 82; Barrett, *The Great Hanging*, 9. Those identified as being present at the first meeting include: William B. Anderson, Benjamin C. Barnes, Barnibus Burch, Henry Cockrum, Arphax R. Dawson, Rama Dye, Hudson J. Esman, James T. Foster, Curd Goss, William W. Johnson, David M. Leffel, John B. Miller, John W. Morris, James A. Powers, and Gilbert Smith, all of whom were later executed, and Obediah B. Atkinson, William Boyles, Robert O. Duncan, Harry Gilman, Moses Powers, S. Snodgrass, John Ware, Isham W. Welch, and John M. Wiley. Frederick W. Sumner may also have been present; he wrote that he and several other Unionists from Grayson County joined a company in Cooke County on the night of October 1 that disbanded after being told the number of militia in Gainesville. See Frederick W. Sumner, "Written by F. W. Sumner During the Civil War, 1860–1865" (Typescript in Sherman Historical Museum, Sherman, Tex.); Thomas Wilson, *Sufferings Endured for a Free Government* (Washington, D.C., 1864), 260.

banded his troopers. Meanwhile, the lieutenant rode hard to reach Gainesville and sound the alarm, whereupon the militia there were assembled into battle formation in the streets and ordered to lie upon their arms all night.[27]

Frightened Confederate sympathizers in Gainesville believed that "nothing but the overpowering numbers" in arms prevented a bloody raid that night, and they welcomed the arrival of reinforcements during the next few days. The first was a Grayson County company from Hugh F. Young's 15th Brigade of state troops, led by Captain John Russell, formerly of the 11th Texas Cavalry. After Lubbock wrote Colonel Douglas H. Cooper, commander of the Confederate troops in the Indian Territory, asking him to send assistance to Gainesville, a pair of partisan ranger companies—which would be mustered into Leonidas M. Martin's 10th Texas Cavalry Battalion on October 23—arrived under the command of Captains Abner M. Marshall and John K. Bumpass on October 5. Captain Nicholas Wilson led Company B of the 29th Texas Cavalry, which was commanded by editor Charles DeMorse, into Gainesville two days later. Several of these units had been recruited on the Forks: Bumpass' company in Grayson and Collin counties, and Wilson's in Cooke and Denton counties. With their support, Bourland soon turned Gainesville into a military camp.[28]

The arrival of reinforcements permitted additional arrests, which continued for thirteen days and nights until no fewer than 150 men had been captured. Many of them were members of Dye's group and other similar cliques, loosely associated through the Peace party network. Some, like Arphax R. Dawson and James A. Ward, had tried to flee the state but found their way across the Red River blocked by unseasonably high water brought on by the deluge of October 1. Others were victims of circumstance. Henry Chiles had told the Chance brothers that communications with the Federal army were conducted through couriers traveling to St. Louis on pretext of

27. Acheson and O'Connell, eds., *Diamond's Account*, 33–34; Barrett, *The Great Hanging*, 8–9. On March 29, 1862, Garrison had been elected captain of a militia company in Hudson's 21st Brigade. See Hudson to Dashiell, May 5, 1862, in AGR.

28. Barrett, *The Great Hanging*, 9; CSR, 5th Texas Partisan Rangers, and 29th Texas Cavalry; Hugh F. Young to Dashiell, June 1, 1862, in AGR; Mamie Yeary, ed., *Reminiscences of the Boys in Gray, 1861–1865* (Dallas, 1912), 70, 99, 100, 134, 351–52, 634–35, 830–32; Wheeler Diary; Acheson and O'Connell, eds., *Diamond's Account*, 32–33; Austin *Texas Almanac Extra*, October 25, 1862; Dallas *Herald*, December 20, 1862; Bradford K. Felmly and John C. Grady, *Suffering to Silence: 29th Texas Cavalry, C.S.A., Regimental History* (Quanah, Tex., 1975), 37, 49, 51, 54, 57; Jacob L. Stambaugh and Lillian J. Stambaugh, *A History of Collin County, Texas* (Austin, 1958), 267; Wright, *Texas in the War*, 31–32.

business. At the time of the arrests, an alleged member of the Peace party was traveling to St. Louis. Bourland's committee assumed he was going to contact Union authorities in Kansas, and he was arrested on his way home by their order.[29]

The prisoners who were brought before the Citizens Court were confronted by a dangerously biased jury from which there was no appeal. The jurors acted unilaterally, relying for authority on the communications from Lubbock and Hebert, the endorsement of the town meeting, and the oaths administered by Piper, a county judge who according to Texas law could hang no one and who had surrendered his courtroom to vigilantes. They chose to convict on a majority vote, an ominous development as more than half of them—as slaveholders and supporters of the Confederacy—had definite biases against the accused. Most of the prisoners were farmers who had never owned slaves, which fostered suspicions that they secretly harbored abolitionist sentiments. Too, a majority of them were eligible for the draft but refused to enlist. While not all the jury were "ultra men," there were at least three who were "rabid secessionists" or "very bitter against the accused." They proved persuasive, and Barrett found himself virtually alone in his determination not to execute anyone. He accepted the appointment, however, because he feared for his own safety; he slept on the floor of a friend's house in Gainesville rather than stay in a hotel.[30]

The jurors were not entirely insensitive to pleas for mercy by family members and friends of the accused. A majority of the men tried by the Citizens Court were acquitted, principally due to the staunch determination of William C. Young—who conducted the examination of prisoners before the jury—to ensure that some standards of justice were upheld. The impassioned speech of Elizabeth Woolsey, a widow who had two sons in the Confederate army and two more at home who had been arrested, particularly moved the jury, and they released her boys. Barrett successfully argued for the release of an unfortunate man who had been drafted to guard prisoners and then found himself mistakenly jailed in the excitement.[31]

29. Acheson and O'Connell, eds., *Diamond's Account*, 46–48; Barrett, *The Great Hanging*, 7, 10–11; Malissa C. Everett, "A Pioneer Woman," *WTHA Yearbook*, III (1927), 64; Austin *Texas Almanac Extra*, October 25, 1862.

30. George H. Ragsdale, "Texas War History Written in 1892" (Typescript in George H. Ragsdale Papers, BTHC); Barrett, *The Great Hanging*, 8–9; William S. Oldham and George W. White, comps., *A Digest of the General Statute Laws of the State of Texas* (Austin, 1859), 79–81, 107.

31. Barrett, *The Great Hanging*, 7, 9, 11; Everett, "A Pioneer Woman," 63–64; Texas

The Citizens Court tried the alleged leaders of the Peace party first, beginning with Henry Chiles, who treated the entire affair with evident contempt. When brought before the jury, he refused Montague's offer of legal counsel, then denied that the Citizens Court had proper jurisdiction. Montague replied that they took their authority from "the unanimous voice of the people," and asked if Chiles was ready for trial. The Unionist countered, "Probably as ready now as I shall ever be," and listened to a long list of indictments read by Montague. The accusations included treason, which Montague defined as colluding with "other evil disposed persons" to incite "open and hostile opposition to the Civil Authorities," and conspiracy, a charge that stemmed from his "advising the killing of good citizens, the destruction of property, [and] the disturbing of the public peace, contrary to the public safety and the peace and welfare of the people" of Texas and Cooke County.[32]

Chiles pled not guilty to all the charges, but damning evidence against him was presented by Newton Chance, who repeated the details of their meeting. Many members of the Peace party, some of whom had clashed earlier with Chance, had chastised Chiles for initiating the brothers, but he continued to believe that they had converted to Unionism. Chiles conversed freely with Chance after his arrest, unaware or incredulous of what was to come, and others appealed to Chance to intervene for them, or asked for his advice on their testimony. Even under the shadow of the hanging tree, some "addressed their last words to him as a friend." The informant was unmoved by their trust; when Chiles cross-examined him, the result only confirmed the determination of the Citizens Court to see the Unionist hang.[33]

Chance's statements were corroborated by a parade of witnesses against Chiles, many of whom testified in the vain hope that they would be spared. Alexander D. Scott, like Chance, had been sworn into the Peace party by Chiles, and he agreed that the defendant had said that the objective of the organization was murder and robbery, if such was necessary to restore the

Comptroller of Public Accounts, Ad Valorem Tax Division, County Real and Personal Property Tax Rolls, 1846–present, Cooke County, in Genealogy Division, TSL; Census of 1860, Cooke Cty., Schedule 1, F.N. 376; Graham Landrum and Allen Smith, *An Illustrated History of Grayson County, Texas* (2d ed.; Fort Worth, 1967), 64.

32. Acheson and O'Connell, eds., *Diamond's Account*, 44; Wheeler Diary; Barrett, *The Great Hanging*, 9, 13.

33. Acheson and O'Connell, eds., *Diamond's Account*, 44, 46–49, 53, 55; Clark, ed., *Recollections of James Clark*, 95, 101.

old Union. Chiles spoke in his own defense, insisting that the Peace party was only for "the purpose of protecting life and property and to prevent the shedding of blood, mobs, Jay-hawking, etc." He denied that it had secret signs, but the jurors did not believe him. He listened "attentively" as they returned a verdict of guilty, then became noticeably lethargic when they sentenced him to death. At his own request, he was permitted to submit a statement recanting most of his previous testimony. A perceptive witness attributed his "strange indifference" to the "novelty of the proceedings" and perhaps a "still buoyant hope of intervention," but noted that the prisoner had not realized the "determined and resolute character of the tribunal."[34]

The Citizens Court sentenced Chiles to be hanged two days after his conviction, on October 4, but he was executed within a few hours of being turned over to the militia. Bob Scott, a trusted slave whose master gave him charge of the family when he left to enlist in the Confederate army, proudly drove the wagon that conveyed the prisoners away from the makeshift jail, down California Street, and to the elm tree outside of town where they were hanged. The cortege bearing Chiles pushed slowly through the "rushing, crowding throngs of people" surrounding the soldiers arranged in a hollow square around the tree. Chiles was pale and trembling as Boutwell, who served as executioner for almost all the hangings, read aloud the order of execution signed by Montague. When he finished, Scott drove the wagon from under Chiles, who swung in the air "while the branches of the obstinate and unyielding elm trembled like an aspen under the weight and shuddering motion of the dying man."[35]

Ephraim Chiles, the unwary Unionist whose imprudent talk had prompted Bourland's investigation, was tried immediately after his brother and just as quickly executed. The jury regarded him as one of the more zealous members of the Peace party, and they entertained no motions to release him. Although he was several years younger than his brother and "decidedly more affable and companionable," he was known for being "dangerous when angry." McCurley and others testified that he was active in spreading the secret signs of the organization, and Henry Chiles himself stated that he initiated Ephraim. After the older brother was suspended for

34. Acheson and O'Connell, eds., *Diamond's Account*, 49–51.

35. *Ibid.*, 52–53, 58; Wheeler Diary, x; Clark, ed., *Recollections of James Clark*, 102, 108–109; Gainesville (Tex.) *Register*, February 2, 1926; A. Morton Smith, *The First 100 Years in Cooke County* (San Antonio, 1955), 37.

an hour, Boutwell cut the body down and hanged Ephraim in his place.[36]

The Citizens Court tried Henry S. Field, a shoemaker, after they condemned the Chiles brothers. Henry Chiles had admitted that he initiated Field, and a neighbor recalled a conversation in which Field unwisely asserted that if conscription were expanded to include men his age, he would rather hang than serve in the army. Field had also intemperately applauded General Benjamin F. Butler's infamous proclamation, made during his occupation of New Orleans, that any female who showed contempt for a soldier of the United States Army would be treated "as a woman of the town plying her occupation," and carried with him a newspaper containing the edict. Field denied being a member of the Peace party but, after being returned before the jury, admitted that he had taken the first degree from Chiles and "afterwards did go through" a full initiation. He insisted he would have confessed earlier, before the arrests, but was afraid.[37]

Because Field was not executed until October 4 he had some time to prepare a will, which he filed the day before his death in the presence of two witnesses, Boutwell and Newton Chance. Field gave some of his livestock to his daughter, Lydia, who had married William A. McCool—soon to be captured by James D. Young—in February, 1861, and left the rest of his possessions to his wife, Mary Ann. For himself, Field requested only that his body be "decently and privately buried in the yard near my residence, with as little expense as may be." Under the elm, he made a long speech, which he addressed to Chance, confessing that he was a full member of the organization. Perhaps reflecting on his own desire for order and security, he declared the verdict against him was fair because the Peace party contained some dangerous elements, and forgave the jury, allegedly saying, "Go on with the work you have so fearlessly begun."[38]

Henry Chiles had been initiated by Harper and testified to that effect in Harper's trial, along with several others. When Harper was taken before the Citizens Court after Field, it became obvious that he had lost control of the Peace party soon after participating in its birth. He knew few of the details of its plans, far less, for example, than Chiles. Harper admitted that

36. Acheson and O'Connell, eds., *Diamond's Account*, 56–58; Wheeler Diary.

37. Acheson and O'Connell, eds., *Diamond's Account*, 64–65; *Congressional Record*, 64th Cong., 1st Sess., LIII, 1018.

38. Cooke County, County Clerk, Probate Record and Minutes, Vol. I: 1849–1871, p. 325, in Cooke Cty. Courthouse; Acheson and O'Connell, eds., *Diamond's Account*, 64–65; Wheeler Diary; *Congressional Record*, 64th Cong., 1st Sess., LII, 1018.

he was a "Union man" who "desired the restoration of the old government," but added, "I was grieved to know that my efforts to resist the march of secession have led to results ruinous to the peace and happiness of the community in which I live." He would not admit that a "desire or an honest effort to reestablish the Union could be termed criminal," but asked clemency for promoting the organization, saying that he did not approve its objectives. Despite his demurrer, the jury condemned him to hang. Harper, shocked by their actions, shed his humble demeanor and shouted defiance at the jurors as he was led from the courtroom. He was hanged after Field on October 4.[39]

Leander W. P. "Jacob" Lock, another organizer of the Peace party, was condemned next by the Citizens Court after many witnesses spoke against him. Jackson H. Mounts testified that he and five others, including William B., George W., and Richard J. Anderson, had been initiated together by Lock. C. F. Anderson said Lock swore him in and then told him that the organization was for mutual protection when the Federal army came, for which they would use the munitions arsenal in Sherman. Lock took the stand in his own defense, saying that he and Mounts had initiated each other in turn and together had organized the Peace party—whose signs and password Lock had devised—as a protective society, not to attack their neighbors.[40]

Lock's testimony was halting and incomplete, indicating that he, like Harper, knew little apart from his own actions and had lost touch with the more radical factions of the organization. For example, he insisted that there was another order, with the same secret signs, with the design of breaking up both armies in the event of an invasion. After he was condemned, he sent for Hamill and Barrett to visit him in the makeshift jail. Several of the prisoners had been pressing Lock to make a confession, perhaps in the hope of expiating themselves, but he hesitated to violate the oaths he had sworn. The two ministers failed to convince him to break the oaths, and he was hanged without further discussion on October 7, demonstrating under the elm tree "that defiance of death that usually seizes hold on the last moments of a depraved, wicked, and abandoned heart."[41]

The next day, October 8, Boutwell hanged William W. Morris. He had

39. Acheson and O'Connell, eds., *Diamond's Account*, 61–63; Wheeler Diary.
40. Acheson and O'Connell, eds., *Diamond's Account*, 66–67.
41. *Ibid.*, 66–68; Wheeler Diary.

pled guilty to the charge of treason and made a statement to the jury in which he confessed that he had been initiated, along with William W. Wernell and Thomas B. Floyd, by Harper, who told them that the organization had begun in the Federal army, then moved south. Like many others introduced to the Peace party by Harper, Morris understood that their objective was to defend themselves using the munitions at Sherman if a Union army invaded North Texas. The ultimate goal, he declared, was to reconstruct "the old Constitution and Union of the United States."[42]

The routine of the Citizens Court was interrupted on October 10 when James T. Foster, a physician who had been imprisoned after the fateful meeting in the Cross Timbers, tried to escape from his guards as he was being escorted from the courtroom. Harvey Howeth, who had enlisted in the 16th Texas Cavalry but returned and joined Roff's company, shot him at close range and the doctor lived for only a few hours. He was not the only prisoner shot while under guard; Floyd, Morris' companion, was also killed as he tried to flee. The excitement did not hinder the proceedings for long; that day Boutwell hanged his seventh prisoner, Edward D. Hampton, who scarcely had time to complete his will before being led to the elm. With his executioner standing nearby as witness, Hampton, "knowing that death is certain," bequeathed half of his estate to Alexander Scott and the remainder to the heirs of the widow Woolsey.[43]

The summary condemnation of seven men horrified Barrett, who had won a few allies as he continued to oppose the hangings. Their efforts had so far been fruitless; as Barrett recalled, they "had as well tried to build a dam across Red River in a time of high water with straw, as to resist and control the excitement in the jury-room." When Barrett proposed surrendering the guilty prisoners to the proper authorities and releasing those who obviously knew little of the organization, other members of the jury tried and failed to have him expelled. He exploded in a melodramatic, if not eloquent, tirade after the sentencing of an eighth man to hang, challenging his fellow jurors either to mend their ways or to hang everyone in the jail and have done with it. He ended in tears, and as he sat down, Long rose to

42. Acheson and O'Connell, eds., *Diamond's Account*, 69; Wheeler Diary.

43. Cooke County, County Clerk, Probate Papers, 1849–present, Box 6, and Cooke County Probate Record and Minutes, I, 331; CSR, 16th Texas Cavalry, C.S.A.; Wheeler Diary; Acheson and O'Connell, eds., *Diamond's Account*, 72, 86, 89; Muster and Pay Rolls of Roff's Company, January 7, 1863, in AGR.

leave. Two others begged Barrett not to break the jury, as that would set in motion a mob reaction that might indeed precipitate the deaths of all of the remaining prisoners.[44]

Barrett and Long agreed to remain if the jurors would assent to convict on a two-thirds vote, which they did on the advice of Piper. The eighth man's sentence was reversed because the jury could not muster a two-thirds vote against him, and he was given over to the military authorities for release. Barrett did not act from pure altruism when he elected to stay. He had already received death threats, and it had become obvious that if a mob did form, he might well become a victim as he had opposed the hangings and had contributed to the release of several prisoners. He did achieve his purpose; after adopting the two-thirds rule, the original jurors for the Citizens Court never again condemned a prisoner to hang.[45]

A confrontation on the streets of Gainesville between Barrett and another man, to whom he referred as "a desperate character, and a man of influence" who wanted all the prisoners hanged, forced the jury to adopt protective measures to shield the stubborn minister and other moderate members. The man tried to remove Barrett from the jury after witnessing his emotional speech following the execution of seven men. Failing in that, he confronted him one evening after a long day of deliberations, intimating that the minister might be taken to the hanging tree soon if he did not cooperate. Barrett reported the incident, and the jury declared that anyone could watch when testimony was given, but when they argued a case or cast a vote the courtroom had to be cleared. The man who threatened Barrett later became a close friend and admitted the wisdom of his attempt to stop the affair, but in the tense atmosphere of October, 1862, the jury could not afford to gamble on a sudden change of heart.[46]

After over a week of testimony the jurors had learned much about the Peace party, but they believed there was more to be divined and were anxious to do so. One of the men who had taken part in the arrests and trials of the suspected Unionists met with the jury and proposed a dastardly plan. He would bring a prisoner who appeared to be prominent in the organization before the jury, who would offer him freedom in return for a confes-

44. Barrett, *The Great Hanging*, 13–14; Missouri Ann Barrett Dustin, "The Early Days of Cook County, Texas" (Typescript in BTHC). Dustin is Thomas Barrett's daughter.
45. Dustin, "The Early Days of Cook County"; Barrett, *The Great Hanging*, 13–14, 15.
46. George H. Ragsdale, "An Incident of the Civil War" (MS in Ragsdale Papers), and "Texas War History Written in 1892"; Barrett, *The Great Hanging*, 15–16.

sion. Once he had given the jurors the information they wanted, he would be set free, and the conspirator pledged to "attend to him before he got home." After the man finished his proposal, Montague asked if the jurors had any comment. There was a tense silence, then Barrett remarked that he had understood the gentleman to say he would kill the prisoner after his release. When the visitor did not respond, indicating the grim truth of Barrett's assumption, the minister angrily declared that he would rather have his right arm amputated than to assent to such a heinous deception. The man withdrew his proposal and left.[47]

The crowds in the streets of Gainesville became hostile over the slow deliberations of the Citizens Court. An informant warned Barrett one evening after supper, as he was returning for a late session, that all of the prisoners in the makeshift jail would be taken and shot that night. Barrett told his fellow jurors, who quickly tried and released over a dozen prisoners in an effort to put them beyond the reach of a mob. While the jury met, a group of men approached the prison and told the doorkeeper that the jury had asked for the prisoners who were inside. He opened the door and told his charges to prepare to go before the jury, but some of the mob broke ranks, apparently losing their stomach for the subterfuge. The guard quickly relocked the door, and others dissuaded the mob from its design. Later that evening a larger group approached and demanded the key. When the guard refused to surrender it, they threatened to break the door down. He drew his pistol, forcing them "after considerable talk and hard words" to withdraw. They found a victim at the less carefully watched town jail. Its sole inmate, accused of being a deserter and a horse thief, was taken from his cell and lynched.[48]

By Saturday evening, October 11, the jurors had reviewed all of the cases before them. Only seven had been condemned to hang; a few had been given to the military authorities, but most had been set free after the shift from a majority to a two-thirds vote for conviction. The excitement outside had apparently subsided, but the jurors decided to retain the rest of the prisoners until the next Saturday, when emotions would have abated even more. An informant leaked the news of their decision, and a mob formed and sent two spokesmen into the courtroom. The pair demanded twenty prisoners to be hanged, or they would kill everyone in the prison. Barrett,

47. Barrett, *The Great Hanging*, 14.
48. *Ibid.*, 15; Ragsdale, "Incident of the Civil War."

ever mindful of the earlier threats against him and observing that the soldiers were doing nothing to protect the jury, held his tongue. Piper gave a list of the prisoners to one of the men. He chose only fourteen names, then handed the list back to Piper to mark them at his dictation. The two men went next to the makeshift jail, called the fourteen condemned men aside, led them to a separate room, and told them they would be hanged the next day.[49]

Once the two had left, the jurors discussed among themselves what should be done. To Barrett and others, it was obvious that they could not defy the mob by sending the prisoners elsewhere; they would be murdered before they left Gainesville. Furthermore, if opposed, the mob might indulge in "wholesale killing," and it had become apparent that military officials such as Bourland, whether they had ordered the hanging of the fourteen (as Barrett suspected) or not, would do nothing to prevent more deaths. None of the prisoners released earlier had been harmed, so it was agreed to leave the rest in jail until the next Saturday as planned, with the expectation that they also would not be molested after the mob had eliminated the fourteen that they apparently believed were the most dangerous. With that decided, the Citizens Court adjourned, and Barrett went home for the first time since the trials began.[50]

The fourteen selected for lynching were a diverse group, united primarily by their refusal to support the Confederacy. Four—C. F. and George W. Anderson, Dye, and William Wernell—had been implicated during earlier trials. Three others had attended the nighttime meeting called by Dye on October 1: Benjamin C. Barnes, Henry Cockrum, and James A. Powers, who may also have been singled out because he was Obediah B. Atkinson's brother-in-law. Abraham McNeese was a captain in Hudson's 21st Brigade who had been quite vocal in opposing secession. William R. Rhodes had left the Frontier Regiment after enlisting in the spring of 1862, perhaps deserting, while Samuel Carmichael had been outspoken against the Confederacy and had refused to march to Fort Cobb in August. A reporter for the St. Louis *Republic* later wrote that Carmichael was a "big, strappin' fellow, not afraid of the devil, and he cussed 'em to the last." Nathaniel M. Clark, like McNeese, had opposed secession, but the last three—Thomas O. Baker, C. A. Jones, and Elliot M. Scott—had apparently done little to single themselves out.[51]

49. Barrett, *The Great Hanging*, 16.
50. *Ibid.*, 16–17.
51. St. Louis *Republic*, March 4, 1894; Acheson and O'Connell, eds., *Diamond's Account*,

Boutwell lynched the fourteen selected by the mob in two groups, three on a chilly Sunday, October 12, the rest on Monday, which proved to be little warmer. The first morning, Jacob Dye, county commissioner and a former treasurer for Cooke County, summoned Barrett to talk to his brother. Rama was spared that day, so Barrett left him and sat on the porch of W. W. Foreman's hotel to watch the condemned go by, a ritual he repeated the next day. He noted that the crowd watching the hangings had shrunk; women, including family members, had been banned from attending executions as their grief had proven too disruptive. Dye wrote a will, leaving all to his wife of little more than a year, Mary Ann, and his three children, and appointing Jacob as his executor. Carmichael sold his horses and mules on October 13 and gave the receipt and a will to Boutwell for filing. He made his wife, Anna, his sole heir and executor and directed her to retain Hughes as a legal representative to collect all his debts from Confederates, a final gesture to his tormentors. Clark wrote to his relatives, asking them to exact no vengeance for his death. His final words reflected resignation: "Prepare yourself to live and die. I hope to meet you all in a future world. God bless you."[52]

Having disposed of what they perceived as an imminent threat from the Peace party, the Citizens Court scattered, along with the troops and vigilantes outside the makeshift courtroom. They had killed twenty-four men in just one week, less than a third of whom were actually condemned by the Citizens Court and none of whom had been adjudged by an established legal authority. Once more, when the people of Cooke County were threatened, they had resorted to vigilantism to restore order and stability. Sadly, the violence during these seven days had only set the stage for subsequent grisly acts, as unexpected events led to the virtual abandonment of formality and the expansion of the Great Hanging from Gainesville into surrounding communities.

75, 76, 77–78; Clark, ed., *Recollections of James Clark*, 16, 52; Noel Parsons to author, April 25, 1989.

52. Clark, ed., *Recollections of James Clark*, 35; Sarah I. S. Rogers, "Memoirs" (Typescript in Morton Museum), 53; Wheeler Diary; Acheson and O'Connell, eds., *Diamond's Account*, 76; Barrett, *The Great Hanging*, 17, 18; Cooke County, County Clerk, Deed Record 1850–present, V, 560, in Cooke Cty. Courthouse; Cooke Cty. Probate Record and Minutes, I, 329–30, 330–31, 338, 343–44; Cooke Cty. Probate Papers, Box 20; Texas Secretary of State, Election Register; Clark, "The Great Hanging," 45–49; Smith, *First 100 Years*, xxxiii.

FOUR

Reaping the Whirlwind

The uneasy peace that settled over Cooke County following the adjourn-
ment of the Citizens Court was shattered by the murder of Colonel
William C. Young on Thursday, October 16, 1862. In the ensuing hysteria,
moderate jurors were replaced, legal formalities were waived, and a more
vengeful Citizens Court reversed the acquittal of nineteen prisoners and
lynched them. Provost marshal James G. Bourland ordered the arrest of
dozens more in adjacent counties before Confederate and state courts intervened to bring a halt to civilian involvement in the Great Hanging. The
killing did not end there, however, but continued under the direction of
zealous Confederate officers such as John S. Randolph and James D. Young,
the late colonel's son. By the time the Great Hanging ran its course, the
effort to restore order and security by vigilantism in Cooke County had
degenerated into a vengeful vendetta that sparked even more dissension
among a substantial proportion of settlers, sowing a legacy of continuing
violence along the North Texas frontier.

In mid-October, 1862, James A. Dickson, a consumptive who was exempt from military service, was hunting with his young brother-in-law and
an older man in the bottoms along Hickory Creek, a tributary of the Red
River, when they saw a man on horseback ride away from them into a
thicket. When the hunters approached, several men fired from ambush,
killing Dickson. The older man told the younger to ride south to bring help
while he rode to the settlement near Young's house to sound the alarm.
Dickson's brother-in-law led a posse back to Dickson's body, which they
found lying under an oak with his hat over his face, his arms crossed, and
his rifle laid across his torso. Without investigating further, they carried the
corpse to his family.[1]

1. John E. Wheeler Diary, 1850–1880 (MS in Morton Museum, Gainesville, Tex.);

Meanwhile, the older man alerted William C. Young, who assembled a group of armed men that included Bourland and led them up the east bank of Hickory Creek, across from where Dickson had been killed. The ground was broken and brushy, perfect for an ambush, and as the posse crossed a ridge a sniper toppled Young from his horse with a shot over his right eye. Allegedly the only reason more of the searchers were not killed in the attack, conducted by as many as twenty or thirty men, was that persistent rain caused many of the attackers' guns to misfire. Young's followers scrambled for cover, allowing the killer to escape. They sent for a wagon to carry Young home, but he died on the way.[2]

Barrett was in Gainesville when the news came of Dickson's death, which everyone believed had been perpetrated by members of the Peace party. The immediate reaction among most of the citizens and soldiers present was to kill the prisoners who were still in the makeshift jail, but Barrett and others dissuaded them. The reports of Young's death did not reach the county seat until the following day, sparking renewed demonstrations of anger and fear. During the trials, Young had tried to limit the violence and had even released three men on his own after the jury adjourned. No one molested the prisoners on Friday when the news came of his assassination, but with Young gone there was no one who could control the vigilantes or their leader, Bourland, if they did come for the hapless men who remained in the makeshift jail.[3]

Young had exercised some measure of control over the hangings by maintaining at least the appearance of legal propriety in the actions of the Citizens Court, which after all had been created to promote security by restoring order. After his death, fear and a widespread desire for vengeance prompted the jurors to set aside many procedures that he had insisted upon. They reconvened on Saturday, October 18, as planned, but three who had

George H. Ragsdale, "An Incident of the Civil War" (MS in George H. Ragsdale Papers, BTHC); Sam Acheson and Julia Ann Hudson O'Connell, eds., *George Washington Diamond's Account of the Great Hanging at Gainesville, 1862* (Austin, 1963), 99; Thomas Barrett, *The Great Hanging at Gainesville* (Austin, 1961), 18–19; Joe T. Roff, *A Brief History of Early Days in North Texas and the Indian Territory* (Roff, Okla., 1930), 8–9.

2. John D. Young to Lilliam Gunter, February 7, 1917, in Cooke County Historical File, Cooke County Library, Gainesville, Tex.; Barrett, *The Great Hanging*, 19; Roff, *A Brief History of Early Days*, 8–9; Buckley B. Paddock, ed., *A Twentieth Century History and Biographical Record of North and West Texas* (2 vols.; Chicago, 1906), I, 233.

3. Barrett, *The Great Hanging*, 18; Lenuel D. Clark, ed., *The Civil War Recollections of James Lemuel Clark* (College Station, Tex., 1984), 100.

opposed the lynchings did not return. Two of their replacements were ruthless men: Newton J. Chance, who claimed the role of foreman from Daniel Montague, and slaveholder William W. Howeth, brother of the man who had shot James T. Foster. Montague and the others who advocated retribution welcomed these additions—expecting they would give them a majority in favor of hanging—as well as a third new juror, James W. McPherson, a trooper who had been recruited off the street for the Citizens Court. They did not realize that McPherson, who had lived among them almost all of his life, was a member of the Peace party.[4]

The reorganized jury voted to renounce the pledge to release the rest of the prisoners. The trials began anew; the suspects were tried again as if they had not been acquitted, but now the jury reviewed only the transcripts of earlier testimony before voting. Chance alone was allowed to recount his story. When McPherson made it clear that he did not believe Chance, Bourland arrested him. Barrett left the courtroom in helpless rage, refusing to serve any longer. He returned only after Bourland released McPherson, and both rejoined the jury. Barrett exploded again after the condemnation of two prisoners; then, realizing it was hopeless, he proposed that six of the worst be hanged and the rest set free. The jury rejected his proposal, so he sat silently while another four were condemned. The seventh man brought before the jury obviously had little connection with the Peace party. When several jurors advocated clemency, Barrett threw his weight into the debate and the prisoner was spared, breaking the domination of those who wanted to execute all of the men in their custody and encouraging undecided jurors to vote for mercy.[5]

The Citizens Court that Saturday freed fifty or sixty prisoners, but condemned nineteen others, a greater proportion than before the death of Young. Like those hanged on October 12 and 13, many had been implicated in earlier testimony. Nine had conspired with Rama Dye to rescue their friends on the night of October 1: William B. Anderson, Barnibus Burch, Arphax R. Dawson, Hudson J. Esman, Curd Goss, William W. Johnson, David M. Leffel, John W. Morris, and Gilbert Smith. Burch, an old man who suffered from arthritis, embellished his confession with a narrative of a dream that he said had convinced him to enlist in the Peace party. The North had overrun the South, and he could see no way for the South to

4. Barrett, *The Great Hanging*, 20–21; Clark, ed., *Recollections of James Clark*, 96–97.
5. Barrett, *The Great Hanging*, 20–21; Clark, ed., *Recollections of James Clark*, 96–98.

escape. The Federals caught him and an officer gave him "the best liquor I ever drank in my life." Esman was more practical; he said little during his first trial, and on October 11 sold his land, anticipating either death or flight. The jury condemned him as readily as they did Smith, who freely confessed knowing the secret signals of the Peace party but maintained he knew nothing of an uprising.[6]

Several of the nineteen condemned on October 18 tried to bargain for their lives. John M. Crisp wrote the jury a letter in which he described an initiation at his blacksmith shop in August, 1862, and offered the names of his accomplices. He said Eliott S. Thomas, a physician, and Thomas O. Baker had come to visit, gone outside to talk, and then returned inside and asked Crisp to initiate Thomas. Crisp refused and said Baker should do it, as they had been inducted together just a week earlier by Alfred McCarty, a doctor from Prairie Point near Wise County who moved to Gainesville in November, 1861. Crisp said Baker could devise a better oath, but Thomas laughingly insisted that Crisp initiate him, so Crisp improvised a suitable oath. A few days later he learned the secret signs, and subsequently swore in Esman and several others. In addition to names, Crisp also provided information about the plans of the Peace party, including the tidbit that either Leander W. P. "Jacob" Lock or Hydeman P. Garrison had gotten gunpowder from a Unionist in the Chickasaw Nation.[7]

The jurors rejected Crisp's overtures and sentenced him to hang. Desperate, Crisp wrote another letter, proposing that he be paroled in the custody "of some of our truest and best Southern men," with his life to be forfeit if he transgressed again. For references he called on Charles L. Roff, William C. West, and Harvey Howeth, among others, to testify about the good service he had performed for the state troops as a blacksmith. His appeals did not win him a reprieve, nor did his position as a deacon in the Church of Christ, Barrett's institution, prove to be of any influence. The jurors were bent on vengeance; testaments and arrangements for custody to ensure good behavior were no longer enough. Crisp hurriedly penned a

6. Acheson and O'Connell, eds., *Diamond's Account,* 70, 78, 79, 81, 82, 84; Wheeler Diary; Malissa C. Everett, "A Pioneer Woman," *WTHA,* III (1927), 64; Cooke County, County Clerk, Deed Record, 1850–present, Vol. IV, 300, 627, V, 795, in Cooke County Courthouse, Gainesville, Tex.
7. Acheson and O'Connell, eds., *Diamond's Account,* 73–74; Edward F. Bates, *History and Reminiscences of Denton County* (Denton, Tex., 1918), 106–107; Catherine T. Gonzalez, *Rhome: A Pioneer History* (Burnet, Tex., 1979), 6–7.

will on October 19, leaving everything to his wife, Ailsey, and their three children, and was taken to the hanging tree.[8]

Thomas, the physician who had been initiated by Crisp at his shop in August, also wrote to the jurors on October 18, asking them to reconsider his case. He named four witnesses, including Crisp, who could clear him if they were allowed to speak, but the jury refused to consider new testimony. Thomas even promised to help implicate others if released, but in vain. He wrote a will on October 19, in which he reflected sadly on the "uncertainty of this frail and transitory life" and left all his possessions to his wife, Susan, and their children, before climbing on the wagon to ride to his hanging.[9]

Unlike Crisp and Thomas, Alexander D. Scott refused to negotiate for his life. When originally summoned before the Citizens Court, he had said, "I am ready to be tried, though I have no defense to make," and he had maintained a fatalistic stance throughout his trial. He affirmed that he understood the objectives of the Peace party were to resist conscription and all other forms of Confederate authority, and to restore the Union through force if necessary. He freely admitted that he believed in the Union and was ready to fight for it. His refusal to save himself by dissembling made him an effective witness against Henry Chiles, despite Scott's request that his statements be used only against himself. After several prisoners had been executed, Scott declined to testify further about the intentions of others. He quietly wrote his will on October 19, leaving everything to his wife, Mary, and their son. Under the elm he exhorted the crowd to continue their work to destroy the Peace party, then watched silently as preparations were made for his execution. He jumped heavily from the wagon as it rolled forward, breaking his neck instantly.[10]

Richard N. Martin did not quietly accept his fate. He had been a recruiter for his brother-in-law, William Boyles, bringing several men to him to be initiated into the Peace party. Boyles eluded arrest, but the jury condemned Martin to hang on the last day of deliberations. Martin made a

8. Acheson and O'Connell, eds., *Diamond's Account*, 73–74; John M. Crisp, Jr., to George M. Crisp, October 20, 1921 (Typescript in Morton Museum); Cooke County, County Clerk, Probate Record and Minutes, I, 329, in Cooke Cty. Courthouse.

9. Cooke Cty. Probate Record and Minutes, I, 324; Acheson and O'Connell, eds., *Diamond's Account*, 73–74.

10. Acheson and O'Connell, eds., *Diamond's Account*, 59, 60; Cooke Cty. Probate Record and Minutes, I, 328; Cooke Cty. Probate Papers, 1849–present, Box 31, in Cooke Cty. Courthouse.

final angry speech from the wagon, boasting that the intent of his comrades was to kill all southern sympathizers, men, women, and children. During his trial, when questioned on the necessity of killing children, Martin allegedly shrugged and delivered the old Indian fighter's maxim, "Nits make lice." Under the elm, he insisted that Boyles had misled him and told listeners where he thought they could find the "author of my ruin," whom Martin wanted "hung to the same limb to which I am hung." Boyles was never caught, but many believed justice had been served when he was murdered in nearby Collinsville a few years later.[11]

The rest of the final nineteen hanged at Gainesville—Richard J. Anderson, John B. Miller, John A. Morris, M. W. Morris, William B. Taylor, and James A. Ward—were apparently selected only for their membership in the Peace party. Like many others, their testimony revealed they knew little of plans for an uprising, but they found security in the fellowship of an association of small farmers. These men shared a strong opposition to the Confederacy but had discussed little more than arrangements for self-defense. A few did profess ideological motives; M. W. Morris told the jury that he had lived as an abolitionist and expected to die as one, while Taylor and Ward declared they had enlisted to support the "old Constitution and Union."[12]

Barrett resumed his seat on the porch of W. W. Foreman's hotel on Sunday, October 19, and watched quietly as Bob Scott shuttled the last group of condemned men to the hanging tree. At least one company of Confederate regulars, Nick Wilson's troopers from the 29th Texas Cavalry, had already left, but their place was taken by a company of partisan rangers commanded by James D. Young, who was intent on avenging his father's murder. The families of all the prisoners had been summoned to take their menfolk home; now nineteen of them stood in horror as their relatives were hanged, beginning at midmorning, when Young adjusted the halter for the first, and continuing at the rate of two each hour until the sun hung low.[13]

11. Acheson and O'Connell, eds., *Diamond's Account*, 83, 93; Roff, *A Brief History of Early Days*, 10.

12. Acheson and O'Connell, eds., *Diamond's Account*, 72, 80; Everett, "A Pioneer Woman," 64; Roff, *A Brief History of Early Days*. 10.

13. Acheson and O'Connell, eds., *Diamond's Account*, 32–33; Barrett, *The Great Hanging*, 21; Clark, ed., *Recollections of James Clark*, 109; Michael Collins, *Cooke County, Texas: Where the South and the West Meet* (Gainesville, 1981), 14–15; Bradford K. Felmly and John C. Grady, *Suffering to Silence: 29th Texas Cavalry, C.S.A., Regimental History* (Quanah, Tex., 1975), 57.

Scott carried the bodies to an empty building next to Bourland's head-quarters on the west side of the town square, where he had earlier placed all the others. A few families claimed the bodies of their menfolk from the warehouse on the square—some of them mutilated by hogs who pushed through a hole in the back wall—but most were left for the county to bury. Slaves were detailed to build rude coffins for the executed men. Frank Fore-man tore down an empty house for lumber, and when that was exhausted, wrapped the remaining bodies in blankets and buried them in shallow graves on the banks of Pecan Creek, near the site of their execution. The next rain washed several corpses from the ground, while the hogs uncovered others and fed upon them. A young girl recalled with horror that she saw a hog dragging her stepfather's arm through the streets of Gainesville.[14]

The poignant testimony of the condemned men illustrated the irony of the makeshift trials in Gainesville, which sought to restore order and secu-rity by eradicating what was believed to be a Union conspiracy that threat-ened the communities within Cooke County. There were a few in the Peace party who professed an ideological commitment to the Union that tran-scended other concerns, but they were a minority in their own organization, as were those who had planned uprisings. The majority of the members had simply sought a method by which they could protect themselves, their

James D. Young allegedly hanged the final nineteen victims of the Great Hanging himself, but he denied this in an interview long after the war, saying he had only helped fix the rope around the neck of the first man hanged on October 19, 1862. See St. Louis *Republican*, March 4, 1894.

14. Clorie A. Gibson to Harry Fogle, n.d., in Great Hanging File, Morton Museum; Pete A. Y. Gunter, ed., "Lillian Gunter Papers on Cooke County History" (Typescript in Morton Museum), 54; Clark, ed., *Recollections of James Clark*, 108–109; Gainesville (Tex.) *Register*, August 30, 1948; A. Morton Smith, *The First 100 Years in Cooke County* (San Antonio, 1955), 37. Freedmen's Bureau agent Anthony M. Bryant asked Federal authorities to exhume and properly reinter the bodies of the Great Hanging victims that had been dumped in a mass grave. This request was denied. Anthony M. Bryant to Charles Griffin, June 1, 1867, U.S. Department of War, Adjutant General's Office, Letters Received, Record Group 94, National Archives. The graves of a few victims of the Great Hanging can still be found in Cooke County. Barnibus Burch lies in an unmarked grave along a fence row on the Marvin Cason farm. A simple headstone marks where James A. Powers is buried at John Ware's ranch, while a more elaborate memorial marks the final resting place of Nathaniel M. Clark in the Clark family cemetery. William W. Wernell is buried on the old James L. Clark farm; his grave is covered with rocks, and a metal marker welded on a post records his name and the date of his death, which is erroneously given as October 16, 1862. See Frances T. Ingmire, comp., *Cemetery Records of Cooke County, Texas* (Gainesville, 1980), 45, 476, 482.

families, and their homes in a frontier environment beset with violence and chaos. Most who joined the Peace party had become convinced by wartime events that the Confederacy could not survive, and they trusted that the Peace party could provide cooperative security until the Federal government could restore order.

The primary goals of the Peace party—to provide for the families of those at war, to protect members from Confederate authority, and to restore the Union—did not greatly alarm the first jury of the Citizens Court, which under the direction of William C. Young focused on ferreting out only the members who planned a violent uprising. Young's queries as prosecuting attorney, however, did reveal the outlines of a terrifying plot. Several admitted that they intended to take possession of North Texas using munitions from militia arsenals in Gainesville and Sherman, each of which contained about four hundred pounds of powder. They had identified Confederate sympathizers and intended to murder them and their families, though they had elected to spare some young daughters because they were "marriageable and handsome." They callously explained that wives had to be killed because they might contest the seizure of their late husbands' estates after order had been restored under the Union, and the children had to be eliminated because the "offspring of bad men must follow in the footprints of their sires." [15]

Those in the Peace party who advocated violence did realize that many of their comrades would not follow them; one man barely escaped a sound thrashing after he revealed the secrets of the second degree to a member who had taken the first degree. To increase their chances of success, they planned to coordinate their attack with the advance of a Federal army, which they admitted trying to contact with couriers. A handful of conspirators, unknown even to most of their fellow plotters, became exasperated with the lack of response from Federal authorities and called upon the disaffected tribes of the Indian Territory for aid, allegedly resurrecting the "free state" proposal that had attracted some support on the eve of secession. If the allied forces could not hold the region, they would have taken all that they could carry, destroyed the remainder, and retreated to Federal lines. A few, when questioned by Young, confirmed the Chance brothers'

15. Acheson and O'Connell, eds., *Diamond's Account*, 16; Barrett, *The Great Hanging*, 10–11. While some of the more radical members of the Peace party may have intended to take the property of their victims in the event of an uprising, there is no evidence that the land of those executed by the Citizens Court was taken by their persecutors.

report that the uprising was to have occurred on the night of September 30, before Bourland could summon reinforcements, but confessed that several factors, especially the untimely deluge, combined to postpone their plans.[16]

Barrett opposed executing any prisoners because "many of those who were duped, imposed upon, and got into this organization, never would have gone into this clan if they had known the dark and bloody intentions of the leaders." Some of his fellow jurors and many others outside the courtroom, though, became concerned with how many members of the Peace party, some of whom were still at large, would follow the leaders in a revolt. Rumor, which was indirectly confirmed by some testimony, set the membership of the Peace party as high as 1,700 along the Forks. Even if only a small proportion of that number took part in an uprising, they could do great damage before being overwhelmed or forced to flee. The class disparity between the jurors and many of the accused prompted the former to identify themselves as potential victims, and their alarm was shared by military officials and other people waiting outside in the streets of Gainesville.[17]

An exchange between Young and a prisoner illustrates the concern many people had. Told by the prisoner of a scheme for destruction, rapine, and murder, Young declared that he had always been kind to his neighbors, including members of the Peace party, and asked what was to have become of him and his property. The man looked at Young for a moment, then confessed that he had often thought about him and had intended to give him the secret signs, but had not. The jurors and those outside the courtroom could only reflect, like Young, on why they had not been provided with protection against an onslaught, and many came to an obvious and unsettling conclusion.[18]

Furthermore, although no slaves were implicated in any testimony before the Citizens Court, the concern of the slaveholders to maintain control over their property probably contributed to an escalation of the violence. The first jury condemned seven prisoners. Only one of these victims, Henry S. Field, owned a slave, while seven of the twelve jurors who judged them were slaveholders, as was Young, the prosecutor, and three of the four

16. Acheson and O'Connell, eds., *Diamond's Account*, 13, 16; Barrett, *The Great Hanging*, 12.

17. Barrett, *The Great Hanging*, 11; Clark, ed., *Recollections of James Clark*, 30.

18. Barrett, *The Great Hanging*, 11.

members of the committee who prescreened their testimony. The slave-holding jurors were not united—Barrett, for instance, owned a slave—but their influence became decisive after the murders of slaveholders Dickson and Young and the addition of slave owner Howeth to the jury. None of the nineteen men executed by the realigned jury were slaveholders. The fourteen nonslaveholders who were lynched earlier without the jury's approval may also have been victims of the same bias; Bourland and most of his committee of investigation were slave owners, as were his son William, who served as the constable for the Citizens Court, sheriff James B. Davenport, Jr., and three captains whose troops were assigned to patrol the streets—John K. Bumpass, Roff, and Wilson.[19]

The myriad fears of the Citizens Court and others in Cooke County were constrained by the stringency of the trials as Young conducted them. These formalities were abruptly violated when more vindictive vigilantes invaded the courtroom, and Young's death removed these boundaries altogether, allowing vengeful leaders such as Bourland a free rein in attacking the accused members of the Peace party. Although only a handful in that organization knew anything about an uprising, all who admitted that they knew its secret signs became suspect. Some members had passed on the signs to friends without an explanation, simply telling them that in an emergency they would bring assistance, thereby condemning many men who later found themselves on trial. It became a moot point whether those prisoners still in custody were responsible for Young's murder or for the previous turmoil in Cooke County; the jurors and others feared what they might do if freed. Moreover, the prisoners became a target for the grief and frustration vented at the death of a respected leader, Young. Bourland and oth-

19. While slaveholding patterns seem to have been of some importance, the decisions of the Citizens Court do not seem to have been greatly influenced by the nativities of those involved. More than two-thirds of both the jurors and the victims that can be identified, 67.7 and 71.4 percent respectively, were born in the Upper South. Too, while there were equivalent proportions from midwestern states in the two groups, 13.3 and 13.8 percent, there was a greater percentage from the Lower South among those who were hanged, 10.7 percent, than among those who served on the jury, 6.7 percent, and more natives of the Northeast among the jurors, 13.3 percent, than among the victims, 3.6 percent. The division within Cooke County that produced the Great Hanging, then, does not reflect that between the Upper and Lower South, but that which divided upper southerners. It is interesting to note also that personal resistance to the draft was apparently not a strong factor in the condemnations of the jury; of the thirty-one victims whose age can be determined, twenty, or almost two-thirds, were too old to be conscripted.

ers were supported in the execution of nineteen previously acquitted men because it served as a catharsis, relieving tension and reaffirming perceptions of security.

In all, forty-one men were hanged in Gainesville in October, 1862, and at least two others (James Foster and Thomas Floyd) were shot in addition to Hiram Kilborn, who was not claimed by the members of the Citizens Court as one of their victims. Under the direction of Bourland, William C. Young, and others, the jury and the mob had greatly reduced the ranks of the Peace party, in the process exterminating almost everyone who had signed Samuel McNutt's petition against conscription. Some, like William Boyles and John Ware, eluded arrest, but overall the operation had proven brutally effective. Most of the prisoners who were freed fled from North Texas, leaving the Eastern Cross Timbers deserted, while a few others, including Jackson H. Mounts and Isham W. Welch, were conscripted into the Confederate army. Ironically, Welch, who had attended Dye's meeting to discuss freeing the prisoners in Gainesville, was captured by the Federal army and imprisoned until the end of the war.[20]

With William R. Hudson absent, leaving the 21st Brigade under the direction of James J. Diamond as adjutant, Bourland was able to continue arresting suspected Unionists within the 21st District. Testimony in Gainesville had implicated physician Alfred McCarty and some of his former neighbors in Prairie Point, a community of emigrants from Missouri near Wise County. Joseph C. Chance lived in that area, and on his confirmation a list was forwarded to John W. Hale, commander of the 21st Brigade troops stationed at Decatur. Hale arrested a number of men in a sweep that continued for several days. They were tried by a commission of two dozen of the "best known and qualified men of the county," who convened in a makeshift courtroom on the second floor of the store that served as Hale's headquarters. The commission was chaired by James R. Bellamy, an

20. Sarah I. S. Rogers, "Memoirs" (Typescript in Morton Museum), 68; Wheeler Diary; Acheson and O'Connell, eds., *Diamond's Account*, 93; Barrett, *The Great Hanging*, 21; Clark, ed., *Recollections of James Clark*, 22, 75; John E. Wheeler to Edmund J. Davis, February 6, 1870, in GOR; Austin *Texas Almanac Extra*, October 25, 1862; Bates, *Denton County*, 115; *Biographical Souvenir of the State of Texas* (Chicago, 1889), 876; Graham Landrum and Allen Smith, *An Illustrated History of Grayson County, Texas* (2d ed.; Fort Worth, 1967), 173. The names of those who were arrested and released were not recorded—unlike the names of those who were executed—nor were the former prisoners inclined to speak for the record later. Thus little analysis of those who were more fortunate can be offered.

itinerant Southern Methodist minister from Virginia who had just organized the first permanent church in Decatur. The tribunal ordered some
prisoners to join the Confederate army, but sentenced five men from Prairie
Point—Ira Burdick, John M. Conn, Jim McKinn, Henry R. Maple, and
another remembered only by his last name, Ward—to hang.[21]

Sheriff Robert G. Cates served as executioner for the condemned
men in Decatur, a "gruesome duty" for an officer reputed to be "one of
the kindest of men." Sitting on their coffins in wagons, the five prisoners
were conveyed from Hale's headquarters to a tree on the western edge of
town, where they were hanged from the wagon beds on October 18. The
sight of them being hauled away on their coffins "almost created a panic"
among the pupils at a nearby school taught by Lutitia Wilson, a former
governess for a prominent family in Wise County who had relocated with
them to Decatur to escape the violence of the Civil War on the Texas
frontier.[22]

After the last hangings in Cooke and Wise counties, the public hysteria
that initiated the Great Hanging began to dissipate. Several men were arrested near Pilot Point in Denton County, but they were all set free because
the "storm of indignation" lost its fury as the "passion of the people
cooled." Some of those tried at Gainesville asserted that several of the
guards at the militia arsenal in Sherman had joined the Peace party and had
supplied its members with weapons and ammunition. Consequently sixteen
men were arrested in Grayson County and tried by a commission of two

21. Stephen P. Beebe to Holton White, July 26, 1865, in Great Hanging File, Wise
County Heritage Museum, Decatur, Tex.; Austin *Texas State Gazette*, October 29, 1862; Bates,
Denton County, 106–107; Gonzalez, *Rhome*, 5, 6–7; Cliff D. Cates, *Pioneer History of Wise
County* (Decatur, Tex., 1907), 81, 117–18, 131–32, 134–35; Mary C. Moore, *Centennial History of Wise County, 1853–1953* (Dallas, 1953), 38, 43–44; Macum Phelan, *A History of Early
Methodism in Texas, 1817–1866* (Dallas, 1924), 335, 482. Conn, a farmer and attorney, had
served as a guard in Gainesville at the outbreak of the Great Hanging. Burdick and McKinn
were also farmers, while Maple was a miller who employed Robert O. Duncan, one of those
present at Dye's meeting on October 1, as a laborer.

22. Austin *Texas State Gazette*, October 29, 1862; Cates, *Pioneer History of Wise County*,
132, 134–35; Gonzalez, *Rhome*, 7; Moore, *Centennial History of Wise County*, 43–44. Cates,
born in 1836 in Tennessee, immigrated to Collin County in 1856, then moved to Wise County
the next year. Elected sheriff for the first time in 1860, he served eleven years in that office.
See Cates, *Pioneer History of Wise County*, 66; Texas Secretary of State, Election Register,
1848–1900, in Archives Division, TSL.

dozen jurors in Sherman, but they were spared through the timely intervention of state district judge Robert W. Waddell and James W. Throckmorton, who had resigned his commission in the 6th Texas Cavalry in May, 1862, and returned to nearby Collin County.[23]

Throckmorton had become the focus of great suspicion when Abraham Lincoln, in an unsolicited assignment, appointed him as United States war tax collector for the "Rebel District of Texas," but he demonstrated that he still enjoyed popular support at Sherman. The former Unionist and Waddell spoke to a crowd numbering more than five hundred, persuading them to send their prisoners to the Confederate district court at Tyler for trial. That action prevented a bloodbath. The commission had already condemned some of the prisoners; one told his guard, Southern Methodist minister John H. McLean, that he had a knife and intended to kill the officer chosen to serve as his executioner and then cut his own throat. McLean persuaded him to abandon the plan, and the man was one of those transferred to Tyler along with Clement C. Wood, at whose house McNutt had held his rally, and prominent physician Richard T. Lively.[24]

Several well-known dissenters fled without waiting for a rescue. Unionist editor J. P. Whitaker and Sherman jeweler Frederick W. Sumner, the alleged leader of the Peace party in Grayson County, left the state, a wise decision as a correspondent wrote that the military had intended to send the latter "up salt river sure." Sumner did not get far. Confederates in Arkansas captured and imprisoned him in an iron cage in Little Rock along with other suspected dissidents; he remained there until that city was captured by Federal forces in September, 1863. He subsequently

23. Barrett, *The Great Hanging*, 11, 32; Jonathan H. Weidermeyer to Jeremiah Y. Dashiell, October 14, 1862, in AGR; Bates, *Denton County*, 107; Claude Elliot, *Leathercoat: The Life History of a Texas Patriot* (San Antonio, 1938), 73.

24. John H. McLean, *The Reminiscences of the Reverend John H. McLean* (Nashville, 1918), 103; Austin *Texas Almanac Extra*, October 25, November 13, 1862; Dallas *Herald*, September 20, 1862; Houston *Telegraph*, November 7, 1862; Clarksville *Standard*, November 1, 1862; McKinney (Tex.) *Courier-Gazette*, August 24, 1906; San Antonio *Express*, May 8, 1867; Sherman (Tex.) *Journal*, August 21, 1862; Elliot, *Leathercoat*, 73–74; Thomas Wilson, *Sufferings Endured for a Free Government* (Washington, D.C., 1864), 261. McLean had been ordained as a Southern Methodist minister by John W. Hamill, a member of the jury at Gainesville. Lively was a Kentucky native, born in 1823, who settled in Fannin County in 1852 and Grayson County seven years later. He reported $4,500 in property in 1860, and was active in founding the Masonic lodge at Whitesboro in February, 1861; interestingly, among the members was John R. Diamond. Census of 1860, Grayson County, Schedule 1 (Free Inhabitants), Family Number [hereinafter cited as F.N.] 665, in Genealogy Division, TSL; Landrum and Smith, *Illustrated History of Grayson County*, 31, 156.

went north, where he became actively involved in publicizing the Great Hanging.[25]

The Confederate district court at Tyler brought the civilians' role in the Great Hanging to an end by rejecting the assertion that the prisoners from Grayson County posed a threat to their neighbors and setting their bail at a paltry two hundred dollars. All of the accused quickly posted bond and scattered; only two, Lively and Wood, returned for a trial on November 13. The court deliberated briefly before acquitting both men. It had little choice in the matter; despite all of the furor, there was apparently very little substantial evidence that the accused were involved in treasonous activities. Too, the court had to take a stand against vigilante proceedings in Gainesville and elsewhere, which violated almost every provision of the Confederate constitution for due process.[26]

Wood quietly returned home, but Lively assailed in print those who had arrested him. His first public letter of protest was published in the Marshall *Texas Republican* on November 22, 1862. He insisted that he had not been fleeing from arrest when he was captured; he had a pass from the provost marshal in Sherman to leave town to obtain clothes for his children, whom he had been left alone to raise after the death of his young wife in October, 1861. A declaration by Lively was also printed in the Houston *Telegraph* on December 3, 1862, recalling that he had been the examining physician for conscripts in Grayson County until he was forced to resign for inadvertently releasing several who were actually fit for duty. When he received official instructions, he realized his errors and that he was not supposed to be examining men from his own county. His honest mistakes, however, had not been overlooked, and "designing men" had implicated him in the Peace party plot. To prove his loyalty to the Confederacy, he pointed out that he had now accepted an appointment as assistant surgeon for the 15th Texas Cavalry. Lively would have done well to let the matter rest; after the war he was shot and killed by pro-Confederate guerrillas.[27]

25. Austin *Texas Almanac Extra*, October 25, 1862; Frederick W. Sumner, "Written by F. W. Sumner During the Civil War, 1860–1865" (Typescript in Sherman Historical Museum, Sherman, Tex.); Wilson, *Sufferings*, 261–62.

26. Houston *Telegraph*, November 7, 22, 26, 28, 1862; H. P. N. Gammel, comp., *The Laws of Texas, 1822–1897* (10 vols.; Austin, 1898), V, 4–5; James Smallwood, "Disaffection in Confederate Texas: The Great Hanging at Gainesville," *Civil War History*, XXII (1976), 358. Few of the official records of the Confederate district court for East Texas survive in the state archives at Austin, and those that do shed little light on this incident.

27. Houston *Telegraph*, December 3, 1862; Marshall *Texas Republican*, November 22, 1862; Landrum and Smith, *Illustrated History of Grayson County*, 156.

The counterattack by the Confederate district court in Tyler was paralleled by that of Waddell in his role as presiding judge of the Twentieth Judicial District of Texas. A former Kentucky legislator who had settled in Collin County, he had been defeated in Cooke County during the 1860 judicial election because he was a staunch supporter of secession, but had gathered enough votes in the other Forks counties within the district to win the campaign. Once in office, he won respect as an "incorruptible and inflexible Judge" who, despite his strong personal opposition to abolitionist agitation, refused to condone vigilante actions and protested against the "reign of terror, the Pryor raid and the vigilance committee bullyism" in the summer of 1860. As he demonstrated at Sherman, he would not "let the Constitution and Laws be trampled under foot by a reckless gang without rebuke."[28]

Waddell's opportunity to lash out against the Great Hanging came when Joel F. DeLemeron was arraigned in his court on November 7, 1862, charged with treason for aiding some of the fugitives from Cooke County in their flight. DeLemeron, allegedly a former resident of the socialist La Reunion colony in Dallas County, had been indicted two days earlier by a Cooke County grand jury that included Citizens Court members Wiley Jones, James B. Stone, and Montague, who served as foreman just as he had done for the first vigilante tribunal at Gainesville. The evidence was strong against DeLemeron. A spy testified that he had visited DeLemeron on October 30, 1862, declaring himself to be a brother of John Miller, who was lynched in Gainesville, and saying he wanted to know where Ware and Boyles were so he could enlist them in his scheme to avenge Miller's death. DeLemeron showed him a path to Ware's house and said that he had repaired a wagon for Ware's wife—contrary to posted orders from Confederate authorities—and had given Boyles' wife a horse so that they could flee to Missouri.[29]

28. J. W. Boyer and C. H. Thurmann, *The Annals of Elder Horn* (New York, 1930), 43, 55–56; Texas Secretary of State, Election Register; Austin *Southern Intelligencer*, October 10, 1860; Bates, *Denton County*, 141; Roy F. Hall and Helen G. Hall, *Collin County: Pioneering in North Texas* (Quanah, Tex., 1975), 278–79; Jacob L. Stambaugh and Lillian J. Stambaugh, *A History of Collin County, Texas* (Austin, 1958), 233.

29. Acheson and O'Connell, eds., *Diamond's Account*, 92–94; Cooke Cty. Commissioners' Court, "Minutes, 1857 to 1878," Vol. I, 109, typescript in Works Progress Administration Historical Records Survey, BTHC; Cooke County, District Clerk, Criminal and Civil Minutes, Sixteenth, Twentieth, and Seventh District Courts, 1857–1871, pp. 186, 199, in Cooke Cty. Courthouse.

DeLemeron compounded his guilt by actively aiding the spy in his apparent preparations to wreak his vengeance on the men who had killed his brother. When the man returned the following day, DeLemeron dropped the facade of neutrality that he previously had maintained and heatedly condemned the Confederacy. He insisted that he and his neighbors would have joined the Peace party but they had not been approached, and he offered to take part in a raid on Gainesville. DeLemeron met the following Sunday night with the spy and others for a rehearsal, but the next night, November 3, proposed that they all flee to the North, taking everyone they encountered as hostages, especially Bourland, whom DeLemeron said he would "shoot . . . and leave . . . kicking" if he refused to come along. If they could find Garrison, they might then be able to muster enough support to attack Gainesville. After DeLemeron had taken an oath to uphold the Union and the Constitution of the United States, his companions dropped their pretense and arrested him on the spot.[30]

The spy's testimony was confirmed by a host of other witnesses, but Waddell was careful in his directions to the jury, reading to them the legal definition of treason, pointing out that "a mere conspiracy or intention to adhere to the enemy, is not treason—actual adherence must be proved." The jurors had to be certain that DeLemeron had joined the association with an intent to overthrow the government, and that he voluntarily took the oath knowing the objective was treasonable. Furthermore, he must have actually furnished weapons or such to agents of the United States "with a traitorous intent." Waddell concluded that if the jury had a "reasonable doubt," then they had to acquit DeLemeron because it was "better that ninety and nine guilty men should escape, than that one innocent man should suffer"—a deliberate reversal of the assertion of the vigilantes in Fort Worth who had hanged William H. Crawford in the summer of 1860.[31]

The jury nonetheless returned a verdict of guilty against DeLemeron on November 8; but the judge refused to sentence him to death despite his obvious participation in a treasonous plot. Waddell sent DeLemeron to the state penitentiary for life, a penalty still permitted under Texas law although a radical faction at the secession convention had attempted to make capital punishment mandatory for treason. Waddell considered a motion for a new

30. Acheson and O'Connell, eds., *Diamond's Account*, 94–96.
31. *Ibid.*, 97–98.

trial from DeLemeron, but after deliberating overnight, he ruled that the evidence was overwhelmingly against DeLemeron and denied the request. DeLemeron was conveyed safely to Huntsville and filed an appeal with the state supreme court from his cell. Although he was not released until after the war, he owed his life to Waddell, who refused to let his court become a stage for another act in the tragedy of the Great Hanging.[32]

Barrett always maintained that all the prisoners in Gainesville should have been turned over to military authorities outside Cooke County rather than be tried by the Citizens Court. He did not realize that other Confederate officers not only condoned the actions of Bourland and the vigilantes, but played an active role in arresting and executing suspected Unionists. Among them was Randolph. He had increased his command to battalion strength by adding new companies, some of which—like the Cooke County unit led by James D. Young—he believed could not be trusted. On October 4, 1862, Randolph wrote to Bourland and William C. Young, asking for the names of any of his troopers who had been implicated in the testimony before the Citizens Court. He added that it would be his "greatest pleasure to arrest them, and if necessary assist you in hanging them."[33]

On October 13, 1862, Randolph led his battalion into Sherman with twenty-seven prisoners in tow, all of them members of his command accused of duplicity in the Unionist conspiracy. Among the group were Jonathan Edmiston, the man who had warned many to flee but had been caught himself; Asbury Edmiston, two years Jonathan's junior and presumably his brother; Alonzo Chiles, possibly related to the brothers hanged in Gainesville; and John M. Cottrell, whose arrest in the summer of 1862 had nearly provoked a riot in Gainesville. Cottrell was in Cooke County on October 1 and, knowing he would be suspected, fled once more with Lucretia Hawley and her daughters. They stopped at the home of a woman who lived sixteen miles east of Sherman and posed as a widower and widow who had recently married. Cottrell left, saying he had business to tend in the Indian Territory

---

32. *Ibid.*; Cooke Cty. Criminal and Civil Minutes, 200, 201, 202–203; Texas Supreme Court, Austin Docket, 1860–1864, pp. 442–43, in Archives Division, TSL; William S. Oldham and George W. White, comp., *A Digest of the General Statute Laws of the State of Texas* (Austin, 1859), 483; Dallas *Herald*, April 24, 1863; Austin *Southern Intelligencer*, February 20, 1862. Presumably DeLemeron was freed in June, 1865, along with all other prisoners held in the Texas penitentiary "solely on account of unfriendly disposition toward the late Confederate authority." See *OR*, Ser. II, Vol. VIII, 659.

33. Acheson and O'Connell, eds., *Diamond's Account*, 33.

and would return soon. Perhaps he intended to rejoin his unit, but he and two others from Randolph's command—William A. McCool, who had deserted from James D. Young's company in September, and A. N. Johnson, Hawley's son-in-law—were captured by James D. Young's troops. Young escorted them to Gainesville to be tried before the Citizens Court, but at their own request they were taken to Randolph's court martial in Grayson County.[34]

Because Hugh F. Young was not present, Randolph was the highest ranking officer present in Grayson County. He presided over a court martial that condemned the three men captured by James D. Young, who then hanged them at his late father's Red River home. Randolph was no more merciful toward many remaining prisoners, indulging in a "wholesale hanging" from which "no man who was proved to belong to the [Peace party] was spared." Like the civilian trials, the court martial ran its course, and Randolph in late November, 1862, turned over Chiles, the Edmistons, and Wilson M. and A. L. Alred to the Confederate district court. His final magnanimity did not win the trust of many of his troops, who "began to desert and scatter like wild buffaloes." Quite a few hid in the brush, waiting for an opportunity to strike back.[35]

James D. Young did not rest until he hanged his father's murderer as well. From his younger brother, he learned that Daniel and Tom Welch had committed the murder. Their father had approached William C. Young shortly before his death, ostensibly to borrow food but also to ask what he

34. *Ibid.*, 88–89; CSR, 5th Texas Partisan Rangers; Barrett, *The Great Hanging*, 18–19; Roff, *A Brief History of Early Days*, 9, 11; Marcus J. Wright, *Texas in the War*, ed. Harold B. Simpson (Hillsboro, Tex., 1965), 31–32. McCool eloped with Henry S. Field's daughter in February, 1861, but apparently they settled nearby. He joined William C. Twitty's company during May, 1861, in Gainesville, but never reported for mustering. He paid taxes in 1862 in Cooke County on two cattle, and that summer joined Randolph's Partisan Battalion. See Acheson and O'Connell, eds., *Diamond's Account*, 89; Muster Roll of William C. Twitty's Company, July 1, 1861, in AGR; Card Index to Confederate Muster Rolls, in Archives Division, TSL; Cooke Cty. Tax Assessor, Tax Roll, 1862, in UNT; Francis T. Ingmire, comp., "Cooke County, Texas, Marriage Records, 1849–1879," p. 5, typescript in BTHC; Smith, *First 100 Years*, 31.

35. George H. Ragsdale, "Texas War History Written in 1892" (Typescript in Ragsdale Papers); Acheson and O'Connell, eds., *Diamond's Account*, 87, 89; Clark, ed., *Recollections of James Clark*, 111; Barrett, *The Great Hanging*, 17. George Fisher encountered five deserters from Randolph's command traveling through Missouri; from them, he obtained the account of hangings and desertions included in *The Yankee Conscript* (Philadelphia, 1864), 244–46. His narrative is substantially borne out by the CSR, 5th Tex. Part. Rangers.

should do with his boys. They had deserted and were hiding near the family home, and one of them had allegedly killed a man in a fight. Young told him to have them return to their unit, the 22d Texas Cavalry. Instead, they heeded the counsel of Garrison, the militant Methodist clergyman, and lashed out against those who threatened them. Tom Welch shot James Dickson, believing that he was Jim Pate, Young's overseer, and Daniel Welch shot Young; whether he did so deliberately or because he took aim at Bourland and missed never became clear. James D. Young tracked Daniel Welch into the Indian Territory, returned with him to the Young home-stead, and hanged him in March, 1863, in front of the late colonel's slaves. Then in a peculiar ritual of vengeance, he burned the body on the site where his father had been killed.[36]

The campaign for vengeance by James D. Young did not end with the death of Daniel Welch. Although Garrison escaped Young's wrath by flee-ing the state, E. Junius Foster, the Unionist editor from Sherman, was nei-ther so clever nor so fortunate. He published a number of editorials about the hangings, including one asserting that the murder of William C. Young was one of the best things that had happened in North Texas in a long time. An evening or two later, Foster was locking up his print shop when three horsemen—Young, Newton Chance, and an unidentified accomplice—accosted him. Young demanded that Foster recant his statement concerning his father's death, but Foster declared that he had printed the comment because it was true. Suddenly one of the men placed a double-barreled shot-gun against Foster's side and pulled both triggers. After the trio rode away, the wounded editor was carried into his office, where he soon died.[37]

Young extended his rampage as a captain in the 5th Texas Partisan Rang-ers, a regiment formed by the consolidation of Randolph's and Leonidas M. Martin's battalions under the command of Martin as colonel. In January, 1864, pressure from his superiors or from his opponents—allegedly Union general James G. Blunt had let it be known that Young would be executed

36. CSR, 22d Texas Cavalry; John D. Young to Gunter, February 7, 1917, in Cooke Cty. Historical File; Gunter, ed., "Gunter Papers," 229; Ragsdale, "Texas War History Written in 1892"; Clark, ed., *Recollections of James Clark*, 100; D. S. Howell, "Along the Texas Frontier During the Civil War," *WTHA Yearbook*, XIII (1937), 85; Roff, *A Brief History of Early Days*, 9, 11. Howell, who joined Bourland's Border Regiment in 1864, recalled that the ferocity exhibited by Bourland against dissenters was due to Bourland's belief that Young was mistak-enly killed by an assassin looking for him.

37. Landrum and Smith, *Illustrated History of Grayson County*, 65.

if caught—impelled him to take leave. A month later he submitted a letter of resignation in which he admitted that his actions had "been adjudged rash by some and perhaps censurable to some extent," but asserted that if he "committed any wrong" it was only "to avenge himself upon the members of an organization banded together in North Western Texas to destroy the lives and property of our people, those who had waylaid and murdered his much loved Father." The missive was forwarded to Confederate general Sam Bell Maxey, who noted in an endorsement that he had "no personal knowledge" of the "course of Capt. Young," but it was "common report" that since the death of his father he had "killed a number" of men alleged to have had "connections with that sad affair." Maxey concluded, and Martin concurred, that Young's "course . . . has been carried too far," and the captain was allowed to leave the service.[38]

The zeal of many Confederate military authorities to punish those implicated in the Peace party plot extended far beyond Texas. In May, 1863, Sumner was joined in his Little Rock cell by Obediah B. Atkinson and John Davidson, who had fled Cooke County. They had enlisted in Company I of the Confederate 6th Missouri Cavalry, commanded by John T. Crisp, the uncle of John M. Crisp, who was hanged in Gainesville on October 19, 1862. John T. Crisp, who had been secretary of the Confederate Senate exiled from Missouri in 1861, had come to Cooke County in the spring of 1862, enrolling his company with the promise that they would be mustered as home guards in Missouri and not in the Confederate army. Many joined with the expectation that they could desert on the march north, but were disappointed when they found themselves drafted into Confederate general Joseph Shelby's cavalry brigade. Atkinson and Davidson had provided only sketchy details of the hangings in Gainesville to their comrades, but several received letters telling them of the death of a relative or friend. When some troops deserted, an investigation resulted in the arrest of Atkinson and Davidson "for conspiracy agains the gov'mt," and of Captain Crisp, in November, 1863.[39]

38. James D. Young to B. E. Benton, February 10, 1864, in CSR, 5th Tex. Part. Rangers; Carrie J. Crouch, *A History of Young County, Texas* (Austin, 1956), 10–11; Larry C. Rampp and Donald L. Rampp, *The Civil War in the Indian Territory* (Austin, 1975), 19–27, 149–50.

39. Clark, ed., *Recollections of James Clark*, 52–75, 77n, 112–15; Sumner, "Written by Sumner During the Civil War." Obediah B. Atkinson and John Davidson are listed on the muster roll of Company I, 6th Missouri Cavalry, C.S.A., taken on September 13, 1862, but contemporary accounts substantiate that they did not join the company until later. See CSR,

Atkinson and Davidson were sent to Little Rock, where they joined Sumner in confinement until the Federal army captured that city in the fall of 1863. Crisp was held pending court martial in a hotel in Russellville, Arkansas. James L. Clark—whose father Nathaniel had been hanged on October 19, 1862—and others went to the hotel and spoke with Crisp. He ordered them to return to the camp, but to pitch their tents on the bank of the river so they could not be surrounded. They were to be watchful and not to surrender to anyone; if necessary, they should "just shoot it out." That night the company raided the regimental commissary, taking all of the ammunition and a few spare muskets. When Shelby heard of the circumstances, he had Crisp released and returned to his unit. Clark later wrote, "Shelby said if he had nown eney thing a bout what tha were doing here in Gainesville, he would a sent a regiment here and killed the hole D out fit, an sent the oald men home to there famleys."[40]

Shelby's rhetoric did not prevent the company's depletion by desertion. While Atkinson and Davidson awaited liberation and their chance to escape north, other members of Company I from Cooke County either fled north or went home. Of the sixty-four remaining troops, six deserted in December, 1862, nine in February, 1863, and four in August, 1863. Among the last four were James L. Clark and John D. Powers, whose brother James was hanged in Gainesville on the same day as Clark's father. They took with them a three-day pass given by Crisp to provide them with a head start. Like his father, Clark opposed slavery and secession; events had now instilled in him a deep hatred of the Confederacy as well. He had joined William C. Twitty's company in 1861 to avoid service in the regular army and participated in the invasion of the Indian Territory, but his father had hired a substitute for him rather than allow him to be sent east. He, Powers, and their two companions now returned to Cooke County, like some of those who had deserted from Randolph's command, to await their opportunity for revenge.[41]

6th Mo. Cav. John T. Crisp served for the duration of the war, then ran unsuccessfully for Congress twice. He was elected to the Missouri senate three times—in 1895, 1897, and 1903, the year of his death. W. Rufus Jackson, *Missouri Democracy* [3 vols.; St. Louis, 1935], I, 639, 641–42, 648–49.

40. Clark, ed., *Recollections of James Clark*, 75–77; Sumner, "Written by Sumner During the Civil War." According to family tradition, Atkinson was put before a firing squad but gave the Masonic sign of distress and was spared by the officer in charge, a fellow Mason. Noel Parsons to author, April 25, 1989.

41. CSR, 6th Mo. Cav.; Clark, ed., *Recollections of James Clark*, 16–18, 77–78; Muster

The purge of dissenters reached high in the Confederate ranks. Suspicion centered on Albert G. Pike, who had resigned from his command in the Indian Territory after a series of angry clashes with General Thomas C. Hindman that climaxed in Pike's refusal to advance against the Federal invasion from Kansas in the summer of 1862. Pike angrily tendered his resignation, then retired to Grayson County to await a decision on the matter. Two men attempted to save themselves during the Great Hanging trials by testifying that Pike was involved in the conspiracy. After an Indian revolt in late October, 1862, Pike imprudently led several companies of Texas cavalry into the Indian Territory without orders and was arrested on November 14. He vigorously defended himself against all charges, including allegations that he was the connection between the Peace party and Kansas abolitionist James H. Lane, but to no avail, especially after it became known that Pike had thwarted the hanging of an accused Unionist by vigilantes in Fannin County, Texas. Although all charges were later dismissed, he lost his commission as a brigadier general and never held another important position for the Confederacy.[42]

Order and security in Cooke County, as elsewhere in North Texas, were not restored by the gruesome deaths of the forty-three men who lost their lives to the Citizens Court or by the similarly brutal execution of many others. The problem of recurring, even escalating, violence in the wake of vigilantism is common, but in Cooke County there was an important contributing factor: the perception by perpetrators of the Great Hanging that a gap in social standing existed between themselves and their victims. Some had maintained, as Throckmorton did in a misguided effort to allay fear, that those who were lynched were only "refugees and suspected persons." As an example, he asserted that Leander W. P. "Jacob" Lock, whom he identified as the leader of the "Association," had been acquitted of murder several years earlier in Lamar County, though most people believed he was

Rolls of Twitty's Co., July 1, October 2, 1861, in AGR. James L. Clark, in his *Recollections*, wrote that John D. Powers was the brother of James A. Powers; but a descendant of Obediah B. Atkinson, brother-in-law of James, contends that John was a first cousin to the man who was hanged in Gainesville. Parsons to author, April 25, 1989.

42. Albert Pike to Andrew Johnson, August 4, 1865, in Amnesty Files; *OR*, Ser. I, Vol. XIII, 918–20, 923–24; Jefferson (Tex.) *Confederate News*, March 28, 1863; Mark M. Boatner III, *The Civil War Dictionary* (New York, 1959), 653; Michael B. Dougan, *Confederate Arkansas: The People and Policies of a Frontier State in Wartime* (Tuscaloosa, Ala., 1976), 90–93; Robert L. Duncan, *Reluctant General: The Life and Times of General Albert Pike* (New York, 1961), 232–52; Landrum and Smith, *Illustrated History of Grayson County*, 65–66.

guilty. To Throckmorton, the lynchings were a "great good to society" because a disruptive group of dissenters had been eliminated.[43]

Truthfully, though, the Citizens Court and others realized that they had cut deeply into their own ranks in their zeal to crush dissent. Many of the victims were not of the lower echelons or fringes of society, but instead could claim to be middle-class. A third of those lynched at Gainesville do not appear in the antebellum records for Cooke or a nearby county, and so could be classified as refugees, but the remainder had settled in the area before the war and acquired property; several had undertaken trades or held county offices. Furthermore, among the third who could be considered refugees were physicians Henry Chiles—who purchased 200 acres from Alexander D. Scott—and James T. Foster, who homesteaded 160 acres. Lock can also be classified as a refugee, but he reported a substantial estate in Lamar County in 1860. Including Chiles and Foster, twenty-four victims owned at least 100 acres; another, Samuel Carmichael, had no farmland but did have five lots in Gainesville. Among those who practiced a trade were Henry S. Field, shoemaker; Henry Cockrum, miller; John M. Crisp, blacksmith; and Eliott S. Thomas, Chiles and Foster, all physicians. Dye, Scott, and Hiram Kilborn had served as road overseers, and Kilborn had also been a school trustee and a poll supervisor.

Shattered family relationships enhanced the bitter divisions left by the Great Hanging. Many of the victims were related to one another, which may have contributed to their being selected for execution. Ephraim and Henry Chiles were brothers, as were M. W. and William W. Morris. James A. Powers, Obediah Atkinson's brother-in-law, attended Dye's meeting with Moses Powers, his uncle; both of James Powers' relatives survived, but Powers did not. Arphax Dawson, Dye's father-in-law, was also present at the meeting that night and was hanged, while Henry Field's lynching preceded that of his son-in-law, William McCool, by only a few weeks. John M. Crisp's desperate attempts to bargain for his life availed him no more than the quiet resignation of his brother-in-law, Hudson Esman. Elizabeth Woolsey successfully pleaded for her sons, but not for her son-

---

43. Richard M. Brown, *Strain of Violence: Historical Studies of American Violence and Vigilantism* (New York, 1975), 68; Clarksville *Standard*, November 1, 1862. Lock may have been one of two brothers involved in a murder in Grayson County in 1859. A woman had fled from her husband and taken refuge with her father, who was the brothers' uncle. Armed with shotguns and concealed in an outhouse, they shot and killed her irate husband when he came to take her back. See Dallas *Herald*, June 22, 1859.

in-law, Alexander Scott. The members of the Citizens Court could point to many among their own number who were related, and thus might easily conclude that familial ties influenced sectional loyalties. They reacted accordingly, leaving sundered families whose grief was often compounded by multiple losses.[44]

The indiscriminate zeal of the vigilantes involved in the Great Hanging, which contributed to the deterioration of that affair into a bloody vendetta, left deep rents in the social fabric of the region. Manhunts like those conducted by John S. Randolph and James D. Young, and the vicious attacks on prominent figures such as Albert Pike only increased resistance to the Confederacy. The consequent chaos further alarmed those settlers who continued to support the Confederacy as the extant authority, and led to renewed violence against anyone accused of undermining order and security by working to restore the Union. It became a repetitive cycle of violence as vigilantes and Confederate officials tried to reimpose order through a campaign of terror along a frontier increasingly alienated by such tactics.

44. Among the relatives involved in the Citizens Court and preceding committees of investigation were James G. and William W. Bourland, Newton J. and Joseph C. Chance, Harvey and William W. Howeth, James M. and William Peery, and William C. Twitty and Daniel Montague.

FIVE

Dark Corner of the Confederacy

While the news of the Great Hanging spread throughout the South, Confederate officials in Texas struggled to maintain order along the Forks. Like most southern newspapermen, those in positions of authority condoned the vigilantes—even if only by remaining silent—and focused on crushing dissent as the solution for the problem of security in North Texas. Instead of reducing chaos and insecurity, however, military officers sent to the region encouraged further disorder by violently attacking dissenters. Hard pressed to defend areas of more immediate importance, Confederate authorities finally gave control of the Forks once more to James G. Bourland. His brutal and often ineffective tactics as commander of the Border Regiment exacerbated disaffection among many settlers, but most continued to support him and other officers as representatives of the extant legal authority. As a result, North Texas remained bitterly divided and wracked with violence; when Katherine Stone moved to the area in 1863, she discovered that "nothing seems more common or less condemned than assassination," and confided to her diary that she loathed this "dark corner of the Confederacy."[1]

The dissemination of reports about the Great Hanging followed a pattern similar to that during the abolition scare in the summer of 1860. Rumors of impending mayhem circulated freely, as well as fears that the Federal army would soon exact revenge for the Unionists hanged on the Forks. In an attempt to allay hysteria, a pair of prominent North Texas editors, Charles DeMorse of the Clarksville *Standard* and Robert W. Loughery of the Marshall *Texas Republican*, printed James W. Throckmorton's letter de-

1. John Q. Anderson, ed., *Brokenburn: The Journal of Kate Stone, 1861–1868* (Baton Rouge, 1955), 226–27, 237.

claring that those who were arrested were nothing but "refugees and suspected persons," and that the Great Hanging was a "great good to society." The letter concluded with a eulogy for the murdered prosecutor, Colonel William C. Young.[2]

Loughery, taking advantage of Marshall's location on a telegraph line, scooped DeMorse by publishing, two weeks before the latter, an article about the Great Hanging that had appeared initially in the Sherman *Journal* before its Unionist editor, J. P. Whitaker, fled north. Drawing on this report and Throckmorton's letter, Loughery wrote an editorial in which he agreed that the victims were mostly "low characters, with here and there a man of limited influence." He added that their conspiracy could not have been extensive, because there were "probably not a thousand Union men (if so many) in the State." Asserting that the Federal army would hardly consider invading such a remote region, Loughery concluded that "thieving and robbing was at the bottom of the affair."[3]

DeMorse closed his later article with a more cryptic comment: "The plot lately developed in Cooke and Grayson has much more importance at a distance than at home." As he thus predicted, newspaper editors in South Texas proved more ready to believe there was a widespread conspiracy among Union abolitionists on the Forks. They had accepted almost unanimously the numerous reports of abolitionist incendiaries in the summer of 1860 and had noted with alarm the vote against secession in the region. Separated from North Texas by distance and poor communications, many of them were convinced that the region was a hotbed of "Black Republicanism," and they endorsed the vigilantes.[4]

Perhaps the most reputable Texas newspaperman at the time of the Civil War was Edward H. Cushing, a Vermont native who as editor of the Houston *Telegraph* supported slavery and secession. He confirmed the rumors of

2. Clarksville *Standard*, November 1, 1862; Robert A. Nesbitt, "Texas Confederate Newspapers, 1861–1865" (M.A. thesis, UT, 1936), 133.

3. Marshall *Texas Republican*, November 1, 1862; Sherman (Tex.) *Journal*, October 9, 1862, quoted in Marshall *Texas Republican*, October 18, 1862. See also Nesbitt, "Texas Confederate Newspapers," 133–34.

4. Sam Acheson and Julia Ann Hudson O'Connell, eds., *George Washington Diamond's Account of the Great Hanging at Gainesville, 1862* (Austin, 1963), xiii–xvi; Austin *Texas State Gazette*, October 1, 1862; Houston *Telegraph*, October 6, 1862; Richmond (Va.) *Enquirer*, October 28, 1862; Robert P. Felgar, "Texas in the War for Southern Independence" (Ph.D. dissertation, UT, 1935), 43, 200–202; William E. White, "The Texas Slave Insurrection of 1860," *SWHQ*, LII (1949), 259–85; Nesbitt, "Texas Confederate Newspapers," 124.

a dangerous conspiracy after an allegedly systematic investigation of the affair. On October 10, 1862, he reprinted a wildly inaccurate account of the hangings from the Natchez, Mississippi, *Courier*. Natchez was on a stage line, and the editor of the *Courier* claimed he had received a "dispatch" from Marshall saying that Texas had been "invaded" through Cooke County by five thousand "Jayhawkers" from Fort Arbuckle in the Indian Territory. Cushing dismissed the story as claptrap, then printed no more for two weeks as he gathered more details.[5]

On October 27, 1862, Cushing revealed to his readers that he had been permitted by Governor Francis R. Lubbock to examine all the official reports on the "secret abolition agency" in North Texas. He asserted that the correspondence revealed that the "pretended" object of resistance to conscription masked a more insidious goal of establishing a spy system for the Federal army in Texas. The organization had begun in the northern states, then had enlisted Union soldiers and members of the Texas militia for its purposes. A mutiny among the state troops was to have been coordinated with a Federal invasion of Texas from the Indian Territory, and the united commands would have marched to Austin and joined with yet another Union army pushing inland from a beachhead at Galveston. Like Loughery, Cushing rejoiced that the guilty had been "nipped" and the traitors had gotten what they deserved.[6]

Like Cushing, editor Willard Richardson of the exiled Galveston *News* was a northerner by birth, but was raised in South Carolina. His newspaper was the most influential and widely circulated in antebellum Texas, but it had been challenged by the development of Cushing's enterprise. Because the most important source for news was the mail, Richardson engaged correspondents throughout the state to keep him apprised of events. Such preparations served him well; H. C. Stone wrote from Gainesville on October 3, 1862, relaying an accurate report of the hangings. Richardson did

5. Natchez (Miss.) *Courier*, October 1, 2, 1862, quoted in Houston *Telegraph*, October 10, 1862; Sam Acheson, *35,000 Days in Texas: A History of the Dallas News and Its Forbearers* (New York, 1938), 50; Earl W. Fornell, *The Galveston Era: The Texas Crescent on the Eve of Secession* (Austin, 1961), 152–53; Marilyn M. Sibley, *Lone Stars and State Gazettes* (College Station, Tex., 1983), 262–64, 335–36; Walter P. Webb, H. Bailey Carroll, and Eldon S. Branda, eds., *The Handbook of Texas* (3 vols.; Austin, 1952, 1976), I, 449; Felgar, "Texas in the War for Southern Independence," 43; Nesbitt, "Texas Confederate Newspapers," 124–26.

6. Houston *Telegraph*, October 27, 1862.

not publish the letter until October 22, under the title "A Lincoln Raid in the Interior," but five days earlier he had published an editorial that indicated that he had the missive. In it, he opined that the Peace party contained the same "abolitionist incendiaries" that were active in the summer of 1860. He claimed that Abraham Lincoln had exposed his support for such operatives with his preliminary emancipation proclamation during September 1862, and recalled that several were hanged in 1860, adding, "We trust the balance will now share the same fate." On October 29 he printed a letter from Samuel Heilbruner, a Sherman merchant, as further evidence of Lincoln's nefarious design.[7]

Other South Texas newspapers also found witnesses to confirm the rumors of conspiracy. Editor I. R. Worrall of the Austin *Texas State Gazette* had been a notary public in Cooke County before the war and knew several people in the region well. On October 29, 1862, he published a letter written just nine days earlier by Jeff W. Hall, who had witnessed the trials in Decatur and the hanging of two men. Hall insisted the Peace party had intended to attack Gainesville, kill the southern sympathizers there, and flee to Kansas with their plunder. He concluded that the trials had begun just in time to avert a bloody tragedy.[8]

On October 23, 1862, the Austin *Texas Almanac Extra*, edited by David Richardson, a member of the Galveston *News* staff but no relation to the editor, published a different letter from Hall. It was accompanied by another eyewitness report from an anonymous traveler entitled "Excitement in North Texas." Richardson wrote that he had warned Paul O. Hebert about the dissidents on the Red River six months earlier, but the general had done nothing. The editor readily accepted assertions that the conspirators would have supported a Federal invasion of Texas, and he applauded the vigilantes, adding, "The loyal citizens of each county have taken the law into their own hands, and are fully determined to give the traitors their just deserts." He later reprinted the Heilbruner letter under the title "More Excitement in Northern Texas," then reported William C. Young's death

7. Galveston *News*, October 17, 22, 29, 1862; Willard Richardson to Andrew Johnson, July 25, 1865, in Amnesty Files; Acheson, *35,000 Days in Texas*, 11, 16–17, 19, 36, 46, 49; Fornell, *The Galveston Era*, 141–42; Sibley, *Lone Stars*, 175–77; Webb, Carroll, and Branda, eds., *Handbook*, II, 470–71; Nesbitt, "Texas Confederate Newspapers," 63, 87, 129–30.

8. Texas Secretary of State, Election Register, 1848–1900, in Archives Division, TSL; Austin *Texas State Gazette*, October 29, 1862; Sibley, *Lone Stars*, 306.

with the observation that the "whole country" was "now fairly aroused" against the plotters and that "there will be but a poor showing for any that remain."[9]

Ironically, the San Antonio *Herald*, which opposed secession under editor James P. Newcomb until a mob compelled him to flee Texas, published the most vitriolic support of the Great Hanging. After earlier reprinting "A Lincoln Raid in the Interior" from the Galveston *News* and an announcement of Young's assassination, the editors on November 15, 1862, wrote: "[The Unionists] think they are unknown. . . . *They are known and will be remembered.* Their numbers were small at first, *and they are becoming every day less. In the mountains near Fort Clark, and along the Rio Grande, their bones are bleaching in the sun, and in the counties of Wise and Denton, their bodies are suspended by scores from black jacks. They were warned in time to leave the country; and, choosing to remain, and rely for protection upon the enemy with whom their government is at war, they must expect to take the consequences of their choice.*" The editorial added that those few Unionists who survived would become "objects of loathing and scorn among heroes and patriots in a free, glorious, and powerful young Confederacy."[10]

As reports of the "Great Hanging" spread quickly throughout the South, assertions that a dangerous Union conspiracy existed in North Texas gained more credence with each retelling. Because Texas had no telegraph connections with any other state in 1862, most southern newspapermen depended on publications available in Houston, the principal clearinghouse for news in Texas, for information. Their perspective, then, became that of hostile editors in the southern part of the state, especially Willard Richardson. The Richmond *Enquirer* was one of the most reputable newspapers in the South. When the paper printed H. C. Stone's letter on November 14, 1862, under the headline "The Tories in Texas," it was accepted as a valid account and lent credibility to Willard Richardson as the editor who first published it. His opinions on the Great Hanging soon appeared in many major southern newspapers, including the Atlanta *Southern Confederacy*, Augusta *Constitutionalist*, Raleigh *Register*, and Wilmington *Journal*. Even citizens in occupied Memphis and New Orleans read his accounts, in the *Bulletin* and *Picayune* respectively.[11]

9. Austin *Texas Almanac Extra*, October 23, 25, 30, 1862; Sibley, *Lone Stars*, 324; Webb, Carroll, and Branda, eds., *Handbook*, II, 732.

10. San Antonio *Herald*, October 25, November 8, 15, 1862; Sibley, *Lone Stars*, 297, 361.

11. Atlanta *Southern Confederacy*, November 12, 1862; Augusta *Constitutionalist*, Novem-

A few newspapers in the South printed other reports of the Great Hanging. The Memphis *Appeal* and Vicksburg *Whig* printed Cushing's studious account. The Charleston *Courier*, the oldest daily in the Carolinas, reproduced Hall's letter under the eye-catching headline "More of the Union Conspiracy in Northern Texas—Twenty Men Hung!" The Mobile *Advertiser and Register*, one of the most widely quoted newspapers in the South, printed Loughery's early article. Most editors, no matter which version they published, agreed with the writer for the Little Rock *True Democrat* who crowed, "By the fortunate discovery of this scheme Texas has been enabled to purge herself of traitors."[12]

Confronted with public support for the vigilantes at Gainesville, the Jefferson Davis administration chose to ignore the affair. Davis had already removed Hebert from command in Texas on October 10, 1862, for his "unwarranted" imposition of martial law and harsh enforcement of the conscription law. Hebert had protested in vain that his officers never interfered with civil courts and always allowed prisoners "to be tried with all the facilities of defense as in the ordinary common law trial." The Great Hanging and similar events elsewhere in Texas, conducted with Hebert's authorization if not his approval, rendered ineffective his pleas and those of Lubbock against his removal and the end of martial law. Davis sent no response to either man's protest, perhaps hoping the event would fade into the background of national memory. Following their chief executive's lead, no further action was taken by high-level Confederate authorities against any of the participants in the Great Hanging.[13]

---

ber 5, 1862; Memphis *Bulletin*, November 20, 1862; New Orleans *Picayune*, November 13, 1862; Raleigh *Register*, November 18, 1862; Richmond *Enquirer*, November 14, 1862; Wilmington *Journal*, November 18, 1862; Acheson, *35,000 Days in Texas*, 50; J. Cutler Andrews, *The South Reports the Civil War* (Princeton, 1970), 25, 26, 27, 34–36.

12. Little Rock *True Democrat*, November 5, 1862; Charleston *Courier*, November 20, 1862; Vicksburg *Whig*, n.d., quoted in Memphis *Appeal*, November 6, 1862; Marshall *Texas Republican*, November 1, 1862, quoted in Mobile *Advertiser and Register*, November 7, 1862; Andrews, *South Reports the Civil War*, 39.

13. *OR*, Ser. I, Vol. IX, 735–36, Vol. XV, 826, Vol. LIII, 828–30, Ser. IV, Vol. II, 39; Francis R. Lubbock to "Hon. Members Composing the Texas Delegation in the Confederate Congress," September 30, 1862, in GOR; H. P. N. Gammel, comp., *The Laws of Texas, 1822–1897* (10 vols.; Austin, 1898), V, 34; San Antonio *Herald*, October 25, 1862; Galveston *News*, November 1, 1862; William M. Robinson, Jr., *Justice in Grey: A History of the Judicial System of the Confederate States of America* (Cambridge, Mass., 1941), 395–98; Felgar, "Texas in the War for Southern Independence," 299.

Davis' silence allowed Texas officials and Confederate officers in the Trans-Mississippi to pursue the course they thought best, which was to crush dissent in North Texas. Lubbock received an official report of the Great Hanging on October 22, 1862, when a courier arrived from William R. Hudson. Texas Adjutant General Jeremiah Y. Dashiell had admonished Hudson the previous day that while "every attempt at a rising by Traitors or disaffected citizens must be crushed out," any "extreme measures" had to be based on "undoubted evidence and not confined to mere suspicion." Lubbock was initially appalled by the lynchings—he expressed doubts to Senator Louis T. Wigfall about the "horrible & speedy" vengeance taken by "loyal citizens" in Cooke and Wise counties—but Young's murder swept aside his early reservations. Dashiell wrote to Hudson again on November 1, asserting that although the hangings were "deplorable," nevertheless the "strictest measures of the sternest justice" had to be imposed on any "Traitors that pollute the soil of our state." He added, "Whenever treason dares to raise its Hydra head it must be crushed." [14]

Lubbock called the legislature into a special session that met on February 2, 1863. In his opening address, he praised Hudson for countering the combined threat of Unionists and Indians in Cooke County, and endorsed Hudson's petition for repayment of his expenses. Confronted with Hudson's assertion that the conspirators had intended to "throw off the veil of secrecy and openly espouse the Federal cause, fully endorsing the abolition administration of Abraham Lincoln, and with fire and sword to devastate the whole country," the legislators approved the appropriation measure. Ironically, its passage in the House was overseen by John W. Hale, Hudson's subordinate, who served as a representative from Cooke County. [15]

14. Jeremiah Y. Dashiell to William R. Hudson, October 21, 1862, in AGR; James Paul to Lubbock, October 23, 1863, Lubbock to Louis T. Wigfall, October 27, 1862, Dashiell to Hudson, November 1, 1862, all in GOR. The issue of states' rights was the bane of Davis' tenure as president of the Confederacy, but it probably served him well in this instance. By allowing the persecution of dissenters to continue along the Forks, Davis allayed the public hysteria in Texas without endorsing any of the proceedings. That he did not greatly object to these activities is evidenced by his appointing Lubbock as a special adviser on the Trans-Mississippi in Richmond after his term as governor expired in 1863. See Dunbar Rowland, ed., *Jefferson Davis, Constitutionalist: His Letters, Papers, and Speeches* (10 vols.; Jackson, Miss., 1923), VI, 276–77; Ralph A. Wooster, "Texas," in *The Confederate Governors*, ed. W. Buck Yearns (Athens, Ga., 1985), 207–208.

15. William R. Hudson, "To the Hon the Legislature of the State of Texas," n.d., in Memorial and Petitions File, Archives Division, TSL; Francis R. Lubbock, *Six Decades in*

Hudson assured the legislators in his petition that dissent had been eliminated on the Forks, but in fact disaffection persisted in the area. Although many opponents of the Confederacy fled the region after the Great Hanging, quite a few remained. They were joined by a growing number of shirkers from the Confederate army. Some of these deserters were returning to families who suffered food shortages due to recurring droughts and a lack of manpower. Impressment and taxation laws passed in the spring of 1863 contributed to greater shortages and inflation. Other deserters had less noble motives; the remote Forks provided a refuge for outlaws who preyed on peaceful families, who were subject to Indian attacks as well. Gainesville became a sanctuary for some refugees, while others fled or built stockades for defense. Amid the turmoil, Confederate officials, isolated on the frontier from either reliable support or close supervision, concentrated on restoring order and security by violently suppressing dissent, thereby encouraging more vigilantism.[16]

The Great Hanging revived attempts to have a garrison stationed permanently along the Forks. James W. Throckmorton wrote to Lubbock on October 25, 1862, urging that a battalion be posted there under his command. He pointed out that such a unit would enlist many malcontents who had joined the Peace party, converting them into a useful home guard. His plan was echoed in another letter from J. B. Wilmette, a retired United

---

Texas, ed. C. W. Raines (Austin, 1900), 463; *Texas House Journal,* Special Session, 1863, xvi, xvl, 1, 7, 12, 45, 75–76, 131, 217*n*; Gammel, comp., *Laws of Texas,* V, 26–27; *Members of the Texas Legislature, 1846–1980* (Austin, 1981), 40.

16. Henry F. C. Johnson to "Delilah," April 10, 1863, in Henry F. C. Johnson Papers, Archives Division, Dallas Public Library; Hudson to Dashiell, March 8, 1863, Charles Freeman to Dashiell, September 24, 30, 1863, all in AGR; Willie Russell, "Sivells Bend Community History" (Typescript in Cooke County Historical File, Cooke County Library, Gainesville, Tex.); Lemuel D. Clark, ed., *The Civil War Recollections of James Lemuel Clark* (College Station, Tex., 1984), 39; William R. Strong, *His Memoirs,* ed. Pete A. Y. Gunter and Robert A. Calvert (Denton, Tex., 1982), 46; Stephen B. Oates, "Texas Under the Secessionists," *SWHQ,* LXVII (1963), 184; Cliff D. Cates, *Pioneer History of Wise County* (Decatur, Tex., 1907), 117–18, 161–62; Mary C. Moore, *Centennial History of Wise County, 1853–1953* (Dallas, 1953), 38, 41–42; Michael Collins, *Cooke County, Texas: Where the South and the West Meet* (Gainesville, Tex., 1981), 18; Jacob L. Stambaugh and Lillian J. Stambaugh, *A History of Collin County, Texas* (Austin, 1958), 67; Felgar, "Texas in the War for Southern Independence," 157, 164; Allan R. Purcell, "The History of the Texas Militia, 1835–1903" (Ph.D. dissertation, UT, 1981), 154–59; Caroline S. Ruckman, "The Frontier of Texas During the Civil War" (M.A. thesis, UT, 1926), 74–75; William R. Geise, "The Confederate Military Forces in the Trans-Mississippi" (Ph.D. dissertation, UT, 1974), 191.

States Army officer commanding a militia regiment in Hugh F. Young's 15th Brigade. Fearing an imminent "invasion of African foe" from Kansas and recalling the "late demonstrations of Jayhawkery and murders [sic] bands within our own borders," Wilmette asked to command a regiment of regular troops assigned to the northwestern frontier.[17]

Lubbock declined both offers and turned instead to a man who already had proved ruthless in countering dissent. At Hebert's suggestion, he appointed John R. Baylor—who had been removed as governor of the Confederate Territory of Arizona and New Mexico for his extermination policies against Indians—to command the state troops along the Forks. To encourage enlistments to defend the northwest border and to retake Galveston, captured by Federal forces during October, 1862, the governor asked Davis to suspend the draft in Texas. Despite Lubbock's assertion that "feverish anxiety" pervaded the "Public Mind" regarding the chance of a "formidable invasion" into North Texas, "where recently great outrages have been committed by Indians & Jayhawkers, as also the discovery of many Home Traitors," the Confederate president did not exempt Texans from conscription. Baylor received just three companies of militia from Hudson's 21st District, commanded by William C. Twitty. These troops remained in the field for nearly three months, a peaceful interlude interrupted only when raiders attacked an Indian agency. The quiet prompted General John B. Magruder, who succeeded Hebert as commander of Texas, to order their mustering out in early January, 1863.[18]

After the dismissal of Twitty's troops, former provost marshal Bourland—idled by the end of martial law—campaigned for the enlistment of a

17. J. B. Wilmette to Lubbock, November 1, 1862, and James W. Throckmorton to Lubbock, October 25, 1862, in GOR. The best account of efforts to defend the northwestern frontier of Texas, though it differs in interpretation from this work, is David P. Smith, *Frontier Defense in the Civil War: Texas' Rangers and Rebels* (College Station, Tex., 1992).

18. Rowland, ed., *Jefferson Davis, Constitutionalist*, V, 369–71, 377–78; James G. Bourland to Paul O. Hebert, November 3, 1862, in CSR, Bourland's Border Regiment; Hebert to Lubbock, November 4, 8, 1862, Lubbock to J. N. Smith, November 10, 1862, Lubbock to Throckmorton, January 4, 1863, all in GOR; Hudson to Dashiell, n.d., General Orders Nos. 12 and 13, Headquarters, 21st Brigade, Texas State Troops, October 27, 30, 1862, Special Orders No. 5, HQ, 21st Brigade, Tex. State Troops, October 30, 1862, Muster and Pay Rolls of Charles L. Roff's Company, January 7, 1863, Muster Roll of William H. Jasper's Company, January 7, 1863, Muster Roll of A. M. Birdwell's Company, January 7, 1863, Muster Roll of Theodore J. Dorsett's Mounted Company C, January 15, 1863, all in AGR; *OR*, Ser. I, Vol. XV, 858–59; Martin H. Hall, *Sibley's New Mexico Campaign* (Austin, 1960), 224n.

permanent garrison from militia in the 21st District. He traveled to Houston and Austin, but received very little encouragement until Indians and "renegade white men," who reportedly had fled in great numbers from North Texas during the Great Hanging, killed as many as a dozen settlers on the Forks in February and March, 1863. The raiders habitually mutilated the bodies of male victims—scalping them and removing the left eye, ear, and hand—and left a piece of red cloth flying on a stick by each victim as a crude flag of no quarter. Lubbock again had Gainesville temporarily garrisoned by companies from the 29th Texas Cavalry, and he persuaded Magruder to enlist a battalion from the 21st District to wage "offensive war against our Indian enemy & the miserable traitors and Jay Hawkers who are inciting them to the butchery of our people." [19]

In response to these raids, Hudson mustered two companies under the command of Twitty; this pair provided a nucleus for the new Frontier Battalion. Twitty recruited two more companies, and the four were sworn into Confederate service for the duration of the war on April 24, 1863, by Bourland. Twitty, as commander of the battalion, fought with Hudson, who resented the usurpation of his authority as commander of the local militia and circulated rumors that Twitty's unit would be sent east, prompting many to avoid enlisting in it. After Twitty traveled to Austin to explain his differences with Hudson to the governor, Lubbock ordered Dashiell to tell Hudson that he would no longer be allowed to muster his troops without orders from Austin, preventing Hudson from using that tactic to disrupt the enlistment of Twitty's companies. [20]

Lubbock assured Twitty that his companies would not be sent away from the frontier and that the creation of a northern subdistrict under the com-

19. Lubbock to Daniel H. Cooper, March 26, 1863, Lubbock to Bourland, March 11, 28, 1863, Lubbock to Josiah A. Carroll, March 21, 1863, Lubbock to John R. Hamill, March 28, 1863, Lubbock to E. Armstrong *et al.*, April 11, 1863, all in GOR; Guy M. Bryan to Lubbock, April 1, 1863, in Francis R. Lubbock Papers, BTHC, John E. Wheeler Diary, 1850–1880 (MS in Morton Museum, Gainesville, Tex.); Joseph Ward to Dashiell, February 14, 1863, Hudson to Dashiell, March 8, 1863, in AGR; *OR*, Ser. I, Vol. XV, 1027–28, Vol. XXII, 799–800; Austin *Texas Almanac Extra*, March 7, 1863; Dallas *Herald*, April 22, 1863; Houston *Telegraph*, March 22, 1863; Geise, "Confederate Military Forces in the Trans-Mississippi," 143–44; Ruckman, "The Texas Frontier During the Civil War," 71–73.

20. Hudson to Dashiell, March 22, 28, April 7, 30, May 29, 1863, Muster Roll of Roff's Co., April 8, 1863, Muster Roll of Roff's Co. of Texas Cavalry . . . Mustered into the Service of the Confederate States by Col. James Bourland, on the 24th Day of April, A.D. 1863 . . . , all in AGR; Lubbock to Bourland, June 24, 1863, in GOR; Clarksville *Standard*, May 2, 1863.

James G. Bourland, as provost marshal for Cooke County, chaired the committee whose investigations led to the Great Hanging at Gainesville during October 1862.

Courtesy *Blue & Gray*, III (April–May, 1986)

Provost Marshal James G. Bourland did little to punish those who attacked dissenters in Cooke County, such as those who lynched Mrs. Hillier, the wife of a local draft-dodger, in the summer of 1862.

Originally published in *Frank Leslie's Illustrated Weekly Newspaper*, February 20, 1864

Obediah B. Atkinson, who founded the Peace Party in Cooke County, is on the far right of this photograph taken in Missouri in the 1890s. To his right is his wife, Dolly; the other man is Obediah and Dolly's son, Lewis, who stands with his wife, Fredonia, and their children: James, Cora and Clayton (left to right).

Courtesy Noel Parsons

William R. Hudson commanded the militia that arrested more than 200 suspected Unionists in October 1862 and occupied Gainesville during the Great Hanging.

Originally published in *The First 100 Years in Cooke County*, by A. Morton Smith. Used with permission.

Daniel Montague served as foreman of the jury for the Citizens Court, which voted to execute twenty-six accused Unionists and allowed at least fourteen more to be hanged at Gainesville during October, 1862.

Originally published in *The First 100 Years in Cooke County*, by A. Morton Smith. Used with permission.

Thomas Barrett, a Church of Christ minister who served as a juror for the Citizens Court, opposed the hanging of the prisoners and later wrote a memoir condemning the affair.

Originally published in *The First 100 Years in Cooke County*, by A. Morton Smith. Used with permission.

The Citizens Court met in a room rented by the county court on the second floor of Rufus F. Scott's store, which is the large building with the cupola in this postwar photograph.

Originally published in *The First 100 Years in Cooke County*, by A. Morton Smith. Used with permission.

John E. Wheeler was among the suspects arrested in Cooke County in October, 1862, but he was released and became a county judge and the mayor of Gainesville after the Civil War.

Originally published in *The First 100 Years in Cooke County*, by A. Morton Smith. Used with permission.

Nathaniel M. Clark was not condemned by the Citizens Court, but he was one of the fourteen prisoners whom the jurors permitted to be hanged on October 12 and 13, 1862. This portrait was made about 1860.

Courtesy L. D. Clark.

Mahuldah H. Clark was Nathaniel M. Clark's wife; this photograph was taken in the 1870s.

Courtesy L. D. Clark.

The gravestone of Nathaniel M. Clark, erected in 1878, includes an inscription of his last words: "Prepare yourself to live and to die. I hope to meet you all in a future world. God bless you all."

Courtesy Michael Clark

William C. Young served as prosecutor for the Citizens Court. His assassination in October, 1862, prompted the jurors to retry and condemn nineteen more accused Unionists.

Courtesy Morton Museum, Gainesville, Texas.

William W. Howeth joined the jury of the Citizens Court after the assassination of William C. Young;. this photograph was taken long after the Civil War had ended and Howeth had opened an abstract office in Gainesville.

Originally published in *The First 100 Years in Cooke County*, by A. Morton Smith. Used with permission.

This fanciful engraving of the hanging tree at Gainesville was based upon an account by Frederick Sumner. In fact, while the victims were all hanged from the same elm, they were executed singly or in pairs.

Originally published in *Frank Leslie's Illustrated Weekly Newspaper*, February 20, 1864.

James W. Throckmorton prevented the lynching of accused Unionists at Sherman in October, 1862. Ironically, his efforts to block the prosecution of Confederates for wartime atrocities contributed to his removal from the governor's office in 1867.

Courtesy Harold B. Simpson Confederate Research Center, Hillsboro, Texas

Henry E. McCulloch, shown here in a postwar portrait, commanded the Northern Subdistrict of Texas from 1863 to 1865. He
tried futilely to suppress disaffection, relying often on the violent
tactics of subordinates such as James G. Bourland in Cooke and
nearby counties.

mand of Smith P. Bankhead would bring a resolution to the controversy with Hudson. In May, 1863, Magruder organized Texas into three subdistricts, then gave Bankhead, his nephew, command of the Northern Subdistrict, which included Cooke County. Bankhead had already been nominated for a brigadier generalship for his operations against disaffected Germans in Central Texas; after appointing him, Magruder told an associate that he knew of "no other officer whom I consider capable." Bankhead increased the number of companies in the Frontier Battalion to six and gave command of it to Bourland, who retained Twitty, Charles L. Roff, James J. Diamond, Samuel P. C. Patton, and other participants in the Great Hanging as subordinates.[21]

The violent persecution of dissenters along the Forks began anew under Bankhead. Ten men in Federal uniforms, most of them from Cooke County, were captured near Fort Arbuckle while attempting to make their way north. Bankhead rejected their contention that they belonged to a scouting party and should be treated as prisoners of war. Instead, he organized a military tribunal and had them tried for treason, desertion, and uttering Union sentiments. All were convicted; three were shot as they knelt on their coffins, and the rest were put to work on the fortifications at Galveston before being exiled.[22]

Such brutality encouraged the resurgence of vigilantism. Three whites and four blacks were lynched in separate incidents in Denton County in the summer of 1863. In August reports surfaced that slaves were congregating at the home of John Beard, a white nonslaveholder from North Carolina who was suspected of being an abolitionist. A vigilance committee was elected in nearby Pilot Point; ominously, they chose a jury before beginning an inquiry. After he and several others were captured, Beard confessed that he had indeed met with blacks at his house. David J. Eddleman, who had been among the militia guarding Gainesville in October, 1862, went to

21. *OR*, Ser. I, Vol. XXII, 977, Vol. XXVI, 13, 20–21, 25, 38, 80; CSR, Bourland's Border Regiment; Bourland to Andrew Johnson, September 18, 1865, in Amnesty Files; William Steele to Smith P. Bankhead, July 11, 1863, in AGR; Lubbock to Bourland, June 24, 1863, and William C. Twitty to Lubbock, August 17, 1863, in GOR.

22. San Antonio *Herald*, August 10, 1863; Clarksville *Standard*, September 17, 1863; Dallas *Herald*, August 19, 1863. Regrettably, the names of the ten men arrested by Bankhead, as well as most of those involved in the renegade bands mentioned in this chapter, have not survived, which precludes a more substantial analysis of the men's origins and motives. The perspective presented here is primarily based upon, and thus has been influenced by, their persecutors' reports, many of which have been preserved.

Bankhead to arrange for transferring the prisoners to Confederate officials for trial. Eddleman was authorized to requisition a company of troops from Hudson, and returned with the men to Pilot Point, where he discovered that one of the white prisoners had been shot to death while allegedly trying to escape. He had the captured slaves whipped and returned to their masters, but in the accompanying chaos, the son of a man implicated by Beard ran past the guards and shot the accused abolitionist dead.[23]

Raids by Indians and white outlaws on the Forks made Bankhead's troops uneasy, but the men received little sympathy from their commander. He sent wagons to take families away from the frontier, but at the same time he disarmed a company who threatened to desert and go home, telling them that if they left he would "follow them up and shoot down every man I caught." He ordered Bourland to sweep the region, then reported to Magruder that the Forks harbored "large numbers of deserters and disaffected men from all parts of the State." After about a month in North Texas, Bankhead, believing most of the populace supported the dissenters, pleaded with his uncle to transfer him from "this God-forsaken country." Like others before him, Bankhead had belatedly realized that along the North Texas frontier, violence only brought more violence, not order and security.[24]

At Lubbock's request, Henry E. McCulloch, now a brigadier general with his own reputation for combating dissent in Central Texas, succeeded Bankhead as the commander of the Northern Subdistrict. Pursuant to a policy promulgated by General Edmund Kirby Smith, McCulloch offered amnesty to shirkers who joined the Confederate army. He enlisted prominent men in North Texas who had opposed secession—such as Throckmorton, Robert H. Taylor, and Benjamin H. Epperson—to persuade dis-

---

23. David J. Eddleman, "Autobiography of the [?]" (Typescript in UNT), 41–42; Census of 1860, Denton County, Tex., Schedule 1 (Free Inhabitants), Family Number 454, in Genealogy Division, TSL; Edward F. Bates, *History and Reminiscences of Denton County* (Denton, Tex., 1918), 107–109, 296–97; Cates, *Pioneer History of Wise County*, 148–49. After the Civil War, the unnamed assassin of Beard was convicted of manslaughter and served a fourth of his ninety-nine–year sentence before being pardoned.

24. *OR*, Ser I, Vol. LIII, 888–91. Bankhead remained in the Confederate army until March, 1865, when he fled to Federal lines in Louisiana and took an oath of allegiance to the United States. Two years later he was killed by an unknown assassin in Memphis, the city in which he had prospered as a newspaper editor and attorney during the 1850s. See Jonathan T. Dorris, *Pardon and Amnesty Under Lincoln and Johnson* (Chapel Hill, 1953), 67; *Elmwood: Charter, Rules, Regulations and By-Laws of Elmwood Cemetery Association of Memphis* (Memphis, 1874), 100.

senters to sign up. To Epperson, he promised that all those who had belonged to commands east of the Mississippi River would be assigned to units in North Texas. He tempered his offer with a promise of violence. If the shirkers did not surrender voluntarily, he would occupy their homes, take their families as hostages, and destroy all of their property.[25]

McCulloch promoted Bourland to lieutenant colonel in October, 1863, and assigned him to command all Confederate troops west of Cooke County's eastern boundary. Bourland's command, which had just 365 effectives in March, 1864, was henceforth the only regular Confederate unit permanently posted on the northwest frontier. He received only sporadic assistance from other Confederate and state units in carrying out his principal mission, which as McCulloch explained was extending "pardon to all that you believe come in voluntarily," arresting "all others dead or alive wherever found," and letting eligible men know "that they must go to the army and stay[,] abandon the country[,] or be killed."[26]

McCulloch's declarations prompted almost fifteen hundred men in North Texas to enlist by January, 1864. One large group came from Collin County. McCulloch wrote to the group's leader, Henry Boren—a deserter from Leonidas M. Martin's 10th Texas Cavalry Battalion—in late October, 1863, reluctantly agreeing to his demand that if his followers returned to service, they would be assigned to the frontier. Boren brought more than five hundred men out of the brush, all of whom were forwarded to Bourland to be enrolled as the Brush Battalion. They knew Bourland and were "afraid of some trick being played on them . . . by which they [were] to be hung or shot," but they were assured that he was a "personal friend" of the Boren

25. Judah P. Benjamin to Henry E. McCulloch, March 18, 1862, in McCulloch Family Papers, BTHC; McCulloch to Edmund P. Turner, September 17, 1863, in James G. Bourland Papers, LC; McCulloch to Benjamin H. Epperson, September 29, 1863, in Benjamin H. Epperson Papers, BTHC; Lubbock, *Six Decades in Texas*, 503; Lubbock to Edmund Kirby Smith, August 31, 1863, Lubbock to McCulloch, September 2, 1863, in GOR; *OR*, Ser. I, Vol. IX, 704–705, Vol. XXVI, 352–53; Austin *Texas State Gazette*, October 23, 1863; Clarksville *Standard*, October 3, 1863; San Antonio *Herald*, September 12, 1863; Robert L. Kerby, *Kirby Smith's Confederacy: The Trans-Mississippi South, 1863–1865* (New York, 1972), 217.

26. McCulloch to Bourland, October 29, December 1, 1863, Special Orders No. 64, HQ, Northern Subdistrict of Texas, October 9, 1863, all in Bourland Papers; Bourland to James E. McCord, October 30, 1863, in James B. Barry Papers, BTHC; Henry F. Bone to Dashiell, November 20, 1863, in AGR; Bourland to Lubbock, October 23, 1863, in GOR; *OR*, Ser. I, Vol. XXII, 1036–37, 1042, Vol. XXXIV, Pt. 2, pp. 932, 1107.

family and that John R. Diamond, who had played no direct role in the Great Hanging, would be their commander.[27]

The Brush Battalion was soon engaged in the distasteful task of hunting dissenters along the Forks. Three of its five companies were assigned to aid Baylor's "Ladies Rangers," sent by McCulloch to help Bourland clear the frontier of shirkers. After losing his command in North Texas in early 1863, Baylor had been elected to the Confederate Congress without the endorsement of his home county of Parker. The tone of his campaign was exemplified by a speech at the county seat, Weatherford, scorning residents for hiding in the brush, feigning illness, or even maiming themselves to avoid service. He called the state troops "flop eared militia," a reference to a dog he had that would bay and then eat all the food when the other dogs gave chase. A correspondent whose byline was "Gray Rover" reported Baylor's return with his rangers to editor Cushing, speculating that they would punish the "soft-shells" who were "eternally harping on the downfall of Vicksburg and our reverses generally" and who had allegedly burned crops to keep them out of Confederate hands.[28]

Baylor agreed with the Gray Rover that "croakers" should be dealt with severely. He led his rangers and some members of the Brush Battalion into Weatherford in early December, established a court martial, and summarily hanged two men. His troopers held others at bay with threats and even looted a few stores before riding on in search of more victims. In Jack County they located the camp of Uel D. Fox, a former resident of Head of Elm in Montague County who had fled to avoid Bourland's dragnet after the Great Hanging. Fox had returned to the region and recruited a company of deserters and draft dodgers, planning to march north in the spring. During his attack on Fox in a mid-December night raid, Baylor took no prisoners; though Fox and a handful escaped, eight of his men were killed

27. McCulloch to Bourland, November 22, 1865, in Bourland Papers; CSR, 5th Texas Partisan Rangers and Bourland's Border Regiment; Eddleman, "Autobiography," 39–40; *OR*, Ser. I, Vol. XXVI, 352–53, 401; McKinney (Tex.) *Messenger*, n.d., quoted in Clarksville *Standard*, November 7, 1863.

28. *Houston Telegraph*, November 25, 1863; Bourland to John R. Diamond, December 13, 1863, and Special Orders No. 142, HQ, Northern Subdistrict of Texas, December [?], 1863, in Bourland Papers; Dallas *Herald*, September 9, 1863; Oran M. Roberts, "Texas," in *Confederate Military History*, ed. Clement A. Evans (12 vols.; Atlanta, 1899), XI, 292–94; H. Smythe, *Historical Sketch of Parker County and Weatherford, Texas* (St. Louis, 1877), 161–62; Ruckman, "The Frontier of Texas During the Civil War," 76–77.

in a savage hand-to-hand struggle. Fox rallied the survivors in Wise County, where his presence worried Confederate officials until he went north early in 1864.[29]

Both McCulloch and Bourland approved of Baylor's operations, but numerous protests led to the disbandment of the Ladies Rangers in January, 1864. While some members of his company were assigned to other regiments in service elsewhere, Baylor was interviewed by Cushing, who praised their work against the "wretches" along the Forks. A more trenchant observer, William Quayle, wondered instead if a "storm" had been raised that would prove difficult to contain. He may have been referring to the Brush Battalion, which at about the same time was implicated in a mutinous conspiracy. McCulloch suggested to Bourland that the "good" ones be weeded out and the rest left to their fate, but this was too difficult to do. In March, 1864, when the unit was finally disbanded and Martin's troopers attempted to escort them to Shreveport, the Clarksville *Standard* demanded execution of the renegades because they would take to the brush again if they could. The writer was correct; many did escape and harassed Confederate sympathizers until long after the war ended.[30]

Bourland received more substantial support from General Sam Bell Maxey, a graduate of West Point and a combat veteran of both the Mexican War and the Civil War east of the Mississippi River. He took command of all Confederate troops in the Indian Territory in December, 1863, and quickly realized that North Texas was a great handicap as the unrest there prevented McCulloch from actively supporting his operations. Too, units mustered along the Forks leaked a steady stream of deserters into that area, draining his effective strength. Finally, the disruption endangered the role of North Texas as a key source of grain and beef; as Confederate general

29. Uel D. Fox to Alex Wilson, November 10, 1862 (Photocopy in Great Hanging File, Morton Museum); Bourland to Diamond, December 13, 1863, in Bourland Papers; William Quayle to Pendleton Murrah, December 27, 1863, in AGR; *OR*, Ser. I, Vol. XXXIV, Pt. 2, p. 911; Houston *Telegraph*, November 25, 1863, January 15, 1864; Clarksville *Standard*, July 13, 1861; Roberts, "Texas," in *Confederate Military History*, ed. Evans, 292–94.

30. Houston *Telegraph*, January 15, 1864; Quayle to Murrah, December 27, 1863, in AGR; McCulloch to Bourland, January 7, 1864, Thomas Lanagin to McCulloch, November 28, 1863, McCulloch to Bourland, December 11, 1863, Bourland to John R. Baylor, January 4, 1864, all in Bourland Papers; CSR, Bourland's Regiment; Kerby, *Kirby Smith's Confederacy*, 219.

William Steele observed, "An enemy in Northern Texas would soon starve out the Trans-Mississippi Department."[31]

Maxey cooperated most effectively by providing troops to police North Texas. Martin was appointed enrolling officer for the Northern Subdistrict in November, 1863, and Maxey assigned Martin's troops to the "conscript business" in December, 1863. A member of Martin's unit later recalled that "gathering deserters was very unpleasant work"; his "tender chords" were "touched by the tears and screams of wives and children." Although to him and some of his comrades "it seemed cruel to make a person do what he did not desire to take part in," they remained at work in North Texas until April, 1864, when they left for Arkansas.[32]

Maxey's troops occasionally clashed with Bourland, whose venality they found frustrating. Bourland ordered a detachment of his troopers into Denton County in January, 1864. Exploring a thicket twelve miles southeast of Denton, on Elm Creek, they found almost 150 well-armed deserters and Unionists led by William Parnell, a resident who had enlisted in the Federal army at the outbreak of the war and had returned home to recruit. He had set up a camp and was preparing to march north in the spring. His followers raided nearby farms for supplies and terrorized slaveholders; one owner of thirty slaves had been accosted by raiders who took his horse, cursed him as a "d——d old secessionist," and told him that in two months they would raise the stars and stripes over Texas. Bourland discounted the boasts but was infuriated to learn that forty members of his own command had visited Parnell's camp and that a dozen subsequently joined him. He made plans to attack, and called for reinforcements.[33]

31 OR, Ser. I, Vol. XXII, 830, 1112, Vol. XXXIV, Pt. 2. pp. 945, 958–59; Samuel B. Maxey to McCulloch, January 8, 1864, in Samuel B. Maxey Papers, TSL; Houston Telegraph, January 15, 1864; Louise W. Horton, "General Sam Bell Maxey: His Defense of North Texas and the Indian Territory," SWHQ, LXXIV (1971), 507, 510–11; Louise W. Horton, Samuel Bell Maxey: A Biography (Austin, 1974), passim; Ernest Wallace, Charles DeMorse, Pioneer Editor and Statesman (Lubbock, 1942), 148–49.

32. Maxey to William R. Boggs, December 26, 1863, Tom P. Ochiltree to Leonidas M. Martin, April 2, 1864, in Maxey Papers; J. W. Boyer and C. H. Thurmann, The Annals of Elder Horn (New York, 1930), 46; OR, Ser. I, Vol. XXVI, 382, Vol. XLI, Pt. 4, p. 1132, Vol. LIII, 923–25; Horton, "General Sam Bell Maxey," 518; Marcus J. Wright, Texas in the War, ed. Harold B. Simpson (Hillsboro, Tex., 1965), 31–32, 125.

33. Ser. I, Vol. XXXIV, Pt. 2, pp. 909–10, 942; Maxey to Charles DeMorse, February 12, 1864, Maxey to McCulloch, February 17, March 5, 1864, all in Maxey Papers.

Maxey assigned a company to aid Bourland, ordering the men to return with all deserters. Maxey's captain attempted to negotiate with Parnell but ran afoul of Bourland, who insisted that he should attack the camp and "take or kill" all of the renegades. Despite the captain's assertion that the deserters were "penitent even to tears" and that he could convince them to surrender, Bourland did attack. Over a hundred renegades were present, but only fourteen were captured while the rest scattered. Maxey protested bitterly about Bourland to McCulloch, surmising that most of the survivors had reached Mexico where they might join Union units. McCulloch did nothing; after all, it was he who had written Bourland before the assault that while it would be a "blessing" if the party left Texas, "it would be a much greater one if we could intercept and kill the last one of them."[34]

Bourland's efforts to secure the northwestern frontier were made more difficult by the intrusion of William C. Quantrill and his irregulars into North Texas in the fall of 1863. McCulloch, at General Kirby Smith's suggestion, assigned Quantrill to hunt deserters in the region, a task in which that raider revealed his penchant for violence by killing numerous dissenters in Collin County. Closer to Bourland's own district, Quantrill peacefully ended a food riot by women in Sherman, but some of his followers terrorized that town and the surrounding countryside. McCulloch repeatedly asked Bourland to help expel the guerrillas, but this was not done until after one of the Missouri intruders killed Major George N. Butts, a Confederate recruiter in Grayson County and an associate of Bourland's. Although Quantrill and many of his marauders fled from Texas shortly thereafter—most of them never to return—other outlaws remained to plague settlers along the Forks.[35]

34. Maxey to McCulloch, February 17, March 5, 1864, in Maxey Papers; McCulloch to Bourland, February 3, 1864, in Bourland Papers.

35. Pete A. Y. Gunter, ed., "Lillian Gunter Papers on Cooke County History" (Typescript in Morton Museum), 386; John T. Darnall to Epperson, June 15, [1864], in Epperson Papers; Throckmorton to Murrah, March 28, 1864, in GOR; George W. Rawick, ed., *The American Slave: A Composite Autobiography: Supplement* (10 vols.; Westport, Conn., 1979), II, 341; *OR*, Ser. I, Vol. XXVI, 382, Vol. XXXIV, Pt. 2, pp. 942, 945, 969, 1197, Pt. 3, pp. 742–43; San Antonio *Herald*, January 23, 1864; Carl W. Breihan, *Quantrill and His Civil War Guerillas* (Denver, 1959), 119–34, 137–44, 158–63; Albert Castel, *William Clarke Quantrill: His Life and Times* (New York, 1962), 122–41, 144–49, 155, 160–68, 199, 201–202, 213; William E. Connelly, *Quantrill and the Border Wars* (New York, 1956), 421, 436–45, 458; Larry C. Rampp, "William C. Quantrill's Civil War Activities in Texas, 1861–1863," *Texas Military History*, VIII (1970), 221–31; Roy F. Hall and Helen G. Hall, *Collin County: Pioneering in North Texas*

Frustrated with North Texas, McCulloch, like Bankhead, begged to be transferred in early 1864. He confessed to Magruder that many of his units refused to obey him and that he could not force them to do so with the few loyal troops he had. He concluded, "The best thing that could happen for the country would be to kill them." Denied a transfer, McCulloch repeatedly threatened to resign, but both Magruder and Kirby Smith insisted that he stay. The former was especially adamant, agreeing that renegades "should be shot without hesitation or mercy" and asking McCulloch to "stick to the ship and do your best, for God's sake; destroy these men whilst you have the means." McCulloch again considered leaving military service in the summer of 1864, but he remained in command of the Northern Subdistrict through the end of the war.[36]

Bourland shared McCulloch's concern, particularly regarding state troops. For some time, Hudson and other district commanders had been telling Austin officials that the militia had disintegrated. Many dissenters along the Forks would not join without guarantees that they would not be drafted to fight elsewhere, and many others organized independent units for home defense and defied efforts to muster for regular service. Bourland attempted to take over the state troops on the Forks in the fall of 1863, but was denied permission to do so by Lubbock. Pendleton Murrah became governor in November, 1863, and at Magruder's insistence ordered a reorganization of the militia as a reserve for the regular Confederate army. The Red River campaign in the spring of 1864 led to the disbandment of the state troops; as they had feared, many militia were sent to Louisiana to combat the Federal forces under General Nathaniel P. Banks. When the legislature finally abolished the militia on May 28, 1864, desertions had almost completely depleted it.[37]

(Quanah, Tex., 1975), 296; Mattie D. Lucas and Mita H. Hall, *A History of Grayson County, Texas* (Sherman, Tex., 1936), 35–37, 118–21; Graham Landrum and Allen Smith, *An Illustrated History of Grayson County, Texas* (2d ed.; Fort Worth, 1967), 2–8, 67, 69; *Ancestors and Descendants: Grayson County, Texas* (Dallas, 1980), 13; Stambaugh and Stambaugh, *History of Collin County*, 68–69.

36. *OR*, Ser. I, Vol. XXVI, Pt. 2, p. 285, Vol. XXXIV, Pt. 3, p. 814, Vol. XXXIV, Pt. 2, pp. 909, 925–26, Vol. LIII, 923–25; Kirby Smith to McCulloch, January 4, June 7, 1864, in McCulloch Family Papers.

37. Hudson to Dashiell, June 19, July 22, 1863, J. P. Hopson to Dashiell, May 26, 1863, Wilmette to Dashiell, July 24, 1863, Hugh F. Young to Dashiell, October 4, 1863, Nathaniel Terry to Dashiell, August 4, 1863, Thomas W. Toler to Dashiell, August 4, 1863, all in AGR;

The abolition of the militia left only the state frontier defense organizations as a refuge for those wishing to avoid the regular Confederate army. Until December, 1863, the Frontier Regiment was the choice of many settlers along the Forks. Because it was a tremendous drain on the state treasury, however, Lubbock tried to have the regiment accepted into regular service. Upon the advice of Magruder, he reorganized it as the Mounted Regiment of Texas State Troops and increased enrollment to ten companies enlisted for the duration of the war, but President Davis hesitated to accept it because of Lubbock's requirement that it not be moved from the frontier. Confederate officials meanwhile criticized the regiment in an attempt to have it dissolved and its troops sent elsewhere, as the militia had been. Bourland inspected Red River Station, where John T. Rowland commanded a small detachment, and reported that most were draft dodgers and none were "vigilant or industrious." He added that "some of our best citizens" believed that quite a few of these men had secretly allied with Federals or "stealling [sic] Indians."[38]

Bourland also said the Mounted Regiment was useless for fighting Indians and chasing deserters, despite several attempts to order them to do so. While it may be true that they were reluctant to enforce the draft, the regiment provided some security for the settlers along the Forks because it was effective against hostile Indians, in spite of a chronic lack of food, munitions, medical supplies, and good horses. As Rowland told James E. McCord, who had assumed command of the regiment in the spring of 1863, if his garrison was removed a "general panic would take place" among the inhabitants along the upper Forks. He pointed out that during an invasion of heavily armed white and red marauders along the Forks in December, 1863, some of Bourland's troops had been surprised and killed. Others of

Lubbock to John S. Ford, September 11, 1863, Terry to Lubbock, August 12, October 25, 1863, Murrah to McCulloch, November 18, 1863, all in GOR; *OR*, Ser. I, Vol. XXII, 1036–37, Vol. XXVI, 159–60; Ila M. Myers, "The Relation of Governor Pendleton Murrah, of Texas, with the Confederate Military Authorities" (M.A. thesis, UT, 1929), 37–39, 42–54.

38. Bourland to McCulloch, November 10, 1863, and Special Orders No. 1, HQ, Mounted Regiment, Tex. State Troops, April 13, 1862, in Barry Papers; Lubbock to Jefferson Davis, November 13, 1862, Terry to Lubbock, August 15, 1863, Lubbock to McCulloch, September 2, 1863, in GOR; *OR*, Ser. I, Vol. XXVI, 166, Vol. LIII, 890–91; Rowland, *Jefferson Davis, Constitutionalist*, V, 454–57; Lubbock, *Six Decades in Texas*, 475; Gammel, comp., *Laws of Texas*, V, 607–608, 856, 860–61; Marshall *Texas Republican*, October 25, 1862; Felgar, "Texas in the War for Southern Independence," 88–89; Purcell, "History of the Texas Militia," 150–51; Ruckman, "The Frontier of Texas During the Civil War," 81–84.

Bourland's command who joined Rowland's men to pursue the raiders fled when told to attack, contributing to the deaths of two members of the Mounted Regiment who stood fast and the wounding of other troopers before the enemy was repulsed.[39]

Convinced of the value of the Mounted Regiment, Magruder accepted it into regular Confederate service and pledged that a battalion from that unit would remain on the Forks. Despite his assurance, the transfer of the Mounted Regiment left many dissenters without a safe refuge from conscription as the battalion could be ordered away just as the state troops could, and would, be. The solution lay in joining a new state frontier defense organization created on December 15, 1863, to be recruited only in frontier counties. Murrah assigned William Quayle, a former chief justice and state senator from Tarrant County who had been lieutenant colonel of the 9th Texas Cavalry, to command the 1st Frontier District, which embraced Cooke and four nearby counties. Quayle had left the cavalry after his eyes failed, but had recovered and taken command of a company formed in Tarrant County to chase deserters. He wanted a more prestigious commission, but he accepted Murrah's offer.[40]

39. John T. Rowland to McCord, January 9, 1864, in AGR; McCord to Barry, May 20, 1863, in Barry Papers; Charles Goodnight, "Autobiography" (Typescript in Charles Goodnight Papers, BTHC), 28–29, 54; James B. Barry, *A Texas Ranger and Frontiersman: The Days of Buck Barry in Texas, 1845–1906*, ed. James K. Greer (Dallas, 1932), 146–48, 153, 155, 166–68; Barry to Dashiell, December 1, 1862, Ward to Dashiell, February 14, 1863, Rowland to Dashiell, April 21, 1863, J. N. Hembre to Dashiell, June 30, 1863, General Orders No. 16, HQ, Tex. State Troops, September 11, 1863, McCord to Dashiell, October 9, 1863, Extract from J. T. Rowland's Scout Report for December, 1863, n.d., all in AGR; *OR*, Ser. I, Vol. XXVI, 531–32; Collins, *Cooke County*, 19–20; J. Evetts Haley, *Charles Goodnight, Cowman and Plainsman* (New York, 1936), 84–85, 96–97. Barry served in the Frontier Regiment during the Civil War.

40. Special Orders No. 233, HQ, Tex. State Troops, February 13, 1863, in Barry Papers; Poll Book of Capt. Quayle's Company for the Election of Colonel, Lt. Colonel + Major for the Second Regiment of the First Brigade of Texas Cavalry, October 2d, 1861, in William Quayle Papers, University of Alabama Library, University, Ala.; Quayle to Murrah, December 27, 1863, in AGR; Lubbock to Dashiell, September 22, 1862, Quayle to Lubbock, July 20, 1863, John B. Magruder to Murrah, November 20, 1863, Murrah to Quayle, January 8, 1864 [mistakenly filed as 1863], Quayle to Murrah, January 15, 1864, all in GOR; Texas Secretary of State, Election Register; Gammel, comp., *Laws of Texas*, V, 677–79, 828; *OR*, Ser. I, Vol. VIII, 5–10, 18–19; Dallas *Herald*, October 16, 1861, July 12, 1862; 5; Smith, *Frontier Defense in the Civil War*, 95–96; Harry M. Henderson, *Texas in the Confederacy* (San Antonio, 1955), 127; *Members of the Texas Legislature*, 37–38; Smythe, *Historical Sketch of Parker County*, 173; Charles I. Evans, "The Service of Texan Troops in the Armies of the Southern Confed-

Quayle completed the muster of twenty companies, a total of 1,517 men, in the 1st Frontier District by late February. Dissenters mingled uneasily with their persecutors in the new organization. One of the companies enlisted from Cooke County was commanded by Cincinnatus Potter; among its members were James B. Stone and Benjamin Scanland, who had served together with Potter on the Citizens Court in October, 1862, as well as Robert O. Duncan, who had attended the ill-fated meeting led by Rama Dye in the Cross Timbers on the night of October 1, 1862. Two other jurors from the Citizens Court, Samuel C. Doss and Thomas Wright, served in another company, while Harvey Howeth was elected first lieutenant of another.[41]

The troops of the 1st Frontier District were bound by oath to turn over to Confederate authorities all men who were avoiding conscription, but they proved lax in performing this duty. Many from the Forks had deserted from Confederate units to enroll in the new organization, while others who lived in nearby counties had slipped across the lines to enlist. Quayle understood the situation, but he frequently assured his superiors that he was not accepting the enlistment of deserters and was chasing them back to their original regiments. The controversy, not settled before the war's end, heightened Confederate officials' suspicions regarding these state troops. Bourland, within whose jurisdiction Quayle's troopers operated almost independently, was especially skeptical.[42]

---

eracy," in *A Comprehensive History of Texas 1685 to 1897*, ed. Dudley G. Wooten (2 vols.; Dallas, 1898), II, 617–18; Felgar, "Texas in the War for Southern Independence," 100; George W. Sergeant, "Early History of Tarrant County" (M.A. thesis, UT, 1953), 155.

41. General Orders No. 6, HQ, Tex. State Troops, February 12, 1864, General Orders No. 4, HQ, Frontier Regiment, August 6, 1864, in Barry Papers; Quayle to David B. Culberson, February 25, 1864, in Quayle Papers; Muster and Pay Rolls of L. F. Whaley's Company, Tex. State Troops, First Frontier District, January 1, 1865, Muster and Pay Rolls, of James O. Hill's Company, Tex. State Troops, 1st Frontier Dist., January 1, 1865, Muster Rolls of Cincinnatus Potter's Company, Tex. State Troops, 1st Frontier Dist., February 13, June 20, 1864, January 1, 1865, all in AGR; A. Morton Smith, *The First 100 Years in Cooke County* (San Antonio, 1955), 42–45; Felgar, "Texas in the War for Southern Independence," 94.

42. Quayle to Culberson, February 4, 1864, and Quayle to McCulloch, February 20, 1864, in Quayle Papers; Quayle to Culberson, January 22, February 10, March 31, 1864, Throckmorton to Jonathan Burke, January 29, 1865, all in AGR; Kirby Smith to Murrah, January 18, 1864, in GOR; Rowland, *Jefferson Davis, Constitutionalist*, VI, 235–36; Gammel, comp., *Laws of Texas*, V, 677–79; *OR*, Ser. I, Vol. XLI, Pt. 3, pp. 986–87, Vol. XLVIII, Pt. 1, pp. 1373–74, 1376, 1378–79; Wooster, "Texas," in *The Confederate Governors*, ed. Yearns, 209–11; Bates, *Denton County*, 110; Felgar, "Texas in the War for Southern Independence," 212, 220–23.

A Union raid deep into the Indian Territory and preparations for their own Red River campaign during the spring of 1864 increased Confederate authorities' concerns about North Texas. Maxey wrote an associate that "traitors behind may make a break for the federal lines any day—keep a lookout," and he also told McCulloch that any suspect organizations had to be crushed. When reports surfaced that some fifteen hundred deserters and Unionists had assembled west of the Forks on the Concho River, Mc-Culloch ordered an attack, even though they had allegedly come together for a peaceful exodus to California. He and Bourland feared that if this plan became known, others would ally with the refugees and perhaps raid into North Texas. Rumors that some of Parnell's former followers had joined the group prompted Magruder to endorse McCulloch's order and Quayle was notified to be ready to combat an uprising.[43]

Confederate suspicions were confirmed when Quayle had an alarming conversation with James M. Luckey. A former constable and town treasurer of Weatherford, Luckey had been a captain in the Parker County militia and had retained that rank in the new organization under Quayle. Allegedly a supporter of secession, he had lost a bitter appeal in the summer of 1863 after goods and accounts held by him and a partner were sequestered, and he was also convicted of issuing illegal currency. Luckey recalled Quayle's opposition to secession, and asked if they could talk as individuals. After Quayle agreed, Luckey declared that he was a Unionist, had voted against secession, and had been quietly plotting to overthrow Confederate rule. He had learned recently that he was marked for elimination by a pro-Confederate organization, the Sons of the South, and he had decided to take action before he was killed.[44]

43. Maxey to Richard M. Gano, March 16, 1864, and Maxey to McCulloch, March 18, 1864, in Maxey Papers; Bourland to Quayle, March 26, 1864, Jonathan P. Hill to Quayle, April 2, 1864, Throckmorton to Quayle, April 4, 1864, all in Quayle Papers; McCulloch to Murrah, March 20, 28, 1864, in GOR; OR, Ser. I, Vol. XXXIV, Pt. 2, pp. 1103–1104, Pt. 3, pp. 726–27; Larry C. Rampp and Donald L. Rampp, "The Phillips Expedition: The Abortive Federal Invasion of Texas," *Military History of Texas and the Southwest*, IX (1971), 23–33; Charles I. Evans, "Military Events and Operations in Texas and Along the Coasts and Border, 1861–1865," in *Comprehensive History of Texas*, ed. Wooten, II, 379.

44. Terry to Dashiell, January 31, 1863, in AGR; U.S. Department of Justice, District Court, Western District of Texas, Austin, Confederate Court Case Files, 1862–1865, Nos. 1895 and 1918: *Confederate States of America* v. *John Shields and James M. Luckey*, in Record Group 21, Federal Records Center, Fort Worth; *Reports of Cases Argued and Decided in the Supreme Court of the State of Texas* (65 vols.; St. Louis, 1848–1886), XXVI, 362–65; OR, Ser. I, Vol. XXXIV, Pt. 3, pp. 772–74; Smythe, *Historical Sketch of Parker County*, 162, 164.

Luckey had more in mind than flight. He asked that Quayle assign his company to hunt deserters in the Indian Territory. There he would organize renegades, establish communications with the Union army, call on the Mounted Regiment to join him—which he believed two-thirds would do—and facilitate a Federal invasion into East Texas by occupying the counties on the northwestern frontier. He insisted that his plan could be effected in twenty days if Quayle would help, and that many of the state troops would join because they believed the oath they had taken was "forced upon them by a mob and not by any legal authority." He gave the names of three other company commanders who would take part, including chief justice J. Wiley Robbins of Jack County.[45]

Quayle sent John W. Hale to report on the conspiracy to Bourland, who proposed that Quayle encourage Luckey in order to learn about other conspirators. To reassure Luckey, Bourland advised that an order be sent to the Sons of the South at Weatherford telling them "to suspend further operations against Luckey." He planned to send a few trusted men to infiltrate suspected companies; when he notified McCulloch of this, the general approved and sent his own spy and more troops to assist in the task. McCulloch also ordered Quayle to "pounce on them and kill or capture the whole of them," adding, "Better kill than capture them." He was more prudent in his directions to Bourland, who as the ranking officer would control the operation. He told him to send all prisoners to Houston for a trial. The suspects were to be moved quickly beyond the reach of their friends, but McCulloch added that it "might be wise" to let it be known that an attempt to free the prisoners "would be fatal to them."[46]

Bourland sent John R. Diamond and a hundred men from his "most reliable companies" to carry out the arrests. As McCulloch had advised, preparations were made in secrecy; Bourland admonished Quayle to "manage this affair in the same way we did in Cooke." No one was told the soldiers were coming, and only the officers knew the destinations before

45. *OR*, Ser. I, Vol. XXXIV, Pt. 3, pp. 772–74, Pt. 4, pp. 634–35.

46. Throckmorton to Quayle, April 12, 15, 1864, Bourland to Quayle, April 14, 1864, McCulloch to Quayle, April 14, 15, 16, 1864, Special Orders No. 99, HQ, Northern Subdistrict of Tex., April 15, 1864, all in Quayle Papers; *OR*, Ser. I, Vol. XXXIV, Pt. 3, pp. 771–72, 782–83. McCulloch was already wary of one conspirator; he had ordered Bourland in October, 1863, to arrest J. Wiley Robbins for urging men not to enlist in the Confederate army and for sheltering deserters, but Robbins had avoided capture. See McCulloch to Bourland, October 29, 1863, in Bourland Papers.

they approached the homes of their quarry, which included both those
Quayle had pointed out and others chosen by Bourland with McCulloch's
approval. Despite all precautions, rumors flew that Confederate troops were
coming to shoot all who opposed the Confederacy. A "stampede" ensued
and hundreds escaped, including Robbins, Henry J. Thompson, and John
Taylor—the last two with more than three hundred followers. Bourland
urged Quayle to pursue the refugees "until the last one is either arrested or
killed." Diamond gave chase but was led astray by the wives of his quarry,
who claimed that a thousand men waited north of the Red River and would
be joined by three times as many Federals. In addition, Thompson's
brother, Alvey, a militia captain, volunteered to guide Diamond, and then
led him in circles.[47]

Bourland told Quayle to send every prisoner to Houston by way of
Gainesville. Instead, Quayle, upon the advice of state district judge J. W.
Ferris, organized a committee to interview all of the prisoners and to for-
ward only the guilty. Chaired by the chief justice of Parker County, A. J.
Hunter, the committee sent just fourteen men, including Luckey, to Houston. Diamond, however, increased the tally by arresting militia captains
Isaac Ward and Charles Adare after their release by Hunter's committee.
Diamond accused the pair, who had taken part in his pursuit, of aiding
renegades in escaping and took them to Gainesville. Texas Adjutant General David A. Culberson wrote Quayle that if he executed prisoners he
would be supported by state authorities, but Quayle surrendered most of
the rest to the Confederate army for enrollment. Only a single fatality was
recorded; Texas legislator John M. Prince, Quayle's adjutant, fell dead from
his horse—apparently the victim of a heart attack—after being betrayed by
Luckey and arrested.[48]

The refusal of other Confederate officials to support Bourland further

47. Bourland to Quayle, April 16, 20, 22, 1864, McCulloch to Bourland, April 15, 1864,
all in Quayle Papers; Affidavits of T. J. Stanfield and Charles Adare, December 19, 1864,
Henry J. Thompson to Andrew J. Hamilton, August 9, 1865, in GOR; OR, Ser. I, Vol. XXXIV,
Pt. 3, p. 792, Pt. 4, pp. 634–35; Austin *Texas State Gazette*, May 18, 1864; San Antonio *News*,
May 28, 1864; Frank H. Smyrl, "Unionism, Abolitionism, and Vigilantism in Texas, 1856–
1865" (M.A. thesis, UT, 1961), 139.

48. Quayle to Culberson, February 4, April 27, 1864, Bourland to Quayle, April 22, 1864,
Culberson to Quayle, April 28, 1864, all in Quayle Papers; Affidavits of Stanfield and Adare,
December 19, 1864, and of F. A. Leach, May 25, 1867, A. J. Hunter to Murrah, May 22, 1864,
J. W. Ferris to Murrah, August 18, 1864, all in GOR; Austin *Texas State Gazette*, May 18, 1864;
San Antonio *News*, May 28, 1864; Smyrl, "Unionism, Abolitionism, and Vigilantism," 139.

reduced the effectiveness of his dragnet operations in Parker County. Upon their arrival in Houston, Luckey and the rest were set free for lack of evidence. Ward was arrested for not having a proper pass as he tried to leave the city. He was enrolled in a coastal defense unit and in December, 1864, was still serving in Houston despite several requests for his release. Adare, a former surveyor and commissioner for Parker County, fared better. He escaped near Dallas and reported to Quayle, then was acquitted by a court martial. William T. Horton remained in a guardhouse at McCulloch's headquarters in Bonham until August, 1864, when he and two others escaped. Bourland's troops shot at him when he tried to reach his mother's house in Wise County, but they failed to kill him. Bourland reminded Quayle that Horton's father-in-law, Arphax Dawson, and his wife's first husband, Rama Dye, were among those hanged at Gainesville in 1862, but Quayle ignored Bourland's directive to shoot the "traitor."[49]

After the arrests in Parker County, Bourland extended the purge to include his own troops. Many dissenters, including some like James L. Clark and John D. Powers who had lost relatives in the Great Hanging, had joined his battalion in order to remain near Cooke County. Diamond reported that about twenty members of a company posted at Head of Elm, which included Clark and Powers, had deserted and that more would bolt in a few days. Bourland dispatched Diamond and a select detachment to solve the problem. They surrounded Head of Elm and opened fire; Clark recalled that they tied one man to a tree and "shot him all to peaces [*sic*]." Clark's squad returned from a patrol about the time the shooting began but were warned to flee by the wife of one of their number. They gathered deserters, women, and children as they went; when they turned for Kansas, their ragged group included over three dozen men. Others from Bourland's battalion fled to Mexico.[50]

Many of his immediate superiors praised Bourland for his efforts. Maxey declared himself satisfied that Bourland's operation, along with Confederate success in Louisiana and Arkansas, had destroyed organized dissent in

49. Bourland to Quayle, August 10, 1864, and Quayle to Elkanah J. Greer, August 25, 1864, in Quayle Papers; Throckmorton to Murrah, December 20, 1864, in GOR; Texas Secretary of State, Election Register; Francis T. Ingmire, comp., "Cooke County, Texas, Marriage Records 1849–1879," p. 7, typescript in BTHC; Smythe, *Historical Sketch of Parker County*, 180–81.

50. Clark, ed., *Recollections*, 78–79, 83, 85–88; Bourland to Quayle, April 18, 1864, in Quayle Papers.

North Texas and "effectually scotched that snake." McCulloch disagreed with Maxey's optimistic view; he and Bourland distrusted the remaining state troops. McCulloch wrote to Culberson that if regular Confederate units were removed from the Northern Subdistrict, "*then* would commence an indiscriminate robbery of our citizens, and a general desertion to the enemy." To a fellow officer, McCulloch confided that what was required was a "good regiment . . . under an energetic, fighting, hanging man," to operate on the frontier "with orders to attack and kill all who are assembled to resist the authorities, and arrest all others who owe service to the country or are disloyal." [51]

McCulloch found his man in Bourland. After a "flying trip" to Gainesville in late April to evaluate the situation, McCulloch asked for troops to upgrade Bourland's command to a regiment. Magruder subsequently assigned four more companies to Bourland, including two carefully selected from among the state troops on the Forks. Bourland became colonel, and John R. Diamond lieutenant colonel, because the former, as McCulloch admitted, "is getting old, is in feeble health, and desires to be relieved from service." Bourland soon recovered his health, though, and campaigned vigorously against dissenters on the Forks, much to the distress of Quayle, who noted that renegades received "but few favors from him[,] which makes them dread to fall into his hands." [52]

Unfortunately for many victims, it became standard procedure for all prisoners to be given to Bourland for transfer to McCulloch's headquarters at Bonham. Bourland often decided who would survive to be tried there. Those whom he condemned were forwarded in the custody of a few trusted men, and would be shot along the way when they allegedly tried to escape.

51. Maxey to Boggs, May 29, 1864, in Maxey Papers; J. H. Earle to Culberson, June 4, 1864, in AGR; *OR*, Ser. I, Vol. XXXIV, Pt. 4, pp. 634–35.

52. *OR*, Ser. I, Vol. XXXIV, Pt. 3, pp. 794–95, Pt. 4, pp. 630–31; Rowland to James B. Barry, May 28, 1864, in Barry Papers; H. A. Whaley to Diamond, n.d., in Bourland Papers; Bourland to Quayle, April 26, 1864, in Quayle Papers; George L. Scott, "History of Early Days in Gainesville" (MS in Cooke County Historical File); D. S. Howell, "Along the Texas Frontier During the Civil War," *WTHA Yearbook*, XIII (1937), 85; *Biographical Souvenir of the State of Texas* (Chicago, 1889), 98; Tom Bomar, *Glimpses of Grayson County from the Early Days* (Sherman, Tex., 1894), 25; John H. Brown and William S. Speer, eds., *Encyclopedia of the New West* (Marshall, Tex., 1881), "Texas," 380, 473; Lucas and Hall, *Grayson County*, 87, 128; Wright, *Texas in the War*, 29, 59, 122, 155; Henderson, *Texas in the Confederacy*, 134. Among the new recruits were Alvin Roff, son of Charles L. Roff, and Citizens Court members Wiley Jones and James B. Stone, who became a company physician.

He was quite candid about his callousness. For example, when an informant reported that seventeen of Rowland's troops had allied with other deserters and set out for Kansas, Bourland badgered Quayle until he sent 250 men in pursuit.The pursuers found three men trying to cross the Red River; one was killed, and the others were sent to Bourland, who later reported that they were shot while trying to escape.[53]

Even McCulloch became upset with Bourland's heartless tactics. On July 14, 1864, he informed the colonel that "complaints are being made that prisoners taken by your command and others turned over to them [have been] killed without trial in cold blood when not trying to make their escape." He pointed out that his orders for the treatment of dissenters were "sufficiently barbarous for any Christian land," and added that he did not intend for men to be shot "after they throw down their arms and hold up their hands nor after they are captured unless they undertake to make their escape." Summary justice would not be tolerated no matter how odious the traitors. Bourland directed his reply to Quayle, with whom the charges apparently originated. He admitted that his men shot prisoners, but only when they ran, not while in custody.[54]

McCulloch tabled the matter, but renewed violence brought it to the forefront once more. After being released in Houston for lack of evidence, Luckey relocated his family to Bell County, where a posse arrested him on August 1, 1864, on a writ from chief justice Hunter after new evidence was uncovered. They escorted Luckey to Parker County and sent him under guard to see Hunter. Meanwhile, a town meeting in Weatherford adopted a resolution forbidding mob violence and pledging that Luckey would get a fair trial. Four men were appointed to tell him of their decision, but upon arriving at Hunter's house, they learned that the escort had allegedly been overpowered by masked vigilantes, who lynched the hapless Luckey.[55]

Luckey's death was followed by more than thirty arrests, some for his murder, others because they were accused of being his allies. District judge Ferris sympathized with the vigilantes—he wrote to Governor Murrah that what they did was no more than what was done to Tories during the "Revo-

53. Rowland to Barry, May 28, 1864, in Barry Papers; Gunter, ed., "Gunter Papers," 231; Bourland to Quayle, May 7, 1864, George Isbett to Quayle, May 11, 1864, Bourland to James Ward, May 20, 1864, all in Quayle Papers.

54. McCulloch to Bourland, July 14, 1864, and Bourland to Quayle, July 19, 1864, in Quayle Papers; McCulloch to Bourland, March 4, 1864, in Bourland Papers.

55. Smythe, *Historical Sketch of Parker County*, 180–84.

lutionary War of our fathers." However, the arresting troops took the prisoners to Quayle; he released all but one, who was ordered to join the Confederate army. Quayle wrote to Culberson that the affair was the work of Hunter's committee, and that troops had been sent to Weatherford to restore order. The conflict soon attracted the attention of Bourland, who sent James S. Moore—a former minister whose independent company had been incorporated into Bourland's regiment—to investigate. As he was passing through Jack County, a sniper mortally wounded one of Moore's men. Moore settled in Jacksboro and began a campaign of retribution that climaxed when he sent a squad to arrest Sheriff A. H. Hancock of Jack County, an alleged Unionist. When the Confederates surrounded Hancock's home, a gunfight erupted that left yet another trooper dying, Hancock and his father wounded, and his mother and a friend dead.[56]

In the wake of the fiasco in Jack County, Moore arrested a number of people. Infuriated, Quayle demanded that they be surrendered to him. Bourland protested in vain that Moore had only done what he had told him to do, which was to use all means necessary to restore order and provide security. Bourland implied that Moore had McCulloch's prior approval for his actions, but the general angrily denied that insinuation and issued a futile order for the arrest of Moore and his men. McCulloch also scolded Bourland, instructing him to stop chasing deserters and Unionists altogether because his troops could not do so without committing "acts of rashness." Henceforth, Bourland was to confine his efforts to defending the frontier against Indians.[57]

McCulloch's chastisement of Bourland brought little reassurance to the people of Jack County; so many departed that the captain in charge of that sector for the 1st Frontier District resigned and followed suit. The Moore affair brought dissaffection to the surface within Bourland's regiment as well. On October 15, 1864, twenty-eight men and officers—including Patton, James J. Diamond, and Twitty (all of whom had taken part in the Great Hanging)—filed formal charges against their commander and demanded

56. Quayle to Culberson, August 19, 1864, Bourland to Quayle, August 26, 1864, James S. Moore to Quayle, n.d., all in Quayle Papers; Affidavits of Mrs. J. H. Hancock and Nancy Speer, September 26, 1864, and of Mrs. N. E. Hancock, September 27, 1864, in Bourland Papers; CSR, Bourland's Border Regiment and 2d Cavalry, Tex. State Troops.

57. Quayle to Moore, September 4, 1864, Bourland to Quayle, September 8, 1864, McCulloch to Bourland, September 12, October 8, 1864, all in Quayle Papers; CSR, Bourland's Border Regiment.

his dismissal. They asserted that he was incompetent to command and, more important, he had demonstrated an impractical venality. They named seven men killed during the previous year while in the custody of guards chosen by Bourland, and recalled others, whose names were not known, that had been executed in a similarly brutal fashion.[58]

McCulloch, confronted with formal charges, ultimately decided to pigeonhole the petition. Indian attacks on the Forks increased alarmingly in the fall of 1864, and Bourland was needed to help defend the frontier. He was given command of all the Confederate troops in eleven contiguous counties, including Cooke, and was ordered once more to confine his attention to operations against Indians. Among the units now under his control was the battalion of the Mounted Regiment that Magruder had assigned to the northwest and within which was Rowland's suspect company. The battalion had been ordered to the Texas coast in September, 1864, but furloughed some men home to organize petition drives for the unit's return to the North Texas frontier. Bourland arrested those battalion members he caught, but Indian raids convinced other Confederate authorities that the troopers were needed. He posted the four companies far out on the frontier, where they could guard against Indians but remained isolated.[59]

The reelection of Lincoln dismayed Confederates along the Forks; as one man wrote his wife, it meant "four more years more war pestilance + famine." State troops posted on the northern frontier were encouraged by the arrival of a new commander; Throckmorton, now a brigadier general in state service, took the place of Quayle, who had served on Throckmorton's Committee on Military Affairs in the Texas senate and who remained

58. Charges and Specifications Preferred Against Jas. Bourland Col. Comdg. Border Reg., P.A.C.S., October 15, 1864, in Quayle Papers; E. M. Crick to Quayle, September 27, 1864, in AGR.

59. McCulloch to Bourland, October 7, 8, 1864, in Quayle Papers; Henry C. Williams, "The Indian Raid in Young County, Texas, October 13, 1864" (Typescript in BTHC); Special Orders Nos. 5 and 20, HQ, Dist. of Tex., New Mexico, and Arizona, September 15, 30, 1864, Special Orders No. 266, HQ, Northern Subdistrict of Tex., October 10, 1864, Special Orders Nos. 67 and [?], Bourland's Regiment, October 15, 16, 1864, all in Barry Papers; General Orders No. 64, HQ, Northern Subdistrict of Tex., October 9, 1864, in Bourland Papers; Isbett to Culberson, October 9, 1864, in AGR; Barry, *A Texas Ranger and Frontiersman*, 174–75, 180, 182–83; Strong, *Memoirs*, 39–41; J. W. Wilbarger, *Indian Depredations in Texas* (Austin, 1889), 449–52; Evans, "Military Events and Operations," in *Comprehensive History of Texas*, ed. Wooten, 562.

as his second-in-command until March, 1865. Throckmorton arrived on the frontier after a stormy term as a state senator. While debating proposals for a negotiated peace, he was told by another senator that "any man who talked of reconstruction would be hanged." He retorted that conscription had caused citizens to be "hunted down like wild beasts." Mocking those who advocated fighting to the last ditch, he painted a verbal portrait of Confederate armies reduced to old men. Even then, Throckmorton said, if a ragged veteran expressed his desire for negotiations to end the carnage, he would "be set upon by a mob of fanatics . . . and be treated to a rope & limb because he dared to express himself as a freeman." In Throckmorton, many dissenters on the Forks believed they had a kindred spirit.[60]

Throckmorton assumed command of the 1st Frontier District at a difficult time. Indians and white raiders cooperated in denuding the area of cattle, often selling them to the Federal army, whose scouts were often sighted patrolling south of the Red River. Deserters from both armies haunted every remote corner, hidden by sympathetic settlers. Many believed, a correspondent from Grayson County wrote to Murrah, that "nothing but bayonets" could impose stability, and an order from McCulloch in late December declared that anyone who resisted arrest would be shot. Throckmorton praised Quayle for his work in "capturing traitors" who sought "to dye their hands in the blood of their own kindred and neighbors," but devoted his attention to cooperating with Bourland in operations against Indians, especially after a band of refugee Kickapoos bloodily repulsed some of their troops on Dove Creek in January, 1865.[61]

60. Throckmorton to Bourland, March 31, 1865, in Bourland Papers; Henry F. C. Johnson to "Delilah," November 27, 1864, in Henry F. C. Johnson Papers; Throckmorton to Epperson, November 3, 1864, in Epperson Papers; Culberson to Quayle, September 26, 1864, and McCulloch to Quayle, March 22, 1865, in Quayle Papers; General Orders No. 1, First Frontier Dist., Tex. State Troops, December 13, 1864, Murrah to Kirby Smith, April 18, 1865, Murrah to John W. Lane, April 18, 1865, all in GOR; Quayle to Culberson, October 7, 1864, in AGR; Gammel, comp., *Laws of Texas*, V, 771–72; Claude Elliot, *Leathercoat: The Life History of a Texas Patriot* (San Antonio, 1938), 84–87; *Members of the Texas Legislature*, 44; Smith, *Frontier Defense in the Civil War*, 130.
61. General Orders No.1, 1st Frontier Dist., Tex. State Troops, December 13, 1864, Throckmorton to Murrah, December 9, 20, 1864, January 13, 1865, C. R. Breedlove to Murrah, November 19, 1864, all in GOR; Throckmorton to Bourland, January 24, 1865, in Bourland Papers; General Orders No. 33, HQ, Northern Subdistrict of Tex., December 29, 1864, in Maxey Papers; Post Returns, First Frontier Dist., Tex. State Troops, January, 1865, Throck-

The declining fortunes of Confederate Texas and the deterioration of Bourland's command brought a halt to joint operations. Mutiny was brewing once more among Bourland's troops. Two subordinates, Patton and James J. Diamond, were arrested by order of McCulloch and subsequently resigned; those who remained were bitterly divided, with a faction opposed to Bourland led by John R. Diamond. To allay tension, Bourland managed to evade an order assigning his regiment to East Texas, and furloughed his men by thirds beginning in February, 1865, to plant corn. By late March, however, when they reassembled, both they and the state troops lacked munitions, and no one had been paid in months.[62]

Throckmorton, who had soon learned that his command included not only Unionists, with whom he might sympathize, but also outlaws with more sanguinary motives, regarded the approach of spring in 1865 with alarm. Renegades were robbing settlers along the Forks "on an extensive scale," while raiders from Arkansas and Missouri in groups of ten to twenty were relieving entire communities of all their horses, specie, and household goods. He believed wholesale arrests and executions could restore order, but his troops were too "feeble" to carry out such a policy. The spring always brought renewed Federal military activity; and if Union forces invaded North Texas, he wrote to an associate, "scenes of atrocity such as you little dream of, will be enacted by men who claim to fight under our banner." Even if Union armies did not arrive, warm weather and good grass would bring more renegades to Texas, and disaffection would continue to spread through "every section and community" as well as Throckmorton's troops.[63]

morton to Burke, January 29, February 22, 1865, Throckmorton to William C. Walsh, February 23, 1865, all in AGR; Barry, *A Texas Ranger and Frontiersman*, 183–96; Strong, *Memoirs*, 30–36; *OR*, Ser. I, Vol. XLI, Pt. 4, p. 1140, Vol. XLVIII, Pt. 1, p. 1358; Dallas *Herald*, March 9, 1865; Wilbarger, *Indian Depredations*, 453–54; Horton, *Samuel Bell Maxey*, 41–42; Kerby, *Kirby Smith's Confederacy*, 232; Geise, "Confederate Military Forces in the Trans-Mississippi," 249–50.

62. McCulloch to Barry, February 16, 1865, Bourland to Rowland, February 17, 1865, Post Returns for Texas Frontier Battalion . . . for March and April 1865, all in Barry Papers; Charles L. Roff to Bourland, February 7, 1865, Whaley to S. J. McKnight, February 12, 1865, Special Orders No. 58, HQ, Northern Subdistrict of Tex., March 14, 1865, Throckmorton to Bourland, March 31, 1865, McCulloch to Bourland, May 23, 1865, all in Bourland Papers; Throckmorton to Dashiell, March 30, 1865, and Hill to Walsh, April 4, 1865, in AGR; *OR*, Ser. I, Vol. XLVIII, Pt. 1, p. 1381.

63. Throckmorton to Epperson, March 12, 1865, in Epperson Papers. The quotations are

The advent of spring did encourage many to renew their attempts to flee from North Texas. Over a hundred deserters assembled on Denton Creek in Wise County. They supplied themselves by raiding nearby homes, then set out to cross the Red River in Montague County on the way to California, Kansas, and Mexico. Throckmorton initiated a pursuit; within a day a combined troop of 134, led by John R. Diamond, were pursuing the refugees. Diamond's troopers stumbled on the renegades' camp on the morning of April 3, 1865. After their attack stampeded the refugees' horses, negotiations ensued that broke off after Diamond was captured by the outlaws, who said they would kill him if their mounts were not returned. When his subordinates refused to comply, Diamond was released after promising to return the horses himself. While he debated what to do, two dozen refugees surrendered to state troopers, preferring Throckmorton's custody to that of Bourland. Diamond finally took in hand over a hundred prisoners and forwarded them safely to Galveston, where they were released at the war's end.[64]

The surrender of Robert E. Lee on April 9, 1865, spawned chaos in the Trans-Mississippi; after the subsequent surrender of Joseph E. Johnston, soldiers in Texas began deserting on a large scale. The pleas of Confederate officials to fight on did not evince a significant response, and the Trans-Mississippi capitulated on May 26, 1865. On the Forks, command of the Mounted Regiment battalion, depleted by desertion, had devolved upon Rowland, who furloughed the unit by thirds to harvest wheat. On May 16, 1865, Bourland ordered Rowland to concentrate his forces with "as little excitement as possible." Union general James G. Blunt was reportedly preparing to invade North Texas, and Bourland planned to give him "a hearty welcome."[65]

---

drawn from two drafts of the same letter, Throckmorton to Crosby, March 19, 1865; one is in the Epperson Papers, and the other in the James W. Throckmorton Papers, BTHC.

64. Hill to Walsh, April 5, 1865, and F. M. Totty to Bourland, April 20, 1865, in AGR; McCulloch to Bourland, April 5, 1865, and List of Prisoners Sent to——in Charge of——, n.d., in Bourland Papers; Throckmorton to Epperson, April 6, 1865, in Epperson Papers; Gunter, ed., "Gunter Papers," 132.

65. Bourland to Rowland, May 16, 1865, Special Orders Nos. 19 and 39, Barry's Battalion, n.d., Rowland to Bourland, May 1, 1865, Bourland to McCulloch, May 8, 1865, T. M. Randolph to Rowland, May 16, 1865, all in Barry Papers; Barry, *A Texas Ranger and Frontiersman*, 201; *OR*, Ser. I, Vol. XLVIII, Pt. 2, pp. 1308, 1313–14; Kerby, *Kirby Smith's Confederacy*, 413–14, 424–31; Charles W. Ramsdell, *Reconstruction in Texas* (New York, 1910), 27–41; Stephen B. Oates, *Confederate Cavalry West of the River* (Austin, 1961), 160.

McCulloch, however, ordered Bourland to surrender. The general, even with his command in ruins, thought principally about trying to "save" North Texas from "anarchy and bloodshed." When it had become obvious that he could do no more, he asked for volunteers to escort him out of the region. In McKinney, a mob gathered to block McCulloch's passage, but when he rallied his small troop of thirty men and advanced, the challengers realized that they were not supported by a majority of the townspeople and allowed him to pass through the town unharmed.[66]

This episode epitomized the Civil War experience for settlers on the Forks. Ruthless persecution of citizens by Confederate officials, coupled with raids by hostile Indians and outlaws, left large areas of the North Texas frontier denuded of people and crops. Many residents fled from the unchecked violence, seeking order and security where they hoped there were no vindicative troopers or vigilantes. The exodus contributed to a collapse of the regional economy; the women whom Quantrill kept from ransacking Sherman for food in 1863 were dismayed to find the Confederate commissary there empty. Although the people on the Forks were greatly reduced in numbers and in resources, many of them chose order over anarchy when an opportunity for revenge arose. That adherence to legality was the key difference between many dissenters and the outlaws for whom Confederate officials frequently mistook them. Sadly, the Federal victory would not bring the lawful vengeance they anticipated. Instead, both Unionists and Confederates, embittered by wartime experiences, would resort to extralegal violence during Reconstruction, continuing the turmoil along the Forks.

66. McCulloch to Bourland, May 23, 1865, in Bourland Papers; Martha D. Lucas, "Interview with William Walsh, November, 1928" (Typescript in Mattie D. Lucas Papers, Sherman Municipal Library, Sherman, Tex.).

SIX

Promises Unfulfilled

As the Civil War came to an end, a substantial number of settlers on the Forks, dismayed at the brutal tactics of the Confederacy's representatives in the region, looked forward to the restoration of the Union. They expected that the return of Federal authority would bring not only order and security but also vindication for those who had been victimized in the Great Hanging and subsequent violence. These people were encouraged by northern leaders who, galvanized by the speeches of refugee Texas Unionist Andrew J. Hamilton, had sponsored several wartime invasions of the state and continued to express concern for the protection of Unionists. Unfortunately, Federal commitment to this goal was diluted by other concerns, and most Texans supported the efforts of state leaders to ignore the past. Not only did the invasions fail, but also it proved impossible either to bring to justice those involved in vigilantism during the war or to prevent the outbreak of new violence in North Texas. Although the presence of Federal troops hindered the organization of vigilance committees, individual and mob violence by frustrated Unionists and their foes contributed to the eventual repudiation of presidential Reconstruction.

Northern interest in Texas antedated the Great Hanging. New England abolitionists had advocated colonizing part of Texas as a free state since its annexation in 1845. After the outbreak of the Civil War, businessman Edward Atkinson began corresponding with Federal officials in Washington, urging them to invade Texas and establish a free state with the aid of Unionists who lived there. The shortage of cotton for textile mills in New England impelled others to join his campaign, adding fiscal concerns to patriotic and humanitarian objectives. As Governor John A. Andrew of Massachusetts wrote to Assistant Secretary of the Navy Gustavus V. Fox, an occupation of Texas would not only provide cotton for New England mills but also bring an end to the persecution of loyal men in that state.[1]

The belief that Texas held a significant number of Unionists also persisted among Federal officials. Proposals were discussed early in the war for an invasion; General George B. McClellan planned a march from Kansas in coordination with a landing on the Texas coast in order to protect the "latent Union and free-State sentiment well-known to predominate in Western Texas." Nathaniel P. Banks, a major general of volunteer troops and a former Massachusetts governor and congressman, offered to enlist fifteen thousand for the seaborne operation, while James H. Lane, the abolitionist senator from Kansas, was promised the command of twenty thousand more for an overland assault. Unionists in North Texas learned of the plan and waited eagerly, but McClellan failed to secure the cooperation of military officials in Kansas and soon turned his attention to the war in Virginia. Although Secretary of War Edwin M. Stanton insisted that he supported a Texas expedition, it was postponed in favor of an attack on New Orleans during the spring of 1862.[2]

While New England was pressing for an expedition to Texas, many refugees from that state settled in New York. News from Texas was sparse in the North due to a lack of effective communications networks, but these Texans at the "hub of American newspaperdom" provided a ready source of information about those left behind. New York *Times* editor Henry J. Raymond published a few anonymous letters detailing the persecution of Unionists in Texas. These caught the attention of an influential sponsor: John A. Stevens, Jr., a New York financier serving as secretary of the National War Committee, an assembly of businessmen and politicians who provided vital support for the Republican party. Stevens and other committee members reviewed a petition from Texas Unionists in September, 1862,

1. *OR*, Ser. I, Vol. XV, 412–13; George W. Smith, "The Banks Expedition of 1862," *Louisiana Historical Quarterly*, XXVI (1943), 343; Ludwell H. Johnson, *Red River Campaign: Politics and Cotton During the Civil War* (Baltimore, 1948), 5–8; John L. Waller, *Colossal Hamilton of Texas* (El Paso, 1968), 42.

2. George B. McClellan, *McClellan's Own Story* (New York, 1887), 104; *OR*, Ser. I, Vol. VIII, 428–29, Vol. LIII, 507–509; Smith, "The Banks Expedition," 341–42; Johnson, *Red River Campaign*, 8–13; Howard C. Westwood, "President Lincoln's Overture to Sam Houston," *SWHQ*, LXXXVIII (1984), 126–27; Nora E. Owens, "Presidential Reconstruction in Texas: A Case Study" (Ph.D. dissertation, Auburn University, 1983), 27–28, 51; William R. Geise, "The Confederate Military Forces in the Trans-Mississippi" (Ph.D. dissertation, UT, 1974), 60.

and declared that no war aim, save the defense of the national capital, should have a higher priority than an invasion of Texas.[3]

Stevens found a perfect spokesman for his cause in Hamilton, a former Texas congressman who had loudly opposed secession and had been forced to flee from his Austin home in the summer of 1862. After his arrival in occupied New Orleans, Hamilton had wasted no time in making his views known. In an emotional speech at Lyceum Hall on September 17, 1862, he claimed that "hundreds and thousands of peaceable men" in Texas had been prevented from voting against secession by "threats and intimidation, liberally used." He added that his home state had no government "except that of a horde of military officers, who have established martial law—a martial law of vigilance committees and petty tyrants [who rule with] unrelenting tyranny." These men, he asserted, had lynched over two hundred Unionists.[4]

Crusty Horace Greeley, editor of the New York *Tribune*, endorsed Hamilton on September 29, 1862, declaring that the Texan should be heard in New York, where reports from his state were eagerly sought. Hamilton had already set sail; he spoke on October 2, 1862, at the Brooklyn Academy of Music, where he revealed to his audience that during the secession campaign "there was no little terror in the prospect of being dragged with a rough rope to the lonely prairie—'To be left a thing, O'er which the raven flaps her funeral wing.'" He delivered another address on October 4 at Cooper's Union Institute. Warming to his subject, he asked amid cheers, "Am I to see my neighbors and friends hung by the neck because they have doubted that the chief business of the Great Ruler of the Universe is not in directing and controlling and maturing and perpetuating the institution of slavery?" He ended by advocating total war against the Confederacy.[5]

3. J. Cutler Andrews, *The North Reports the Civil War* (Pittsburgh, 1955), 8, 10–11; Clippings of "Tombigbee" to "Editor, New York *Times*," July 27, August 14, 1862 (Scrapbook in John L. Haynes Papers, BTHC); New York *Tribune*, February 7, 1863; National War Committee of New York, *Report of the Committee Appointed to Take into Consideration the Condition of Western Texas* (New York, 1862), 1–9; Smith, "The Banks Expedition," 347–48; Westwood, "President Lincoln's Overture to Sam Houston," 128; *Dictionary of American Biography*, IX, 616–17.

4. Memphis *Bulletin*, October 7, 1862, quoted in Houston *Telegraph*, October 20, 1862; Frank H. Smyrl, "Texans in the Union Army," *SWHQ*, LXV (1961), 240–41; Waller, *Colossal Hamilton*, 36–37.

5. New York *Herald*, October 4, 1862; Henry O'Rielly, ed., *Origin and Objects of the Slaveholders' Conspiracy* (New York, 1862), 7–9; Houston *Telegraph*, October 29, 1862; New York

When Greeley printed reports of the Great Hanging as evidence of the Texan's assertions, others followed suit. In the New York *Independent* on October 9, 1862, Greeley lauded Hamilton as a hero and demanded help for the Unionists in Texas. A little over a month later, on November 12, 1862, he printed conclusive evidence of Confederate atrocities in Texas—Galveston *News* editor Willard Richardson's report on the Great Hanging entitled "A Lincoln Raid in the Interior." New York *Times* editor Raymond, rather than copy his mentor, searched for another version of the Great Hanging. In February, 1863, he published on his front page the bellicose article from the San Antonio *Herald* underneath the alarming headline "Important from Texas: Evidence of the Existence of Union Feeling—Barbarities Perpetuated by the Rebels on the Unionists." The Washington *National Intelligencer* reprinted Robert W. Loughery's article under the explicit title "Murder of Union Men in Texas." In the West, the St. Louis *Republic* printed eyewitness H. C. Stone's letter and lamented that "hundreds are now chased like wild beasts through the wilderness of North-western Texas, and succumb because of the most horrid tortures, their fate never being known to their fellow men."[6]

Stevens, preparing to go to Washington with other members of the National War Committee to lobby for a Texas invasion, included Hamilton as the centerpiece of the group. In Washington, Stevens secured an invitation for Hamilton to dine with Salmon P. Chase and Stanton at Chase's home on October 5, 1862. After hearing Hamilton speak about conditions in Texas, both men agreed something must be done. The next morning William H. Seward went with Hamilton to the White House to arrange an interview with Abraham Lincoln. Their meeting went well, and with the aid of Stevens's delegation and another led by Governor Andrew, Hamilton also secured the support of cabinet members Stanton, Edward Bates, Sew-

---

Tribune, September 29, October 2, 1862; Andrews, *North Reports the Civil War*, 9; Waller, *Colossal Hamilton*, 37.

6. O'Rielly, *Origin and Objects of the Slaveholders' Conspiracy*, 1–2; San Antonio *Herald*, October 25, 1862, quoted in New York *Tribune*, November 12, 1862; San Antonio *Herald*, November 15, 1862, quoted in New York *Times*, February 25, 1863; Richmond *Enquirer*, November 14, 1862, quoted in St. Louis *Republican*, December 14, 1862; Frank Moore, ed., *The Rebellion Record: A Diary of American Events* (12 vols.; New York, 1865–1866), VI, "Poetry, Rumors, and Incidents," 49; Marshall *Texas Republican*, November 1, 1862, quoted in Washington *National Intelligencer*, December 11, 1862.

ard, and Montgomery Blair, leading him to believe that Texas would soon be invaded.[7]

Hamilton and his supporters were quickly disappointed. Stanton appointed Banks to lead an invasion, and signed an appointment for Hamilton as military governor of Texas, but unrest in the Midwest undid these careful plans. Lincoln decided that the campaign to reopen the Mississippi River should receive top priority. His general-in-chief, Henry W. Halleck, told Banks of his new goal on November 8, 1862, but Stanton still supported the scheme for an invasion of Texas. No one told Hamilton or his allies, and when delegates from the National War Committee led by Stevens handed Lincoln a petition endorsing an invasion of Texas on November 10, the president said nothing of his change of heart. Hamilton arrived in New Orleans with a trunk filled with Texas maps—gifts from Stevens in anticipation of a triumphant return to his home state—and was infuriated to learn that the troops had been reassigned to the campaign for Vicksburg. To placate him, Banks ordered a poorly supported landing at Galveston in October, 1862, but this tiny Federal force was overwhelmed on New Year's Day, 1863.[8]

After the recapture of Galveston, Halleck ordered Banks to devote his attention to the capture of Vicksburg, and the Senate allowed Hamilton's appointment as military governor to expire in March, 1863. The Texan refused to give up, however, and stumped the North seeking support for another Texas invasion. He constantly stressed the number of loyal men in Texas and their plight. The Loyal League of Union Citizens organized at Cooper's Union on March 20, 1863, with a rally that featured Hamilton repeating his accusation that "hundreds" of Texas Unionists had been

7. Speech of Andrew J. Hamilton, March 21, 1865, in Andrew J. Hamilton Papers, BTHC; Roy P. Basler, ed., *The Collected Works of Abraham Lincoln* (10 vols.; Rutgers, 1953), V, 492; David Donald, ed., *Inside Lincoln's Cabinet: The Civil War Diaries of Salmon P. Chase* (New York, 1954), 166–68; National War Committee of New York, *Report of the Committee Who Visited Washington on the Affairs of Western Texas* (New York, 1862), 9; Smyrl, "Texans in the Union Army," 240–41; Waller, *Colossal Hamilton*, 38–39; Johnson, *Red River Campaign*, 14–16.

8. Appointment of Andrew J. Hamilton as Military Governor of Texas, November 14, 1862 (photocopy), and John A. Stevens, Jr., to Hamilton, November 28, 1862, in Hamilton Papers; *OR*, Ser. I, Vol. XV, 590; Mobile *Advertiser and Register*, November 14, 1862; Smyrl, "Texans in the Union Army," 241–42; Smith, "The Banks Expedition," 356–57; Westwood, "President Lincoln's Overture to Sam Houston," 127; Johnson, *Red River Campaign*, 20–24, 28; Waller, *Colossal Hamilton*, 42–44.

lynched. Hamilton's preparations for the fall, 1862, invasion had forced him to decline invitations from Governor Andrew and Congressman Alex H. Rice to speak at Faneuil Hall, but a subsequent request from the Boston Committee of Invitation—signed by such luminaries as industrialist Amos Lawrence—could not be ignored. Hamilton's speech was well received and reprinted for distribution.[9]

In the late summer of 1863, renewed preparations for an invasion of Texas forced Hamilton to decline speaking invitations from James G. Blaine, then chairman of the Union State Committee of Maine, and a group of New England businessmen, including Atkinson and Lawrence. Strong support for Hamilton in the North had persuaded Lincoln to postpone plans for an invasion of Mobile, despite angry protests from General Ulysses S. Grant and Admiral David Farragut. The chief architect of the campaign for Texas was Stevens, about whom Hamilton would recall, "There was no man in New York or elsewhere in the North to whom the refugees from Texas were so much indebted." Stevens badgered decision makers and gathered political intelligence for another foray to Washington by Hamilton in July, 1863. The Texan avoided confronting Seward or Halleck, both of whom now opposed his idea, and persuaded Lincoln and Stanton that occupying Texas would save many Unionists, as well as further divide the Confederacy, block cotton exports through Mexico, and send a warning to the French who had occupied that country.[10]

Lincoln told Stanton on July 29, 1863, that "no local object" was "more desirable" than an invasion of Texas. Despite the protests of both Stevens

9. New York *Tribune*, March 21, 1863; Alexander H. Rice to Hamilton, October 20, 1862, John A. Andrew to Hamilton, October 27, 1862, James L. Little *et al.* to Hamilton, February 10, 1863, James Wadsworth *et al.* to Hamilton, April 14, 1863, "Salem Union League" to Hamilton, April 22, 1863, all in Hamilton Papers; *Speech of Gen. A. J. Hamilton, of Texas, at the War Meeting at Faneuil Hall, Saturday Evening, April 18, 1863* (Boston, 1863), *passim*; OR, Ser. I, Vol. XV, 656–57; Smith, "The Banks Expedition," 359; Smyrl, "Texans in the Union Army," 241–42; Waller, *Colossal Hamilton*, 42–45, 47.

10. Speech of Hamilton, March 21, 1865, Edward Atkinson *et al.* to Hamilton, July 10, 1863, James G. Blaine to Hamilton, August 8, 1863, Andrew to William A. Buckingham, May 28, 1863, Stevens to Hamilton, February 19, March 11, July 31, 1863, n.d., all in Hamilton Papers; Hamilton to Abraham Lincoln, July 25, 1863, in Abraham Lincoln Papers, LC; John G. Nicolay and John Hay, eds., *Collected Works of Abraham Lincoln* (12 vols.; New York, 1905), IX, 64–65; OR, Ser. I, Vol. XXVI, Pt. 1, p. 680; Richard B. Irwin, "The Red River Campaign," in *Battles and Leaders of the Civil War*, ed. Robert U. Johnson and Clarence C. Buel (4 vols.; 1886; rpr. New York, 1956, IV, 345–47; William L. Barney, *Flawed Victory: A New Perspective on the Civil War* (New York, 1975), 24; Waller, *Colossal Hamilton*, 47–48.

156

and Hamilton, Banks was again chosen to lead the expedition. The president himself wrote to express his hope that the national flag would soon be planted in Texas, but Stevens and Hamilton believed Banks was not as concerned as he should be about the plight of the Unionists in Texas. Hamilton, remembering his experience in the fall of 1862, remained hostile and suspicious. When Lincoln wrote in August, 1863, to inquire politely whether he wished to nominate a Texan for admittance to West Point, Hamilton exploded: "While the loyal fathers of such young men . . . are being daily murdered or driven into exile, and their families plundered and subjected to daily insult, I do not think that any one of them would be likely to thank me for so dangerous a compliment, but would rather look upon it as a bitter and cruel jest." Warming to his subject, he added, "I have *hoped*, *implored*, and *prayed* [that the Federal government] would give deliverance to the suffering loyalists of Texas—and a few days past I thought I had reason to indulge renewed hope." But after Stanton refused to see him, and a messenger reported that the president had *"nothing to say to me,"* he had concluded that "nothing was likely to be done for Texas."[11]

Chase intervened to save the Texas expedition from its mentor's temper. He addressed a note, endorsed by Lincoln, to Hamilton, apologizing for the president's inattentiveness and assuring him that the request for the nomination of a cadet was "prompted by pure kindness and respect for you." Chase confided that he also wished that Lincoln was "differently constituted and would take hold of affairs such as those of your state more effectively," but added "the President leaves (too much I fear) all matters connected with the prosecution of the war to others." Chase spoke with Lincoln on September 17, and was told that Hamilton had been invited for an interview and would "probably return to Texas, as Brigadier General and Military Governor."[12]

Two days after Chase talked with Lincoln, Hamilton received his new appointments and orders to report to Banks at New Orleans. That same day Lincoln wrote Banks, urging him to invade Texas as soon as possible and endorsing Hamilton as a "man of worth and ability." Banks, ignoring

11. Stevens to Hamilton, February 19, July 31, 1863, John L. Haynes to Hamilton, June 13, 1863, Hamilton to Lincoln, August 22, 1863, all in Hamilton Papers; Nicolay and Hay, eds., *Collected Works of Lincoln*, IX, 47–48; Basler, ed., *Collected Works of Lincoln*, VI, 465–66; *OR*, Ser. I, Vol. XXVI, Pt. 1, p. 664; Waller, *Colossal Hamilton*, 47.

12. Salmon P. Chase to Hamilton, August 27, 1863, in Hamilton Papers; Donald, ed., *Inside Lincoln's Cabinet*, 198.

Halleck's advice to advance up the Red River, had already tried to land on the Texas coast at Sabine Pass, but the Federal force of four thousand troops and a naval escort were driven off by fewer than fifty Confederates. After Hamilton arrived, Banks continued to probe along the coast, and in November occupied Brownsville in an attempt to staunch the flow of cotton to Mexico and to provide a safe enclave for Texas Unionists.[13]

Pleased with Banks's capture of Brownsville, Hamilton established his headquarters there on December 1, 1863. Three days later he promulgated an "Address to the Citizens of Texas" declaring that "three thousand" Texans had been "hung, shot, and butchered" for loving "good Government and peace and order in society." Others had been "tortured, in many instances, beyond anything known in savage Warfare." He added that the "thresholds of many homes are still red with the blood of Husbands & Fathers who were shot in the presence of their Wives and children because they loved the Flag under which they were born and the Govt. that had ever blessed them." Under his administration, he pledged, all "murderers, assassins, and robbers now infesting the Country" would be forced to "seek some other Country in which to ply their vocation or be brought to answer for their misdeeds." While he remained in Brownsville he continued to harangue the Confederates for persecuting dissenters and called for Unionists to join him, but his words were not published in Texas and few there heard them.[14]

Halleck, angered by Banks's dilatory tactics, ordered him to make a push up the Red River into Texas. The defenses at Brownsville were stripped in preparation for the campaign, and Hamilton left for Louisiana to take part. The operation, begun in March, 1864, proved to be a disaster for the Federals, prompting Hamilton to return again to the lecture circuit in the North. An account of the Great Hanging and other atrocities in North Texas had reached a larger audience in early 1864 through the efforts of Frederick W. Sumner of Sherman, who had finally reached the safety of Federal lines. His sensationalist report was printed in *Frank Leslie's Illus-*

13. Edwin M. Stanton to Hamilton, September 19, 1863, in Hamilton Papers; Basler, ed., *Collected Works of Lincoln*, VI, 465–66; Donald, ed., *Inside Lincoln's Cabinet*, 200; *OR*, Ser. I, Vol. XXVI, Pt. 1, pp. 673, 683; Irwin, "The Red River Campaign," 345–47; Smyrl, "Texans in the Union Army," 241–42; Johnson, *Red River Campaign*, 37–39; Waller, *Colossal Hamilton*, 44, 48–49.

14. Address to the Citizens of Texas by Andrew J. Hamilton, December 4, 1863, in Hamilton Papers; Smyrl, "Texans in the Union Army," 242; Waller, *Colossal Hamilton*, 50–52.

trated Weekly on February 20, 1864, under the title "Rebel Outrages in Texas." His undeniably authentic tale was enhanced by lurid engravings of the lynching of Mrs. Hillier, and of the events that comprised the Great Hanging itself. Sumner's stories reappeared later that year in *Sufferings Endured for a Free Government; or, A History of the Cruelties and Atrocities of the Rebellion*, a collection published in Washington by Thomas Wilson. Northern audiences, primed with such material, greeted Hamilton with sympathetic cheers whenever he spoke.[15]

Despite Hamilton's proselytizing, plans to invade Texas were not renewed until after the Civil War had ended in the East. General Philip H. Sheridan was appointed to command the Military Division of the Gulf—which included Texas—on May 29, 1865, and worked quickly to establish his army in that state. He believed it was imperative to do so because Confederates in Texas were preparing to continue resisting. Matters appeared especially serious in North Texas, where according to a Confederate deserter, Henry E. McCulloch had mustered over seven hundred men at recruiting camps in Gainesville and Fort Belknap. Too, rumors abounded that the Sons of the South, a chapter of which had initiated the violence in Parker County during April, 1864, had reorganized at a meeting in San Antonio and vowed to undertake guerrilla operations against anyone who attempted to restore Federal authority.[16]

Diplomatic considerations soon overrode Sheridan's concern for the protection of Texas Unionists; when Federal troops landed at Galveston on June 19, 1865, most of them were hurried to the Rio Grande for a demonstration against Mexico. Only a few soldiers were posted inland, and none could be spared for remote regions such as North Texas. The problem was compounded by the small number of troops available for an occupation; only 52,000 were initially sent into Texas, and this force was soon reduced to one-tenth that number. On the Forks, the paroling of Confederates was

15. *Frank Leslie's Illustrated Weekly*, February 20, 1864; New York *Tribune*, October 14, 1864; Thomas Wilson, *Sufferings Endured for a Free Government* (Washington, D.C., 1864), 258–64; Johnson, *Red River Campaign*, 40–41; Waller, *Colossal Hamilton*, 54–55; Allan C. Ashcraft, "Texas 1860–1866—The Lone Star State in the Civil War" (Ph.D. dissertation, Columbia University, 1960), 203–204, 207, 210–11.

16. *House Executive Documents*, 39th Cong., 2d Sess., No. 1, p. 45; *OR*, Ser. I, Vol. XLVIII, Pt. 2, p. 375; Robert W. Shook, "The Federal Occupation and Administration of Texas, 1865–1870" (Ph.D. dissertation, University of North Texas, 1970), 45; William J. Ulrich, "The Northern Military Mind in Regard to Reconstruction, 1865–1872: The Attitudes of Ten Leading Union Generals" (Ph.D. dissertation, Ohio State University, 1959), 146, 148.

assigned to James G. Bourland who, in compliance with Federal orders, established his headquarters in Bonham and paroled all who applied, regardless of their record.[17]

Resentment among Unionists at being abandoned led to violence in North Texas. Members of a Union league occupied Decatur in the summer of 1865, intending to lynch tax collector Charles D. Cates, his brother Robert G. Cates—the sheriff who hanged five men during the Great Hanging—and everyone else who had participated in that affair. Their first sortie was repulsed, but they returned with reinforcements a few days later. They replaced the flag over the courthouse with a banner of their own and then scattered, capturing the sheriff but failing to overpower his brother. The situation appeared hopeless until Joe Henry Martin, apparently drunk, began haranguing the invaders. Many of them gathered in an empty lot to watch him and were trapped by a few defenders led by Charles C. Thompson, a former Confederate captain. He told the raiders that if they resisted, "more damned men would be killed in a minute than a wagon could haul away in a day." They left and did not return, but Charles D. Cates and others petitioned for Federal cavalry to "restore peace and good order."[18]

A solution to such conflicts would have to be found by Hamilton, who after interviews with President Andrew Johnson and his cabinet was appointed provisional governor of Texas on June 17, 1865. His main task was to organize a government to manage state affairs until an administration could be elected under a revised state constitution, but he soon discovered that the persecution of dissenters in Texas had created a "major psychological barrier to political restoration." Dissenters' bitterness toward their persecutors was more than matched by the latter's conviction that Unionists

17. James G. Bourland to Andrew Johnson, September 18, 1865, in Amnesty Files; *House Executive Documents*, 39th Cong., 2d Sess., No. 1, p. 48; *OR*, Ser. I, Vol. XLVIII, Pt. 2, p. 929; *Dallas Herald*, July 1, 1865; Charles W. Ramsdell, *Reconstruction in Texas* (New York, 1910), 39–41; William L. Richter, *The Army in Texas During Reconstruction* (College Station, Tex., 1987), 23–24; James E. Sefton, *The United States Army and Reconstruction* (Baton Rouge, 1967), 92.

18. Cliff D. Cates, *Pioneer History of Wise County* (Decatur, Texas, 1907), 124, 149–51, 321–22; R. F. Halsted to Charles D. Cates, August 14, 1865, in U.S. Department of War, Letters Sent by the Department of Texas and the Fifth Military District, 1865–1870, Record Group 397, NA; Floyd F. Ewing, "Unionist Sentiment on the Northwest Texas Frontier," *WTHA Yearbook* XXXIII (1957), 69–70; Mary C. Moore, *Centennial History of Wise County, 1853–1953* (Dallas, 1953), 46.

endangered order and stability by their agitation. Confronted by this on-going conflict, Hamilton proved ineffectual, adopting a haltingly methodical approach that provided almost no protection for former opponents of the Confederacy.[19]

Hamilton's belligerent assertions upon assuming power in Texas provided an initial surge of hope for those who had opposed the Confederacy. He landed at Galveston on July 21, 1865, and five days later issued an angry "Proclamation to the People of Texas," asserting that the "dark spirit at whose bidding the fires of civil war were lit and the South [was] transformed from peaceful States to one broad theater of bloody deeds and 'irremediable woes'" had to be immediately "exorcised." He delivered a similar speech at Houston, then yet another upon his arrival at Austin on August 2. Court dockets in Texas became crowded with petitions for redress of Confederate persecution. Hamilton's appointment did not make clear his judicial authority, but General Horatio G. Wright, commanding the Department of Texas, urged him to open the courts, further encouraging those who wanted legal vengeance.[20]

Hamilton made judicial appointments as rapidly as possible with the advice of those who had opposed secession. For North Texas, he relied on James W. Throckmorton, unaware that Throckmorton believed the restoration of order and security should be trusted to those who had supported the Confederacy. After Hamilton's speech in Austin, Throckmorton wrote to Benjamin H. Epperson, "There are but few Union men here who are equal to the occasion, & with the same spirit of persecution heretofore carried on by secessionists." The August, 1865, lynching of a former member of John R. Baylor's Ladies Rangers in Jack County further hardened Throckmorton against dissenters along the Forks, and he advised appointing many ex-Confederates as local officials in North Texas. These men, Throckmorton must have believed, had only acted as he did—performed

19. Appointment of Andrew J. Hamilton as Provisional Governor of Texas, June 17, 1865 (photocopy) in Hamilton Papers; Howard K. Beale, ed., *Diary of Gideon Welles* (3 vols.; New York, 1960), II, 315; Carl H. Moneyhan, *Republicanism in Reconstruction Texas* (Austin, 1980), 18–19; Richter, *The Army in Texas During Reconstruction*, 23; Waller, *Colossal Hamilton*, 58.

20. Proclamation to the People of Texas by Andrew J. Hamilton, July 25, 1865, in Hamilton Papers; Hamilton to Johnson, July 24, 1865, Christopher C. Andrews to Johnson, July 28, 1865, in Andrew Johnson Papers, LC; Horatio G. Wright to Hamilton, October 10, 1865, in Lets. Sent, Fifth Mil. Dist., RG 397, NA; Ramsdell, *Reconstruction in Texas*, 77–78; Richter, *The Army in Texas During Reconstruction*, 22; Waller, *Colossal Hamilton*, 61–63.

their duty to Texas by working to maintain order and security during the war, regardless of personal convictions—and would continue to do so.[21]

Hamilton rejected some of Throckmorton's suggestions, but many ex-Confederates were appointed because the governor's information was incomplete. Johnson in August, 1865, asked his provisional governors, including Hamilton, about rumors that Unionists were passed over in favor of former Confederates. Hamilton responded that such a report was an "unmitigated and malignant falsehood." Two days later he added, "If I could have been so *base* I could not have been so great a *fool.*" Despite these disclaimers, the governor was more deliberate in making his appointments after he received Johnson's inquiry. In Cooke County, his selections included judicial newcomer Nathaniel T. Bomar as chief justice and William T. G. Weaver— who like Throckmorton had served as a Confederate officer but had opposed disunion—as judge for the district court. In addition, the president's query and protests from settlers along the Forks prompted removals of earlier appointees such as chief justice Daniel Howell of Wise County who, according to more than two hundred petitioners, served on the vigilance committee that condemned the five men hanged by Robert G. Cates.[22]

Hamilton's uninformed judicial appointments impeded efforts in the fall of 1865 to prosecute those responsible for the Great Hanging. Bourland, James D. Young, and all twelve jurors of the Citizens Court were indicted for murder on November 11, 1865. Threats by Bourland and his followers that they would use arms stored at his home to block the arrest of anyone involved in the 1862 affair apparently impressed the judicial appointees along the Forks. It was alleged that Weaver, in whose court the indictments were returned, deliberately issued faulty writs; he denied this, but it is true that they were not served until a week after his court adjourned, permitting

21. James W. Throckmorton to Benjamin H. Epperson, August 6, 1865, in Benjamin H. Epperson Papers, BTHC; Throckmorton to Hamilton, August 20, 1865, in GOR; Ramsdell, *Reconstruction in Texas*, 59–60; Waller, *Colossal Hamilton*, 65–66.

22. Hamilton to Johnson, September 21, 23, 1865, Johnson to Hamilton, August 22, 1865, all in Johnson Papers; Texas Secretary of State, Election Register, 1848–1900, in Archives Division, TSL; F. M. Millican *et al.* to Hamilton, August, 1865, Henry J. Thompson to Hamilton, August 9, 1865, John Babb *et al.* to Hamilton, August 29, 1865, C. B. Ball *et al.* to Hamilton, August 29, 1865, Henry Plaster *et al.* to Hamilton, August 29, 1865, Lewellen Murphy *et al.* to Hamilton, September 8, 1865, Throckmorton to Hamilton, September 16, 1865, John S. Chisum to Hamilton, November 1, 1865, John T. Nelson *et al.* to Hamilton, November 10, 1865, all in GOR.

many of the guilty to escape. Thirty-seven residents of Cooke County, including Obediah B. Atkinson and John Davidson, who had survived their imprisonment in Little Rock, sent a petition to Hamilton in October, 1862, asking him to remove their county officials. He replaced everyone on November 10, 1865, but not in time to prevent a debacle.[23]

The petitioners in Cooke County also asked for Federal troops to restore order, echoing demands from others in the area. Weaver's own grandfather, Mansell W. Matthews—an itinerant Disciples of Christ minister who had been jailed several times during the war as a Unionist, including a harrowing experience in Cooke County—reported to Hamilton that "nothing short of military force will secure the faithful execution of the law and give security to this part of the country." Christopher C. Binkley, a prominent attorney and Unionist who had been forced to flee his home in Sherman by a "howling mob" during the war, added his voice as well to the rising chorus along the Forks in the fall of 1865.[24]

Hamilton received requests for protection not only from Unionists but also from ex-Confederates asking to be defended from Indians "frequently incited and aided by whites more barbarous than the savages themselves." The presence of hundreds of outlaws from the irregular units that had preyed upon North Texas during the war added to the danger for all settlers

23. Pete A. Y. Gunter, ed., "Lillian Gunter Papers on Cooke County History" (Typescript in Morton Museum, Gainesville, Tex.), 384; Lemuel D. Clark, ed., *The Civil War Recollections of James Lemuel Clark* (College Station, Tex., 1984), 40; A. T. Howell to Hardin Hart, February 6, 1866, John C. Magee *et al.* to Hamilton, October 2, 1865, John N. Redmon to Hamilton, February 6, 1866, all in GOR; Cooke County, District Clerk, Judge's State Docket [Civil and Criminal], Sixteenth, Twentieth, and Seventh District Courts, 1857–1871, Case No. 250, in UNT; Cooke County, District Clerk, Criminal and Civil Minutes, Sixteenth, Twentieth, and Seventh District Courts, 1857–1871, p. 245, in Cooke County Courthouse, Gainesville, Tex.; Michael Collins, *Cooke County, Texas: Where the South and the West Meet* (Gainesville, 1981), 11.

24. Mansell W. Matthews to John Hancock, August 15, 1865, Nancy Hill to Hamilton, September 16, 1865, Magee *et al.* to Hamilton, October 2, 1865, Christopher C. Binkley to Hamilton, September 2, 1865, Nelson *et al.* to Hamilton, November 10, 1865, Benjamin F. Barkley to Hamilton, October 4, 30, 1865, Matthews to Hamilton, October 4, 1865, all in GOR; John M. Crisp to George M. Crisp, October 20, 1921 (Typescript in Great Hanging File, Morton Museum); John H. McLean, *The Reminiscences of the Reverend John H. McLean* (Nashville, 1918), 106; Joseph C. Terrell, "Reminiscences of Early Days of Fort Worth" (Typescript in Texas Writer's Project: Fort Worth History Notes, Vol. I, Pt. 2, pp. 284–86, BTHC); Binkley to Johnson, August 24, 1865, in Amnesty Files; *House Executive Documents*, 39th Cong., 2d Sess., No. 116, p. 56. For more about Matthews, see Walter P. Webb, H. Bailey Carroll, and Eldon S. Branda, eds., *The Handbook of Texas* (3 vols.; Austin, 1952, 1976), II, 160.

along the Forks. These "Renegade Texans," unable to return to their homes in Missouri and Arkansas, remained in North Texas and supported themselves by robbery. They preferred those accused of Unionism, but many did not refrain from attacking anyone, regardless of politics.[25]

Concerned, Hamilton asked General George A. Custer to dispatch some troopers to restore "order, peace, and a just regard for constitutional authority" in North Texas. Custer agreed to send two hundred commanded by a "most prudent and discreet officer," Lieutenant Colonel Thomas M. Browne. After settling in Sherman, Browne sent a company to Cooke County on December 23. Many of those indicted for the Great Hanging surrendered, confident of the outcome of a civil trial, but some fled. County officials refused Browne's offer to pursue the fugitives, and the troopers departed on Christmas Day, frustrating those who had anticipated legal redress. John N. Redmon, who had delivered the petition that prompted the removal of the first slate of county officers, complained to the governor again in February, 1866, that a majority of the "murderers" and "mobbers" were still at large. Asserting he had "never . . . seen so one sided a thing in all of my life," Redmon wrote, "Widdowes And orphans wants those mobbers Brot to Justice," adding, "If we can get the power we will hunt them close or catch some of them."[26]

Despite the apparent impotence of the military, Hamilton worried that the occupation forces would be reduced further. President Johnson reassured him in December, 1865, that no more troops would be withdrawn, but Hamilton wrote Sheridan that simply discussing a reduction filled him with "apprehension." He explained that such actions "would be disastrous to the Union men of the State and to the interests of the Govt.," because "violence and outrage" would be inflicted upon Unionists and freedmen on a scale that would shock the "moral sense of the entire Country." Sheridan endorsed the governor's missive to Grant: "I very much fear that Gov. Hamilton has not in the least exaggerated in this letter."[27]

25. A. Gilbert *et al.* to F. W. Emery, July 29, 1865, Thomas N. Toler *et al.* to Emery, July 29, 1865, Otis G. Welch to Jesse M. Blount, September 20, 1865, all in GOR.

26. George A. Custer to Hamilton, November 23, 1865, and Redmon to Hamilton, February 6, 1866, in GOR; John E. Wheeler Diary, 1850–1880 (MS in Morton Museum); Thomas Barrett, *The Great Hanging at Gainesville* (Austin, 1961), 22; Wright to George Lee, January 5, 1866, in Lets. Sent, Fifth Mil. Dist., RG 397, NA; Philip Lindsley, *A History of Greater Dallas and Vicinity* (2 vols.; Chicago, 1909), I, 69–70.

27. Hamilton to Philip H. Sheridan, January 17, 1866, with Endorsements of Sheridan,

Despite Sheridan's pleas to the contrary, Custer's commission as a major general of volunteers was allowed to expire, and at the end of January, 1866, he was recalled from Texas to his regular army post as a captain in the 5th Cavalry. Wright, on January 6, 1866, had asked Custer to send more troops to North Texas after receiving new complaints about "lawlessness" and "resistance to civil authority," and had proposed that Custer be promoted to the command of a division so that he could conduct military trials. These proposals, in spite of urgent requests from Unionists, were canceled; only a small force remained along the Forks under the distant command of General James Shaw, Jr., in San Antonio.[28]

Renewed violence against Unionists on the Forks revived attempts to provide military protection for them. Prior to the fall, 1865, session of the district court in Weatherford, vigilantes disguised as Indians terrorized Unionists to force them to abandon plans to obtain legal redress for wartime excesses. The raiders fled when the court convened, but to emphasize their point, they returned one night and pulled down the United States flag that flew over the courthouse. The members of the jury understood all too well; they refused to convict sixteen men indicted for the murder of James M. Luckey, the militia captain and conspirator who had been lynched in 1864. Luckey's widow and one of the men who had been conveyed to Houston with Luckey filed civil suits seeking $100,000 apiece in damages, but these were dismissed as well.[29]

After the district court adjourned, the renegades returned in full force. Sheriff D. B. Luckey of Parker County, the brother of the slain militia captain, begged Hamilton to have Federal troopers sent, admitting that the ruffians were too numerous and too well armed for him to confront alone and that he could not muster a posse. D. O. Norton, who had been

<hr />

February 2, 1865, Ulysses S. Grant, February 16, 1865, and Stanton, February 29, 1865, in Johnson Papers; Wright to Hamilton, August 14, September 2, 1865, Johnson to Hamilton, December 1, 1865, all in GOR.

28. Anthony M. Bryant to Hamilton, January 29, 1866, in GOR; Wright to Custer, January 6, 1866, in Lets. Sent, Fifth Mil. Dist., RG 397, NA; Mark M. Boatner III, *The Civil War Dictionary* (New York, 1959), 736; Jay Monaghan, *Custer: The Life of General George Armstrong Custer* (Boston, 1959), 264.

29. R. W. Scott to Hamilton, October 3, 1865, D. B. Luckey to Hamilton, October 16, 1865, D. O. Norton to Hamilton, October 17, 1865, Barkley to Hamilton, October 30, 1865, all in GOR; H. Smythe, *Historical Sketch of Parker County and Weatherford, Texas* (St. Louis, 1877), 183–84.

Tainted Breeze

arrested with James Luckey in April, 1864, echoed the sheriff's pleas in a separate letter to the governor, adding that those who had opposed the Confederacy in Parker County were terrorized by raiders who cursed them as "God damned Union dogs," beat them, and stoned their houses. Many were leaving, and more would do so if they could not get effective protection.[30]

The arrival of Custer's troops on the Forks in December, 1865, had forced the raiders in Parker County to lay low, but violence began anew after their departure when a Unionist in Weatherford killed an ex-Confederate who assaulted him. The victim's son, who had already killed a Unionist and a former slave in previous encounters, fled the town but soon returned with two younger brothers and initiated a reign of terror against the Unionists. Luckey resigned as sheriff and was followed in rapid succession by three subsequent appointees, preventing any attempt to convene the district court and try the son, who had been indicted for two murders. Petitions to Wright for assistance were signed by many prominent Unionists, including Luckey, Norton, former chief justices J. Wiley Robbins and Henry J. Thompson—who had been appointed by Hamilton but resigned in October, 1865—and Alvey J. Thompson, who had saved his brother's life and many others in 1864 by leading John R. Diamond astray.[31]

The allegations from Weatherford were verified by Lieutenant Colonel Browne's final report. He confirmed that North Texas was infested with outlaws, including former members of William C. Quantrill's company. The Unionists could not defend themselves; for example, Frederick Sumner of Sherman was shot when he attempted to raise a homemade banner over his home, where he had returned at the close of the war. He survived, but he lost an eye. Many who had aided Browne left when his troops departed because they were marked for elimination. Browne stated that "Grayson, Cook, and Fannin counties were the theatre of the most unparalleled and atrocious outrages during the war. . . . Hundreds of cold-blooded butcheries" were perpetrated on "men guilty of no offense but their devotion to their country." In a direct, but inaccurate, reference to the Great Hanging, he wrote: "Mob juries, without authority of civil or military tribunals, con-

30. Luckey to Hamilton, October 16, 1865, Norton to Hamilton, October 17, 1865, Barkley to Hamilton, October 30, 1865, all in GOR; *House Executive Documents*, 40th Cong., 2d Sess., No. 57, p. 24.
31. Secretary of State, Election Register; *House Executive Documents*, 40th Cong., 2d Sess., 24.

166

demned the suspected without evidence and hanged them speedily and mercilessly"; more than fifty were hanged "upon *one limb*" in Gainesville, thirty in one day. He concluded, "Certainly in no portion of Texas are troops so badly needed." [32]

Alarmed, Wright talked with General Samuel D. Sturgis, Browne's brigade commander. They agreed, in light of the threat to loyal Union men and freedmen on the Forks, to increase the force there to four companies: two at Sherman, one at Weatherford, and one in Jacksboro. In response to demands from Hamilton that Austin be secured for a state convention, however, Wright delayed sending additional troops to North Texas. He did order a company posted at Pilot Point to patrol in Parker County, but told them not to interfere "in matters of crimes committed before the occupation of the state by Federal troops," a clear signal to the Unionists that they could expect no action from Federal officials against those responsible for the Great Hanging and similar affairs. [33]

Escalating violence in Parker County prompted Wright to send four companies of the 6th Cavalry to North Texas as planned at the end of March, but by the time they arrived the Unionists had already taken the law into their own hands. Robbins led thirty men in pursuit of renegades who had robbed his store and killed another Unionist in Weatherford. Robbins' band occupied the county seat on April 10, 1866, and caught G. N. Boyles, an accomplice in the murder. They enjoyed the turn of events, cursing their prisoner as a "(damned) Rebel" and threatening to kill all ex-Confederates who opposed them. Too, they declared that "the days of vigilance committees had passed," asserting that "it was their time now and they be damned if they was not going to have things their own way awhile." They released their captive unharmed, but later many of the mob—including Robbins, Luckey, Henry J. and Alvey J. Thompson, and W. Frank Carter, chief justice of Parker County—were indicted for their acts. Apparently, the determination to put wartime violence and its aftermath in the

32. *House Executive Documents*, 40th Cong., 2d Sess, No. 57, pp. 22–23; B. R. Sanders to Bryant, January 2, 1866, with endorsement of Thomas M. Browne, January 14, 1865, in GOR; *House Reports*, 39th Cong., 1st Sess., No. 30, Pt. 4, p. 74.

33. Wright to George L. Hartsuff, March 13, 1866, and H. Whittelsey to Shaw, March 23, 1866, in Lets. Sent, Fifth Mil. Dist., RG 397, NA; Samuel D. Sturgis to Hamilton, March 19, 1866, and James Shaw to Hamilton, March 26, 1866, in GOR; *House Executive Documents*, 40th Cong., 2d Sess, No. 57, pp. 21–22, 27; Richter, *The Army in Texas During Reconstruction*, 48.

past intervened in their favor. None were convicted, and General Joseph J. Reynolds dismissed charges against the last two, the Thompson brothers, in October, 1867.[34]

The demands of Unionists for redress became the topic of heated debate during the constitutional convention that met at Austin in February, 1866. The assembly was dominated by ex-Confederates; prominent among the Forks delegates were James W. Throckmorton and John K. Bumpass, who had commanded a company at Gainesville in October, 1862. Also present from Cooke County was James M. Lindsay, whom the Quitman *Clipper* claimed had taken part in the Great Hanging, too. Journalist Benjamin C. Truman wrote to President Johnson that the Unionist delegates from North Texas, among whom was Robert H. Taylor, were "among the ablest" at the convention, but Hamilton admitted that they were opposed by "violent & intracticable [*sic*] men." Throckmorton and Taylor, who had been allies against secession, were the respective leaders of the opposing factions. The latter had hidden in the brush to avoid being arrested by McCulloch and now wanted retribution. The former, elected president of the convention, asked them to "bury, upon the altar of our common country, all the recent past, with all its painful associations and recollections."[35]

The specter of wartime persecutions precluded factional amity. A proposal to repudiate the entire civil debt acrued during the war was championed by those who argued that much of this indebtedness was incurred in the unlawful persecution of persons loyal to the United States. This measure prevailed only with the support of others who believed that warrants had been issued in violation of the 1845 constitution of Texas, that they

34. A. J. Hunter to Throckmorton, May 24, 1867, Affidavit of G. N. Boyles, May 24, 1867, Affidavit of B. L. Richey, May 24, 1867, all in GOR; Wright to Shaw, March 30, 1866, and Wright to Hartsuff, May 2, 1866, in Lets. Sent, Fifth Mil. Dist., RG 397, NA; Throckmorton to John J. Good, April 29, 1867, Throckmorton to William T. G. Weaver, April 29, 1867, Throckmorton to Charles Griffin, April 30, May 28, 1867, all in Texas Secretary of State, Executive Record Book, Archives Division, TSL; Shook, "Federal Occupation and Administration of Texas," 186.

35. Ben C. Truman to Johnson, February 8, April 9, 1866, Hamilton to Johnson, February 12, 16, 1866, all in Johnson Papers; Throckmorton to Epperson, April 17, 1866, in Epperson Papers; *Journal of the Texas State Convention, Assembled at Austin, February 7, 1866* (Austin, 1866), 4, 5, 6–7, 369, 379; *House Reports*, 39th Cong., 1st Sess., No. 30, Pt. 4, pp. 136–37; Quitman (Tex.) *Clipper*, n.d., quoted in Austin *Southern Intelligencer*, June 14, 1866; Claude Elliot, *Leathercoat: The Life History of a Texas Patriot* (San Antonio, 1938), 105–14; Moneyhan, *Republicanism in Reconstruction Texas*, 228.

were held primarily by speculators, and that to pay them would financially cripple the state. The arguments over the debt, however, paled in comparison with the furor raised by the introduction of Ordinance Number 11, which mandated that no one was to be prosecuted or sued for any acts performed under Confederate authority. Unionists recalled the Great Hanging—condemning William R. Hudson as a "fiend in human shape"— and accused Throckmorton of obstructing justice. But this time the desire for restoring order by burying the past won out, and the convention adopted the objectionable act.[36]

Informed of the passage of Ordinance Number 11, Hamilton angrily addressed the delegates on March 31, 1866. He denounced them for "legislating wholesale robbery and murder throughout the land." Scorning those who referred to it a "measure of peace," he asked, "Does it bring peace to the bereaved hearts made desolate by such deeds?" He confronted the delegates, saying: "You have an account to settle before the people yet. You have not done with this. You shall confront them, and shall answer to them, and if God spares my life, I pledge myself to go before the people of the state and draw these men up and make them answer." As applause rippled through the galleries, he added, "I may not get through, but the same precautions will not be necessary as two years ago. The ready rope and convenient limb will not be used as they were then."[37]

Hamilton's plans were undone by the triumph of Throckmorton and his conservative allies during the postconvention election in the summer of 1866. The diehard Unionists nominated Elisha M. Pease—the former governor who had tried to organize a party in 1861 to thwart secession—to run for governor against Throckmorton, Epperson for lieutenant governor, and Binkley of Grayson County for attorney general. Binkley had loudly opposed Throckmorton's election to the convention; Throckmorton responded by excoriating Binkley in a letter to Epperson as one of those who had "skulked from danger and drew no sword in defense of either belligerent and who now flock around the slain carcass like filthy beasts and vul-

36. *Journal of the Texas State Convention*, 46, 66, 116, 160, 355–57; *The Constitution, as Amended, and Ordinances of the Convention of 1866* (Austin, 1866), 42–43; Clipping from San Antonio *Express*, n.d. (Scrapbook in Haynes Papers); Austin *Texas State Gazette*, February 15, 1866; Moneyhan, *Republicanism in Reconstruction Texas*, 40–41; Ramsdell, *Reconstruction in Texas*, 102–103; Waller, *Colossal Hamilton*, 90–91, 93.

37. Austin *Southern Intelligencer*, May 24, 1866; Ramsdell, *Reconstruction in Texas*, 105; Waller, *Colossal Hamilton*, 91.

tures." Epperson subsequently declined to be on the ticket with Binkley. Campaigning as a Union man who had served in the Confederate army primarily to preserve order and protect others, Throckmorton outpolled Pease more than three to one.[38]

Throckmorton, having secured election through the creation of a conservative coalition that turned its back on wartime excesses, did nothing to protect Unionists in regions like the Forks, where violence continued. Advocating a minimal amount of interference by the national government in Texas, he clashed constantly with Federal military officers in the state, especially Sheridan. On August 20, 1866, President Johnson encouraged Throckmorton and his supporters, who had won a majority in the legislature, by declaring the rebellion at an end in Texas, the last state freed from military rule during presidential Reconstruction.[39]

Under Throckmorton's rule, violence against Unionists and blacks increased. Former Confederates in remote areas such as the Forks waged a campaign of intimidation unchecked by "any fear of retribution." The number of homicides in Texas more than doubled from 1866 to 1867; in Cooke County alone during the first two months of 1867 seventeen murders were committed. General Edgar M. Gregory in his final report as the commander of the Freedmen's Bureau in Texas, submitted in June, 1866, stated that Unionists as well as freedmen were "trembling for their lives and preparing to leave the state," and that their persecutors were almost always acquitted by the courts. His lament was sadly accurate; though 550 people were killed from June, 1865, through December, 1867, only 249 suspects were indicted and only 5 were convicted.[40]

The lassitude of the Throckmorton administration even encouraged violent defiance of Federal authority. D. W. Steadham, who had fled Texas with his son in October, 1862, to avoid being hanged by the tribunal in Sherman, was appointed internal revenue assessor and collector for Cooke

38. Throckmorton to Epperson, January 21, 1866, in Epperson Papers; Austin *Southern Intelligencer*, April 19, June 7, 1866; Elliot, *Leathercoat*, 103–104; Ramsdell, *Reconstruction in Texas*, 108–12; Waller, *Colossal Hamilton*, 92–93; Ernest W. Winkler, *Platforms of Political Parties in Texas* (Austin, 1916), 95, 98–99.

39. Elliot, *Leathercoat*, 120–29; T. R. Fehrenbach, *Lone Star: A History of Texas and the Texans* (New York, 1968), 401–403; Ramsdell, *Reconstruction in Texas*, 112–13, 126; Richter, *The Army in Texas During Reconstruction*, 54; Shook, "Federal Occupation and Administration of Texas," 161–64.

40. R. L. Bullock to Throckmorton, February 16, 1867, in GOR; Ramsdell, *Reconstruction in Texas*, 134–35; *Senate Miscellaneous Documents*, 40th Cong., 2d Sess., No. 109, pp. 2–5.

and Montague counties during the fall of 1866. He took a room at W. L. Fletcher's hotel in Gainesville; that night, Samuel Davidson stood in front of the establishment, cursing the Federal government and shouting that an "honest man" would not allow such people in his hotel. Davidson was so drunk he "tottered," but he did have a pistol, which made him a threat to be taken seriously. When Steadham's son and a friend walked toward Davidson, he ran into a shed. They waited at the door for him with drawn pistols, but he came from around a corner and got the first shot. When the two returned his fire, Davidson again retreated, shouting that his gun's cylinder would not revolve.[41]

The older Steadham, who had watched the entire scene, was shaken by the exchange of gunfire. The sheriff and other officials were solicitous; all three men were arrested, but only Davidson had to post a bond while the other two were set free without bail. The sheriff also offered to provide an escort for the tax collector, but Steadham decided to leave instead. He recovered his nerve and returned in a week, but again his son entered an altercation on the porch of Fletcher's hotel. They left once more, and this time returned only to take depositions on what had occurred, with an escort of United States soldiers. Throckmorton, alerted to these threats against a Federal official, refused to intervene. He received a petition from Cooke County asking him to remove the Unionist because he was a "very obnoxious officer" who slandered the citizens there by reporting them to be disloyal, and insulted them by traveling with an escort. State district judge Weaver concurred in this advice, but for different reasons; he asserted that Steadham was in danger because of his earlier association with the Peace party. By refusing to act, the governor satisfied Steadham's detractors, because the Unionist soon left North Texas for good.[42]

Former Confederates grew bold under Throckmorton's rule, openly using the courts to thwart efforts to avenge wartime atrocities. In Cooke County during the fall of 1866, Weaver presided over the acquittals of the first six jurors from the Citizens Court brought to trial—Samuel C. Doss, Reason and Wiley Jones, Benjamin Scanland, William J. Simpson, and Thomas Wright. Rumors circulated that a substantial amount of hush

41. J. A. Smith and Thomas P. Ferrell to Throckmorton, September 1866, and Weaver to Throckmorton, September 21, 1866, in GOR; Galveston *News*, October 23, 1862.
42. Smith and Ferrell to Throckmorton, September 1866, Weaver to Throckmorton, September 21, 23, 1866, J. H. Howell *et al.* to Throckmorton, September 20, 1866, all in GOR; Collins, *Cooke County*, 17.

money was paid, but it was more likely that a jury to convict them could not be mustered from among the many residents who had supported the Confederacy's attempts to impose order and who now wanted to put the war behind them. In this, they were encouraged by General Wright's orders not to interfere in wartime matters, Ordinance Number 11 from the state convention absolving Confederate officials, and the amnesty proclamation of Johnson himself, issued on May 29, 1865.[43]

Sheridan watched these developments closely, waiting to intervene whenever an opportunity arose. He was especially concerned with Throckmorton's plan for ten ranger companies to protect settlers from the attacks of Indians and "wicked and reckless white men & negroes." Numerous petitions from frightened citizens, memorials from the legislature, and a rising death toll did provide solid evidence of a problem that needed to be addressed. Hamilton had enlisted "county police" units without incident in the fall of 1865, but Sheridan regarded the proposed new organization with alarm because of the large number of former Confederates in the ranks. All of its ten captains, including John T. Rowland, had served in the Frontier or Mounted regiments; would they, Sheridan wondered, include Unionists among the "reckless white men" against whom they would campaign, as they had during the war? With Commander-in-Chief Grant's endorsement, Sheridan ordered Throckmorton not to muster the companies, though he was compelled by a sympathetic Stanton to provide for the establishment of Fort Richardson in Jack County with a permanent garrison of six companies from the 6th United States Cavalry.[44]

43. Thomas Barrett, *The Great Hanging at Gainesville* (Austin, 1961), 22; Cooke Cty., Dist. Clerk, Criminal and Civil Minutes, 289–90; Cooke Cty., Dist. Clerk, Judge's State Docket, Case No. 250; Moneyhan, *Republicanism in Reconstruction Texas*, 51. For a substantial analysis of Johnson's amnesty proclamation of May 29, 1865, and its lenient application, see Jonathan T. Dorris, *Pardon and Amnesty Under Lincoln and Johnson* (Chapel Hill, 1953), *passim.*

44. Hamilton to Johnson, March 1, 28, 1866, in Johnson Papers; Throckmorton to Stanton, August 5, 1867, in James W. Throckmorton Papers, BTHC; Wheeler Diary; William R. Strong, *His Memoirs*, ed. Pete A. Y. Gunter and Robert A. Calvert (Denton, Tex., 1982), 36; Magee *et al.* to Hamilton, October 2, 1865, W. Frank Carter to Hamilton, December 20, 1865, Nathaniel T. Bomar to Hamilton, January 19, 1866, Weaver to Throckmorton, August 2, 1866, J. H. Cost to Throckmorton, September 4, 1866, Thomas L. Stanfield *et al.* to Throckmorton, September 12, 1866, Samuel F. Mains et al. to Throckmorton, September 16, 1866, F. E. Piner *et al.* to Throckmorton, September 20, 1866, James M. Lindsay to Throckmorton, October 6, 1866, S. Shannon to Throckmorton, October 7, 1866, George B. Pickett to Throckmorton, October 25, 1866, Sheridan to Samuel P. Heintzelman, October 15, Novem-

Sheridan's angry suspicions were heightened when Throckmorton defied his order and urged Cooke County commissioner Thomas L. Mosby to proceed with the muster of volunteer rangers. Rowland's company patrolled North Texas, as did another commanded by John R. Diamond, who enlisted many former members of the 11th Texas Cavalry. This defiance infuriated Sheridan, but his attempt to intervene proved futile due to the determination of residents on the Forks to impose order in their own fashion. When a petition from Diamond's company to be allowed to remain in the field was rejected on the grounds that many of the signatures were in the same hand—despite the explanation that most of the troops were illiterate and someone had to sign on their behalf—Weaver gave protest speeches that resulted in his arrest for sedition. He spent a few days in Austin, but when he was freed, he returned home to resume efforts to retain the company. A lieutenant in the 6th United States Cavalry agreed to swear the volunteers into service, and Diamond led them on patrols through the winter of 1866.[45]

For Sheridan, the campaign to increase the number of troops along the frontier, which many Unionists in fact endorsed, demonstrated Throckmorton's lack of concern for loyal men. From the beginning he had suspected that the governor was more interested in reducing the police role of the military than in protecting settlers. A tour of the frontier by a trusted aide reaffirmed Sheridan's belief that Throckmorton exaggerated the dan-

---

ber 6, 1866, Sheridan to Throckmorton, October 16, 1866, A. J. Yount to Throckmorton, November 26, 1866, Oliver Loving *et al.* to Emery, n.d., all in GOR; W. W. Brady *et al.* to Texas House of Representatives, July 27, 1866, in Memorial and Petitions File, Archives Division, TSL; Wright to Throckmorton, August 14, 1866, Heintzelman to Throckmorton, October 25, 1866, George B. Potrim to R. M. Hall, October 25, 1866, Potrim to H. I. Ransom, November 12, 1866, in Lets. Sent, Fifth Mil. Dist., RG 397, NA; *House Executive Documents*, 40th Cong., 2d Sess., No. 57, pp. 39–40, 43–44; H. P. N. Gammel, comp., *The Laws of Texas, 1822–1897* (10 vols.; Austin, 1898), V, 928–30; Austin *Southern Intelligencer*, March 1, October 18, 1866; *Texas Senate Journal*, 1866, pp. 25, 32; Collins, *Cooke County*, 20–21; Elliot, *Leathercoat*, 137–42; Ramsdell, *Reconstruction in Texas*, 68; Richter, *The Army in Texas During Reconstruction*, 54, 67, 69; Allen L. Hamilton, *Sentinel of the Southern Plains: Fort Richardson and the Northwest Texas Frontier, 1866–1878* (Fort Worth, 1988), *passim*.

45. "Interview with Thant Gorham, March 27, 1925" (MS in Lillian Gunter Papers, UNT); Strong, *Memoirs*, 47; Throckmorton to Thomas L. Mosby, November 26, 1866, and to Stanton, August 5, 1867, in Throckmorton Papers; Throckmorton to John T. Rowland, December 3, 1866, Lindsay to Throckmorton, December 15, 1866, William Cloud to Throckmorton, December 15, 1866, all in GOR; Elliot, *Leathercoat*, 137–38, 144–46.

ger. He confronted the governor in January, 1867, writing, "There are more casualties occurring from outrages perpetrated upon Union men and freedmen in the interior of the state than occur from Indian depredations on the frontier." In an angry reply, Throckmorton compounded his culpability by not only denying the accusations but also adding that most of the "outraged Union men" were rogues who cried wolf to get military protection for their own evil purposes. This "howling crowd of canting, lying scamps," he wrote, initiated much trouble, then complained when they met with rough treatment.[46]

To demonstrate his point, Throckmorton on February 9, 1867, sent a printed circular to the justices of the county courts and other officials, asking them to report on the administration of justice in their jurisdictions. Without exception, they insisted that most of those who complained sought the protection of the Federal government only after they had committed a crime. Sheridan was unconvinced and wrote to Grant: "The condition of Freedmen and Union men in remote parts of the State is truly horrible. The Government is denounced, the Freedmen are shot, and Union men are persecuted if they have the temerity to express their opinion." He asserted once more that Throckmorton was trying to get troops removed to the frontier to prevent their interference in these "fiendish actions." Grant forwarded Sheridan's letter to Stanton with his endorsement, adding that martial law should be declared in Texas. Although the secretary of war did not authorize such a drastic action, he endorsed Sheridan's choice of General Charles Griffin to take command of the Department of Texas.[47]

Griffin had scarcely settled into his new headquarters when more reports came of violence on the Forks. Albert Evans had resigned as the Freedmen's Bureau agent for Grayson County after repeated threats against his life, but remained in the area and reported on February 28 that the "slaughter" of Unionists and freedmen had reached unprecedented levels. When the district attorney also quit, Throckmorton appointed James M. Hurt, a former Confederate officer and conservative delegate to the 1866 convention, telling him to demonstrate "that violence, rascality and breaches of the law

46. *House Executive Documents*, 39th Cong., 2d Sess., No. 1, pp. 46–48; *OR*, Ser. I, Vol. XLVIII, Pt. 1, p. 301; Throckmorton to Sheridan, January 28, 1867, in Texas Secretary of State, Executive Record Book; Ramsdell, *Reconstruction in Texas*, 134–35; Richter, *The Army in Texas During Reconstruction*, 70–71.

47. *House Executive Documents*, 40th Cong., 2d Sess., No. 57, pp. 34–35; Robert Wilson to Throckmorton, March 13, 1867, in GOR; Ramsdell, *Reconstruction in Texas*, 135–36; Richter, *The Army in Texas During Reconstruction*, 71, 73–74.

must cease . . . or that punishment will follow." But Hurt accomplished little.[48]

Reports of the lawlessness in Texas infuriated many northerners. John A. Stewart, president of the United States Trust Company, had been an adviser to Lincoln and an assistant treasurer of the United States during the war. He wrote to Throckmorton in February, 1867, denouncing him as a "whipper in of blood hounds" and asserting, "All good men will quit your state or drive you and all murderers out." He dismissed the Texan's allies as "lawless thieves and murderers" who possessed "neither character, credit or money." He concluded his note with a threat: "Your teritory [sic] belongs to us and unless you govern yourselves you will be governed by your owners. Andy Johnson & James Buchanan occupy the same nich [sic]—Throckmorton may come next, in the utter detestation of the people."[49]

Not all northerners were as enraged as Stewart, but their demands for a remedy were heard just as clearly in Congress. No less than six officers and five civilians testified about the plight of Texas Unionists before the Joint Committee on Reconstruction, which, as the sounding board for congressional Republicans, was "particularly receptive" to reports of persecution. Custer, with Sumner's flag on his lap, told the committee on March 10, 1866, that loyalists were murdered in North Texas during the war, and that it was not safe for those who had fled to return without the protection of troops. He reported on his operations in the area, and included an account of Sumner's loss of an eye. Truman subsequently corroborated all that Custer said in his interview with the committee. Senator-elect Oran M. Roberts of Texas, who was denied his seat, recalled that when he arrived in Washington the question he was most often asked was whether his home state was safe for loyal men.[50]

---

48. Throckmorton to James M. Hurt, February 27, 1867, in Throckmorton Papers; Throckmorton to James H. Bell, September 1, 1865, and Leonidas M. Martin to Joseph B. Kiddoo, September 2, 1865, in GOR; Throckmorton to J. W. Wood, February 28, 1867, in Texas Secretary of State Executive Record Book; Wright to Heintzelman, July 19, 1866, in Lets. Sent, Fifth Mil. Dist., RG 397, NA; Albert Evans to Kiddoo, January 18, February 1, 28, 1867, in U.S. Department of War, Bureau of Refugees, Freedmen, and Abandoned Lands, 1865–1869, Records of the Assistant Commissioner for Texas, Record Group 105, NA; *House Miscellaneous Documents*, 40th Cong., 2d Sess., No. 127, p. 12; James Smallwood, *A Century of Achievement: Blacks in Cooke County, Texas* (Gainesville, 1975), 15; Webb, Carroll and Branda, eds., *Handbook*, II, 869.

49. John A. Stewart to Throckmorton, February 9, 1867, in Epperson Papers; *DAB*, IX, 619.

50. Oran M. Roberts, "The Experiences of an Unrecognized Southern Senator," *SWHQ*,

The alarming evidence from North Texas contributed to the revolt in Congress against the conservatism of Johnson's Reconstruction policies, which hindered effective intervention on behalf of the Unionists. For many congressmen, claims by the Texas legislature and Throckmorton that the rumors of violence were all untrue were invalidated by the reports of Sheridan. Observing the reaction of Congress to accounts from Texas and elsewhere, Secretary of the Navy Gideon Welles wrote in his diary: "The entire South seem to be stupid and vindictive." On March 2, 1867, Congress passed the First Reconstruction Act, placing Texas in the 5th Military District under the direction of Sheridan.[51]

Griffin remained commander of the Department of Texas for only four days after passage of the bill but implemented changes on the Forks. On his last day, in response to requests for assistance in quelling the disturbances in Grayson County, he suspended the operation of General Orders Number 5—which had directed military authorities to defer to civilians—in that region. The garrison in Sherman was placed at the disposal of the Freedmen's Bureau agent there (Unionist and former chief justice Anthony M. Bryant accepted an appointment on April 1) for the arrest of any person accused of a crime against Unionists or freedmen. Bryant was to detain them "until such time as a proper judicial tribunal may be ready and willing to try them."[52]

Unfortunately such measures did not end the assaults on Unionists and freedmen along the Forks. Griffin was outraged that charges were not filed in the numerous cases reported in North Texas, and repeatedly demanded the removal of Throckmorton and all disloyal officials. He declared that

---

XII (1908), 138; *Senate Executive Documents* 39th Cong., 1st Sess., No. 43, pp. 3, 6, 12–13; *House Reports*, 39th Cong., 1st Sess., No. 30, Pt. 4, pp. 39–40, 43–45, 46–50, 72–74, 86–91, 122–25, 129–32, 136–37, 147, 152–53; Dan T. Carter, *When the War Was Over: The Failure of Self-Reconstruction in the South, 1865–1867* (Baton Rouge, 1985), 37–39; Shook, "Federal Occupation and Administration of Texas," 206–207.

51. Beale, ed., *Diary of Gideon Welles*, II, 420, 568; Throckmorton to Oran M. Roberts, December 22, 1866, in Texas Secretary of State, Executive Record Book; *Texas Senate Journal*, 1866, pp. 25, 32; Ramsdell, *Reconstruction in Texas*, 146, 149–51; Richter, *The Army in Texas During Reconstruction*, 72–73, 90; Shook, "Federal Occupation and Administration of Texas," 166–68; Ulrich, "The Northern Military Mind in Regard to Reconstruction," 163.

52. *House Executive Documents*, 40th Cong., 2d Sess., No. 57, pp. 23–24; A. H. M. Taylor to Commanding Officer, 6th Cav., U.S.A., February 6, 1867, in Lets. Sent, Fifth Mil. Dist., RG 397, NA: Austin *Southern Intelligencer*, March 21, 1867.

though he had called the governor's attention to "outrages and murders" perpetrated on "loyal men, white and black," there was not a "single instance in which the offender has been punished." His denunciations were sent, with Sheridan's and Grant's endorsements, to Attorney General Henry Stanbery, in whose office they were filed awaiting his attention. With Griffin's missive thus pigeonholed, Grant wired Sheridan to postpone plans for the removal of any civil officials in Texas, as his authority to do so was not clear.[53]

Griffin could not wait until a decision was made in Washington. A petition from Unionists in Jack and Parker counties brought new charges against A. J. Hunter, the wartime chief justice of Parker County who had regained his seat in the summer of 1866. Hunter was accused of allowing ex-Confederates who terrorized Unionists to go unpunished, while he prosecuted to the full extent of the law Unionists who retaliated. Griffin wrote to Throckmorton on April 26, 1867, that "such grave charges of maladministration if false, should be disproved without delay, if true, the remedy must be swift and effectual." The governor did nothing more than admonish Hunter and Weaver, who presided as state district judge over the two counties, to "redouble, if possible, your vigilance and energy in matters of this kind." Throckmorton also could not resist repeating earlier assertions that although the Unionists had suffered, some of them "were not guiltless themselves."[54]

Anticipating Throckmorton's inaction, Griffin on April 26, 1867, issued his Circular Number 13, which required all jurors to take an "iron-clad oath" that they had never borne arms against the United States or supported the rebellion in any way. As he later explained to Sheridan, he intended to fill the juries in Texas with loyal men to protect Unionists from the "unjust acts of the courts." Grant approved Griffin's measure and adopted it for use elsewhere, but in Texas it proved a failure because Throckmorton allowed local officials to nullify the circular by ignoring it or by refusing to convene courts.[55]

53. *House Miscellaneous Documents*, 40th Cong., 2d Sess., No. 127, pp. 9, 12, 17, 21; *Senate Executive Documents*, 40th Cong., 1st Sess., No. 14, pp. 194–95; Edward D. Townsend to Grant, April 2, 1867, in Johnson Papers.

54. Griffin to Throckmorton, April 26, 1867, and Throckmorton to Weaver, April 29, 1867, in Throckmorton Papers; Hunter to Throckmorton, May 24, 1867, in GOR; Throckmorton to Hunter, April 29, 1867, Throckmorton to Griffin, April 30, May 28, 1867, all in Texas Secretary of State, Executive Record Book.

55. *Senate Executive Documents*, 40th Cong., 1st Sess., No. 14, pp. 208–10, 221–22;

The idea of removing Throckmorton himself was actively pressed by the Texas Republican party, which was founded to provide a forum for more effective politicking by angry Unionists and freedmen. Morgan C. Hamilton, brother of the former provisional governor, wrote Pease during the fall of 1866 that the number of Unionists left in Texas was dwindling, but those who remained could provide the "mucilage" of a "very respectable and efficient party." Hamilton continued to urge his idea, pointedly reminding correspondents of the plight of Texas Unionists in a court system that was little more than a "legalized vigilance committee."[56]

Hamilton found a kindred soul in John L. Haynes, the firebrand former colonel of the 1st Texas Cavalry, U.S.A., who had been appointed collector of internal revenue in Austin upon the recommendation of Governor Hamilton. In early 1867, Haynes assumed the presidency of the Texas Loyal League of Union Citizens—which by 1866 had established chapters in many counties, including Cooke, Jack, and Wise—and used it as a base for the creation of a Republican party in Texas. He skillfully mustered the support of Unionists; along the Forks, he recruited Sumner and James L. Clark, whose father had been lynched at Gainesville and who had narrowly escaped being executed at Head of Elm in 1864. When a Republican executive committee for Texas was organized in late 1867, Haynes served as its first chairman.[57]

Haynes initiated a vicious media campaign against Throckmorton in which he referred to the attack on D. W. Steadham and to other more gruesome atrocities along the Forks. He ridiculed Throckmorton's claims that Unionists had nothing to fear, writing, "Whilst red handed murder stalks abroad in every county of the State, there he sets at Austin like an old hen on a bad egg, clucking away about 'occasional' crimes." He struck a nerve when he recalled the Great Hanging and implied that Throckmorton had endorsed the lynchings. Throckmorton wrote to James J. Diamond on

---

William H. Horton to J. T. Kirkman, June 3, 1867, in AGR; Sefton, *The United States Army and Reconstruction*, 142–43.

56. Morgan C. Hamilton to Elisha M. Pease, November 9, 28, 1866, in Elisha M. Pease Papers, Austin History Center; Morgan C. Hamilton to Alexander J. Hamilton, January 8, 1867, in Hamilton Papers.

57. Throckmorton to Epperson, April 25, 1866, in Epperson Papers; John L. Haynes to Pease, November 28, 1866, in Pease Papers, Austin History Center; Frederick W. Sumner to James P. Newcomb, August 31, 1871, and James L. Clark to Newcomb, October 19, 1872, in James P. Newcomb Papers, BTHC; James A. Baggett, "Birth of the Texas Republican Party," *SWHQ*, LXXVIII (1974), 7, 14–15.

May 25, 1867, asking him to publish a rebuttal in the Houston *Dispatch*, which Diamond had established after the war along with his brothers, William and George. The governor recounted how he had prevented the execution of several men in Sherman, including Steadham, and requested that Diamond, as one who had also been there, tell the truth. George, who had the transcripts of the Citizens Court, did begin writing an account of the affair for publication, but he did not finish before Throckmorton was removed from office, and eventually gave up altogether on the project.[58]

The Diamonds' failure to clear Throckmorton's name in the matter of the Great Hanging added a heavy weight in the balance against him. Shortly before a supplemental Reconstruction act on July 19, 1867, bestowed full powers of removal and appointment upon the military district commanders, Epperson wrote to Throckmorton from Washington that he considered it a "settled fact that your head goes off." On July 30, after receiving another letter from Griffin asking him to remove Throckmorton and appoint Pease in his place, Sheridan did so, explaining that the incumbent was an "impediment to the reconstruction of that state under the law."[59]

Sheridan also replaced many other ex-Confederates elected in the summer of 1866. In Cooke County eight were removed, including James E. Sheegog, who had served on the Citizens Court. Among the new appointees was Obediah B. Atkinson. Chief justice Wheeler was allowed to remain in office; a slaveholder whose two sons served in the Confederate army, he nonetheless had opposed secession and was arrested and brought to Gainesville during the Great Hanging. He was released, but in the excitement his horse fell on him, leaving him a cripple for life. He fled from Cooke County in 1863, but returned and was elected in 1866. Sheridan's decision to retain him must have been quite satisfying.[60]

58. Austin *Southern Intelligencer*, May 31, 1866; San Antonio *Express*, March 20, 1867; Clipping from San Antonio *Express*, n.d. (Scrapbook in Haynes Papers); Throckmorton to James J. Diamond, May 25, 1867, in Throckmorton Papers; Sam Acheson and Julia Ann Hudson O'Connell, eds., *George Washington Diamond's Account of the Great Hanging at Gainesville, 1862* (Austin, 1963), xi–xii.

59. Ramsdell, *Reconstruction in Texas*, 168–69; Special Orders No. 105, Headquarters, Fifth Military District, July 30, 1867, in Throckmorton Papers; Sefton, *The United States Army and Reconstruction*, 142–44; Ulrich, "The Northern Military Mind in Regard to Reconstruction," 170.

60. Wheeler Diary; Strong, *Memoirs*, 46; John E. Wheeler to Edmund J. Davis, February 6, 1870, in GOR; Secretary of State, Election Register; A. Morton Smith, *The First 100 Years in Cooke County* (San Antonio, 1955), 24, 35; Walter N. Vernon, *Methodism Moves Across North Texas* (Dallas, 1967), 130–31.

The day after his removal, Throckmorton wrote to Epperson, "I go out of office more endeared to the great mass of the people than any man ever did in Texas. . . . The time will yet come when right and justice will be vindicated." Sheridan's actions did raise a storm of protest in the national press, but it was due to his preemption of civil authority rather than any sympathy for Throckmorton. Concern for Johnson's failure to protect loyal men remained strong. When the president exiled Sheridan, the officer who had intervened for Union men in Texas, to Missouri on August 17, 1867, Johnson added substantially to the growing resentment against himself, and he only narrowly avoided being removed from office.[61]

Sheridan, like Hamilton before him, left many pledges unfulfilled when he was forced to relinquish control over Texas. Unionists along the Forks had waited with mounting impatience through the war years and presidential Reconstruction for vindication, and in the end they were disappointed. The national impetus for conciliation in the postwar period paralleled the desire for security through the restoration of order among a majority of Texans, including those on the Forks. Officers such as Sheridan who attempted to redress the balance were themselves removed as impediments to the achievement of the majority's goals. To be abandoned was galling to the Unionists on the Forks, but nevertheless they had ultimately been ignored in the rush to put the disruption of the Civil War in the past.

61. Throckmorton to Epperson, July 31, 1867, in Throckmorton Papers; *House Executive Documents*, 40th Cong., 2d Sess., No. 57, p. 5; Sefton, *The United States Army and Reconstruction*, 144, 156; Ulrich, "The Northern Military Mind in Regard to Reconstruction," 160, 173–78.

Epilogue

Congress seized control of Reconstruction in 1867, but along the Forks this made little difference. Before, during, and after the Civil War the primary goal of a majority in the region had been to maintain order and security. This had impelled them to oppose secession, then to attack those who apparently did not support the Confederacy, and finally to stifle the disruptive postbellum demands of wartime dissenters for legal retribution, an effort that continued after 1867. The last trials of those involved in the Great Hanging ended with acquittals, and the assaults on families accused of Unionism continued unabated. Ironically, it was the passage of time that imposed order and security, not deliberate efforts by either faction to do so. Widows remarried, while an influx of newcomers pushed the frontier far to the west and obscured wartime social divisions. These divisions, however, never entirely disappeared; although accounts of the Great Hanging were suppressed and the Confederacy was publicly venerated in an attempt to impose order on the past, accusations occasionally resurfaced, revealing the indelible imprint of that affair on the Forks.

The period of presidential Reconstruction ended in Texas with a few members of the Citizens Court still untried. Among them was Thomas Barrett, the Disciples of Christ minister who had opposed many of the lynchings in October, 1862. He had remained at home in Cooke County for over a year after the Great Hanging, but the accelerating conflict between Unionists and Confederates made him fear for his life. He left in the fall of 1863, settling first in Mount Vernon, Titus County—later the seat of Franklin County—then in June, 1865, relocating to Bell County, where James M. Luckey had futilely sought refuge. Realizing that Federal troops would learn that he had been a juror for the Citizens Court, he left an affidavit with the chief justice of Bell County to be given to any soldiers who came after him. In it, he declared he would return peacefully to Gainesville only if he was promised a fair trial and was allowed to call witnesses who would be immune from arrest while testifying. Furthermore, he should be allowed to travel on his own to Gainesville, not under arrest. As security for his appearance in court, he offered a bond of $100,000.[1]

Having provided a statement for the pursuers he believed were close behind, Barrett prepared to flee, packing his belongings while friends stood guard. When Federal soldiers were reported in Bell County, Barrett hid overnight in a thicket near his home. The next afternoon, when he returned to his house for a meal, his son told him that at least seven men had been arrested during the night. Barrett fled to nearby Salado where a friend operated a hotel, although for safety's sake he again slept in the brush at night. While he was absent, soldiers did search his home, but left without a clue to his whereabouts.[2]

The soldiers' visit terrified Barrett, but he was determined not to be taken before a military court. He spent a total of three weeks in the woods near his home in January, 1866. Afraid to build a fire, he had his son bring food and news every day until a friend let him take shelter in a thicket near his tanning yard in Williamson County, about twenty-five miles from Barrett's house, and arranged for him to be fed. In his self-imposed exile, Barrett heard frightful rumors that the Federal soldiers in Cooke County had been bushwhacked, and that the Citizens Court jurors who had surrendered thinking they would get a civil trial had been taken before a court martial. To mislead any pursuers, his family and friends let it be known that Barrett had escaped to Mexico. When they told him that many civilians had been imprisoned in Austin awaiting a court martial, however, he decided to leave Texas.[3]

Taking his son with him, Barrett traveled by night and arrived at his brother's house in Mount Pleasant, Mississippi, on February 16, 1866. He

1. Thomas Barrett, *The Great Hanging at Gainesville* (Austin, 1961), 21–23.
2. *Ibid.*, 23–25.
3. *Ibid.*, 25–27. In fact, only sixteen members of a vigilance committee had been arrested in Williamson County near where Barrett was hiding. Eight of them testified for the state and were freed after showing authorities where fourteen of an estimated thirty executed Unionists lay buried together. Barrett was later told by another man jailed in Austin that the remainder of the prisoners were subsequently released as well, allegedly on General Philip H. Sheridan's order. See Barrett, *Great Hanging*, 26; Thomas North, *Five Years in Texas* (Cincinnati, 1871), 191–92.

stayed only two months before moving on to Giles County, Tennessee, where he visited with another brother before moving again to Franklin, Tennessee, to be with other relatives. Unable to stay put, he returned to his brother's home in Giles County in August, 1866, then on November 13, 1866, started for Cooke County. He reunited with his family there on December 12, 1866, his wife having sold the house in Bell County and returned to their home near Gainesville.[4]

Inexplicably, Barrett did not have his day in court until almost two years later, on December 5, 1868. He was tried together with fellow Citizens Court juror J. Pope Long in Gainesville before Judge Hardin Hart of the new Seventh District. Like Barrett, Long had left Cooke County during the war, but only after he and three relatives had been indicted for "assault with intent to kill" on November 7, 1863, in regard to a mysterious incident. Hart was not concerned about the second indictment against Long— he would subsequently dismiss the case altogether—but he did have a special interest in the charges relating to the Great Hanging. He had been appointed by Governor Elisha M. Pease on December 7, 1867, in place of William T. G. Weaver to try those responsible for atrocities against Unionists. He seemed a good choice for the job; his brother Martin had raised a company for the Federal army in North Texas and was lynched in Arkansas by Confederates who accused him of being a guerrilla. Too, Hardin had been a stalwart Unionist in the 1866 convention, and he had acquitted himself well as a Freedmen's Bureau agent.[5]

Hart took special care in the selection of a jury to try Barrett and Long, but to no avail. Two veteran attorneys with much influence on the Forks, especially among ex-Confederates, defended Barrett: former governor James W. Throckmorton and former district judge Weaver. Only two witnesses appeared for Barrett's brief trial; after his attorneys declined either to cross-examine these men or to deliver closing arguments, the jurors did

4. Barrett, *Great Hanging*, 27–30.

5. Cooke County, District Clerk, Judge's State Docket [Civil and Criminal], Sixteenth, Twentieth, and Seventh District Courts, 1857–1871, Case Nos. 229, 250, in UNT; Cooke County, District Clerk, Criminal and Civil Minutes, Sixteenth, Twentieth, and Seventh District Courts, 1857–1871, pp. 320, 322, in Cooke Cty. Courthouse, Gainesville, Tex.; New York *Times*, March 11, 1868; C. A. Bridges, *History of Denton, Texas: From Its Beginning to 1960* (Waco, 1960), 109–10; Graham Landrum and Allen Smith, *An Illustrated History of Grayson County* (2d ed.; Fort Worth, 1967), 70–71; Ernest W. Winkler, *Platforms of Political Parties in Texas* (Austin, 1916), 95. Additional material on Hardin and Martin Hart provided by Dr. Cecil O. Harper, Jr., of North Harris County Community College, Houston.

not even retire to deliberate before delivering a verdict of not guilty. They also acquitted Long in a similarly precipitous manner. Barrett later recalled, "I thought if ever the mountain of labor brought forth a mouse, we had it in this case about which there had been such a splutter." To reassure himself, he had his jubilant attorneys and Hart endorse a certificate attesting to his acquittal.[6]

Hart also revived an 1865 indictment against James G. Bourland, defying Ordinance Number 11—which provided immunity under state law for acts committed under Confederate authority—and ignoring the fact that a Federal pardon had been granted to him by President Andrew Johnson under his amnesty proclamation of May 29, 1865. Bourland had applied on September 18, 1865, admitting only that he owned at least $20,000 in property, which brought him within one of the specified exceptions to the general amnesty, while not mentioning his role during the war. Texas governor Andrew J. Hamilton wrote Johnson in August, 1865, that he would not endorse the applications of those whose "sins have been enormous," and he did not sign Bourland's petition. Johnson, however, disregarded this advice and approved Bourland's request on November 30, 1866.[7]

The outcome of Bourland's trial was predictable, given that he could claim immunity under Ordinance Number 11 and that he had the distinction of having received a presidential pardon. Just a few days after Barrett's acquittal, Hart presided while another Cooke County jury, convened at his request, refused to convict the former provost marshal for instigating the Great Hanging. Bourland subsequently disappeared from public life and retired to his Red River home. This house, which was well supplied with arms, was built with a lookout tower and a hidden passage that led underground from the front hall to a nearby creek bottom. Although Bourland lived as a recluse there until his death on August 20, 1879, he was not forgotten. When John H. Brown and William S. Speer published *Encyclopedia of the New West*, a collection of biographies, in 1882, they took the opportunity to dispute those who disparaged Bourland as a bloodthirsty tyrant. His actions, they said, were identical to those taken against the Tories by American patriots during the Revolution, and were just as necessary.[8]

6. Barrett, *Great Hanging*, 31; Cooke Cty., Dist. Clerk, Judge's State Docket, Case No. 250; Cooke Cty., Dist. Clerk, Criminal and Civil Minutes, 322.

7. Andrew J. Hamilton to Andrew Johnson, August 30, 1865, in Andrew Johnson Papers, LC; James G. Bourland to Johnson, September 18, 1865, in Amnesty Files; *House Executive Documents*, 39th Cong., 2d Sess., No. 116, p. 55.

8. Pete A. Y. Gunter, ed., "Lillian Gunter Papers on Cooke County History" (Typescript

Among the key witnesses at Bourland's trial in December, 1868, was Citizens Court juror James Jones. A subpoena had been issued for Jones in November, 1865, after Bourland's original indictment, but he had already fled to the Indian Territory. Before he left, though, he caused a minor sensation in Gainesville by announcing that he intended to kill Alexander Boutwell, the former sheriff who served as executioner for the Great Hanging. Boutwell got a gun and sat down on a wooden box on the southwest corner of the town square, halfway out into the street, challenging Jones to come after him, but nothing happened. Boutwell also moved to the Indian Territory in 1865. In return for his testimony against Bourland, Jones was given immunity from prosecution both for his role in the Great Hanging and for an unrelated murder indictment against him and six others on November 7, 1863.[9]

Jones was also called to be a witness against James D. Young, the hotheaded son of the late Colonel William C. Young. Although he was indicted with Bourland in November, 1865, Young remained at large until 1871, after Hart had turned over his bench to another Unionist, Christopher C. Binkley. On December 20, 1871, a jury declared Young to be not guilty of several charges, the primary one of which was involvement in the killing of E. Junius Foster. No one would testify regarding the identities of the three men who had shot the editor, and the case collapsed due to a lack of substantial evidence. After his acquittal, Young settled in Cooke County, where he became a respectable, if not well-respected, citizen.[10]

in Morton Museum, Gainesville, Tex.), 384; "Chronological History of James G. Bourland" (Typescript in Bourland Family File, Sherman Municipal Library, Sherman, Tex.); Cooke Cty., Dist. Clerk, Judge's State Docket, Case No. 253; Cooke Cty., Dist. Clerk, Criminal and Civil Minutes, 447; Pete A. Y. Gunter, "The Great Gainesville Hanging, October, 1862," *Blue and Gray*, III (April–May 1986), 53; *Biographical Souvenir of the State of Texas* (Chicago, 1889), 98; John H. Brown and William S. Speer, eds., *Encyclopedia of the New West* (Marshall, Tex., 1881), 233–34; Buckley B. Paddock, ed., *A Twentieth Century History and Biographical Record of North and West Texas* (2 vols.; Chicago, 1906), II, 233–34; Michael Collins, *Cooke County, Texas: Where the South and the West Meet* (Gainesville, 1981), 11.

9. William R. Strong, *His Memoirs*, ed. Pete A. Y. Gunter and Robert A. Calvert (Denton, Tex., 1982), 46; Cooke Cty., Dist. Clerk, Judge's State Docket, Case Nos. 230, 253; Cooke Cty., Dist. Clerk, Criminal and Civil Minutes, 209, 294, 343, 352, 356, 391, 447.

10. Cooke Cty., Dist. Clerk, Judge's State Docket, Case Nos. 250, 253; Cooke Cty., Dist. Clerk, Criminal and Civil Minutes, 294, 567, 578, 581–82; St. Louis *Republic*, March 4, 1894. Hardin Hart traveled with a military escort at his own request, but he was ambushed in September, 1869, and badly wounded. He made his way to a farmhouse, where a doctor saved his life but amputated his arm. T. C. Griffin to Joseph J. Reynolds, August 18, 1868, in U.S.

Newton J. Chance, the infiltrator who had betrayed many members of the Peace party to the Citizens Court in 1862, had earlier been identified by several people as one of Young's accomplices in the assassination of Foster. After the war, Chance moved to southern Illinois, whence United States Deputy Marshal John F. Rittenhouse contacted Governor Throckmorton on January 29, 1867, offering to extradite him to Texas if the offer of a reward was confirmed. Throckmorton did not respond and Chance was not arrested until 1885, after he had returned to Wise County and established himself as a minister of the Christian church. His trial proved sensational, especially when Young made a surprise confession in court that he killed Foster. Because Young had been acquitted earlier and could not be tried again, both men went free.[11]

The dismissal of charges against Chance ended the trials of those involved in the Citizens Court. The primary judicial effort had been directed against the jurors, nine of whom—Barrett, Chance, Samuel C. Doss, Reason Jones, Wiley Jones, Long, Benjamin Scanland, William J. Simpson, and Thomas Wright—had been acquitted by a lawful jury. Jeremiah E. Hughes, like Bourland, had been given a presidential pardon. Because of his service as postmaster and tax collector for the Confederacy, Hughes was not included in the general amnesty, but with the recommendations of Weaver and Throckmorton, he was pardoned in May, 1867, and charges against him were later dropped. James Jones was given immunity, but inexplicably, no records remain of dispositions for John W. Hamill, William W. Howeth, James W. McPherson, and Daniel Montague. Howeth remained in Gainesville, but Hamill and McPherson may have followed Montague into exile. The latter remained in Mexico from 1865 until 1876; he returned to his daughter's home in Cooke County, which she shared with her husband, William C. Twitty, and died within a few months of his arrival.[12]

<hr/>

Department of War, Bureau of Refugees, Freedmen, and Abandoned Lands, Records of the Assistant Commissioner for Texas, Record Group 105, NA; Reynolds to Elisha M. Pease, September 23, 1868, in U.S Department of War, Letters Sent by the Department of Texas and the Fifth Military District, 1865–1870, Record Group 397, NA; Allen W. Trelease, *White Terror: The Ku Klux Klan Conspiracy and Southern Reconstruction* (New York, 1971), 138.

11. Sam Acheson and Julia Ann Hudson O'Connell, eds., *George Washington Diamond's Account of the Great Hanging at Gainesville, 1862* (Austin, 1963), 26n; John F. Rittenhouse to James W. Throckmorton, January 25, 1867, in GOR; St. Louis *Republic*, March 4, 1894; Landrum and Smith, *Illustrated History of Grayson County*, 65.

12. Jeremiah E. Hughes to Johnson, August 25, 1865, Throckmorton to Henry Stanbery,

Montague need not have stayed away so long. It was obvious that no Cooke County jury would try to resurrect the unpleasant past by convicting him, especially as most of them had supported his efforts and those of others to maintain order and security both during the war and afterward. A majority of the people in Cooke County had supported community leaders during the Great Hanging in 1862 and in their subsequent measures against the threat of dissent. They would not later turn their backs on these men when to do so was to risk not only the disruption of inviting further legal retribution but also the personal turmoil of admitting that they had been wrong. Confronted with an uncomfortable choice, the juries chose the security of endorsing what had been done and confirming the established order of local leadership, not raising questions whose answers could be quite disturbing.

Frustrated, quite a few former Unionists during the Reconstruction period turned to the Republican party for support. Frederick W. Sumner, after recovering from the loss of an eye, remained an active campaigner for the Republicans in North Texas, canvassing Grayson County in 1871 for funds. Republican efforts along the Forks, however, collapsed after the triumph of conservative Democrats in the 1872 elections. Federal troopers remained in Sherman until 1876, but the "redemption" of Texas four years earlier effectively ended Reconstruction there.[13]

James L. Clark was among the North Texas Republicans set adrift in 1872. After fleeing Head of Elm in 1864, he returned to Cooke County at the end of the war as a scout for a Union regiment from Kansas. At home, he found "some of the oald rebbles still on the warpath." He later wrote in a memoir that "we stayed with them until tha got cool," adding, "Tha was not but a fiew big fooles a mong them eney way." But a letter written by him in October, 1872, recorded a more activist stance. In it, he reported to James P. Newcomb, Republican secretary of state, that he had delivered the commissions Newcomb sent, removing several former Confederates from office and installing Unionist John E. Wheeler once more as chief justice of

---

February 26, 1867, in Amnesty Files; Cooke Cty., Dist. Clerk, Judge's State Docket, Case No. 250; Cooke Cty., Dist. Clerk, Criminal and Civil Minutes, 343; Gunter, "The Great Gainesville Hanging," 53; Mattie D. Lucas and Mita H. Hall, *A History of Grayson County, Texas* (Sherman, Tex., 1936), 41–42.

13. Frederick W. Sumner to James P. Newcomb, August 31, 1871, D. Mackay to Newcomb, September 15, 1871, April 23, 1872, all in James P. Newcomb Papers, BTHC; Sherman (Tex.) *Courier*, May 11, 1876.

Cooke County. Clark crowed that "the Rebles hated to give it up," but Wheeler had set to work and soon "the Business [would] be Brewing up as directed." He added, "I glory in Beeting the Roten handed villiones in Evry Start tha make[.] Keep thumping them." The collapse of Republican efforts in Texas crushed Clark. He tried his hand at vengeance, but when he trapped a man he knew had chosen his father to hang, he could not shoot after the former vigilante begged for his life. Clark gave up and retired to his farm.[14]

Most relatives of those hanged in 1862 gave up long before Clark. Some widows had family members with whom they found refuge; for example, John M. Crisp's wife and children settled in Montague County with his father. Many women left, but a few remarried in Cooke County, probably because their resources left them no other choice. Mary Miller, who had been married to John B. Miller only two years before he died, remarried in April, 1863. Mary Ann Dye, the young bride of Rama Dye, married twice in 1863, the second time to William T. Horton, who almost lost his life to Bourland's troopers in the summer of 1864. Two others remarried in 1863 as well—Mary Ann Field, widow of Henry S. Field, and Mary E. Goss, whose first husband was Curd Goss—but Mary Scott, the wife of Alexander D. Scott, did not remarry until June, 1865. In Wise County, Susan M. Conn—the widow of John M. Conn, who was hanged at Decatur—married Stephen P. Beebe, a Unionist delegate to the Texas secession convention. Other women who lost male kin in the Great Hanging found security in matrimony as well: William C. Young's widow, Margaret Ann, married Citizens Court juror Long in March, 1865, and one of Young's daughters wed former sheriff James B. Davenport, Jr.[15]

The travails of the women who chose to brave the certain storm of retribution alone were especially poignant. Susan Leffel, widow of David M. Leffel, who had been lynched during the Great Hanging, wrote to Governor Edmund J. Davis in June, 1869, asking for help. Since the end of the

14. Lemuel D. Clark, ed., *The Civil War Recollections of James Lemuel Clark* (College Station, Tex., 1984), 41–42, 88–91; James L. Clark to Newcomb, October 19, 1872, in Newcomb Papers.

15. Stephen B. Beebe to Holton White, July 26, 1865, in Great Hanging File, Wise County Heritage Museum, Decatur, Tex.; John M. Crisp to George M. Crisp, October 20, 1921, in Great Hanging File, Morton Museum; Francis T. Ingmire, comp., "Cooke County, Texas, Marriage Records 1849–1879," pp. 6–8, typescript in BTHC; *Biographical Souvenir of Texas*, 233–34; A. Morton Smith, *The First 100 Years in Cooke County* (San Antonio, 1955), 32.

war she and others who had lost relatives in that affair had been plagued by attacks. Male members of their families had been arrested "without a line of a rit [sic] or any showing of any legal authority whatever." Conversely, when she was robbed by her tormentors, no one was arrested. Nevertheless, "thinking we would get protection after a while," she remained at her home where, two weeks earlier, a dozen men came to arrest her son on a charge of horse stealing. After he fled amid a shower of bullets, one of the party dragged her onto the floor from her sickbed and pistol-whipped her younger son. She sadly concluded, "I with maney others have lost hopes of protection from that party's abuse by the beloved country and government that we loved so dearly. . . . What to do, or where to go to hide from them I can not tell." [16]

To the west, a violent act begun during the war came to a bloody climax in Parker County. Allen C. Hill, a settler who lived near Spring Hill, was lynched as a Unionist in the winter of 1863, but his family unwisely chose to remain in the county. Hill's eldest son was killed in 1869 or 1870 following an altercation in nearby Palo Pinto County. Hill's oldest daughter, who allegedly had a "bad character" and was a "disturbing element in the community," fled her home in 1872 after being warned that a posse was coming for her, but she was overtaken and hanged near the line between Clay and Wichita counties. A few days later two other daughters, also grown women, were taken from their home and lynched as well. Within a few more days the widow's house was burned, forcing her to flee with her four remaining children. They too were ridden down by a posse, and the widow and her two older daughters were shot and killed in a deliberate execution near Agnes, in Parker County. They remained unburied until two Texas Rangers defied public opinion and interred them in a local cemetery. [17]

The plight of accused Unionists along the Forks was made worse by frequent Indian attacks, which continued into the early 1870s with many casualties and captives taken on both sides. A single raid in 1868 claimed the lives of fifteen settlers in Cooke and neighboring counties. In early November of that year a militia company from Gainesville set out in pursuit

16. Susan Leffel to Edmund J. Davis, June 11, 1869, in GOR.

17. Ida L. Huckaby, *Ninety-Four Years in Jack County, 1854–1948* (Austin, 1949), 95–96; Rupert N. Richardson, *The Frontier of Northwest Texas, 1846–1876* (Glendale, Calif., 1963), 175–76. Lydia C. Jones recalled that the skull of a "woman thief by the name of Nancy Hill," who had been hanged, was brought to her house by a male friend. Gunter, ed., "Gunter Papers," 65.

of a group of Comanche who had stolen some horses, but the Texans were arrested by troopers from the 6th United States Cavalry at Fort Richardson. Left without effective self-protection, the settlements were raided often that winter. Only the decisive defeat of the Kiowa and Comanche in 1875 during the Red River War ended the disruptive raids for good.[18]

The continuing violence and Indian raids retarded the population growth along the Forks during the 1860s. The expansion of agriculture on the Forks, paced by the rapid development of the cattle industry, revived settlement during the next decade; Cooke County's population, for example, exploded from 5,315 in 1870 to 20,391 in 1880. Many of the cattlemen who gave the high plains of West Texas its distinctive character first established their operations in the Cross Timbers before expanding west. The railroad reached Gainesville in 1879 and soon extended across the Forks, fostering more diverse agriculture as the area was transformed almost overnight from a peripheral region to a threshhold for new economic growth.[19]

The flood of newcomers and economic development pushed the era of frontier vigilantism further into Gainesville's past, but memories of the Great Hanging lingered among the people along the Forks. Barrett in an effort to correct some vexing misconceptions—most of which ascribed to him more responsibility for the lynchings than he deserved—penned an account of what had transpired in 1862. When he traveled through the region in 1885 trying to sell his pamphlets, he encountered opposition based on the enduring animosities between Unionists and ex-Confederates and the desire of many people to let the past lie undisturbed. It became

18. John E. Wheeler to Johnson, January 17, 1868, in Johnson Papers; Levi Perryman, *Thrilling Indian Raids into Cooke and Montague Counties* (Forestburg, Tex., 1917), *passim;* Strong, *Memoirs,* 36; William C. Holden, "Frontier Defense, 1865–1889," *Panhandle Plains Historical Review,* II (1929), 54; Collins, *Cooke County,* 20–23; Charles N. Jones, *Early Days in Cooke County* (Gainesville, 1936), 25–36; Joseph C. McConnell, *The West Texas Frontier* (Jacksboro, Tex., 1933), *passim;* Mary C. Moore, *Centennial History of Wise County, 1853–1953* (Dallas, 1953), 48–59; Robert M. Utley, *The Indian Frontier of the American West, 1845–1890* (Albuquerque, 1984), 19, 112–13, 174–78.

19. Collins, *Cooke County,* 23–27; Francis W. Johnson, *A History of Texas and Texans,* ed. Eugene C. Barker (5 vols.; Chicago, 1914), II, 843–45; David W. Meinig, *Imperial Texas: An Interpretive Essay in Cultural Geography* (Austin, 1969), 68, 75; Richardson, *The Frontier of Northwest Texas,* 251–67; A. W. Spaight, *Resources, Soil, and Climate of Texas* (Galveston, 1882), 72.

unsafe to have a copy of his publication, and the few copies that existed were secreted away. Nonetheless, popular curiosity about the Great Hanging endured; when a storm uprooted the hanging tree in the early 1880s, an "enterprising individual" carved it into walking sticks, which "sold like hotcakes" because of their grim history.[20]

Barrett himself, after his unpleasant experiences on the stump, became closemouthed about the Great Hanging, as did many of those involved in the event. He told the Gainesville historian George H. Ragsdale, who spoke with him twice during the early 1890s, that it was not yet safe to reveal all he knew, and wept openly as he related a few details about the affair. After he told Ragsdale that the "military were determined to execute the ringleader but intended to make a cats paw of the Civil Courts," the interviewer wrote William C. Twitty, asking for additional information, but was coldly rebuffed.[21]

Despite the obvious reticence of many residents to discuss the Great Hanging, the story occasionally resurfaced. On March 4, 1894, a reporter for the St. Louis *Republic* published an account that included material from an interview with James D. Young. It attracted little notice, but in 1916 the subject emerged again during an exchange in the United States House of Representatives. The previous year a bill limiting immigration, and including a literacy test, had passed, but Woodrow Wilson vetoed it. During an attempt to revive the measure, Representative John H. Stephens of the Thirteenth Congressional District of Texas, in which Cooke County lay, printed in the *Congressional Record* a speech that included anti-Catholic remarks. Representative James A. Gallivan of Massachusetts, an opponent of the literacy clause, retaliated by attacking not only Stephens but his constituents as bigots. He read aloud passages from Barrett's book, a copy of which he found in the Library of Congress, to corroborate his assertions, and later called for an appropriation of $100,000 to build a monument to the "martyrs" of Gainesville. Stephens published a lengthy defense in the

20. "Gainesville" (MS in Cooke County Historical File, Cooke County Library, Gainesville, Tex.); Barrett, *The Great Hanging*, i–ii, 17; Clark, ed., *Recollections of James Clark*, 44; Decatur (Tex.) *Messenger*, April 4, 1885; St. Louis *Republic*, March 4, 1894. Only three copies of Barrett's pamphlet were known to exist when the Texas State Historical Association began reprinting it in 1961.
21. George H. Ragsdale, "Historical Note, 7/29/92," "An Incident of the Civil War," and "Texas War History Written in 1892" (MSS all in George H. Ragsdale Papers, BTHC).

Record, reiterating that those who were lynched were dangerous renegades, but he was politically hurt and was not reelected that fall.[22]

The exchange in Congress briefly reignited the controversy along the Forks. James L. Clark, having read in local newspapers that the men who were hanged had been vagabonds and criminals, wrote his version of what had happened in a letter to Congress on May 12, 1916, but he never mailed it. The other point of view had proponents as well. On February 7, 1917, John G. Young, who had been with his father, William C. Young, when he was assassinated, wrote to local historian Lillian Gunter: "You say that *beast* of a *Bostonian Representative* Proclaimed in Congress that they were *union men.* . . . From what I have always heard [that is] *a wilful lie.*" He asserted that the condemned had been tried by a "jury of just citizens" after being indicted by a grand jury and that the "evidence was plain against them. . . . As to being union men and for the union, They intended *murdering* women and children, as well as men, that did not belong to their dastardly *clan.*" Like Clark, Young had no impact on the debate in Congress, but three letters from other constituents along the Forks, including one from B. T. Parr, who had witnessed the hanging of Henry S. Field, were cited as evidence by Stephens.[23]

The opinions expressed by Young, Parr, and others who supported Stephens were simply additional manifestations of the majority sentiment in favor of imposing order on the past by denying the excesses of the Confederacy. Such denial was symbolized by the inscription on the base of a monument to the Confederacy, erected on the lawn of the county courthouse in Gainesville:

> God holds the scales of Justice;
> He will measure praise and blame;
> And the South will stand the verdict,
> And will stand it without shame.
>
> Oh, home of tears, but let her bear
> This blazoned to the end of time;

22. *Congressional Record*, 64th Cong., 1st Sess., LIII, 5026–28, 5272, Appendix, 1016–19; St. Louis *Republic*, March 4, 1894; Clark, ed., *Recollections of James Clark*, 93–94; Walter P. Webb, H. Bailey Carroll, and Eldon S. Branda, eds., *The Handbook of Texas* (3 vols.; Austin, 1952, 1976), II, 667.

23. John D. Young to Lillian Gunter, February 7, 1917, in Cooke County Historical File; *Congressional Record*, 64th Cong., 1st Sess., LIII, Appendix, 1018; Clark, ed., *Recollections of James Clark*, 94–102.

> No nation rose so white and fair,
> None fell so free of crime.

However, despite the best efforts of the majority, those who had opposed the Confederacy refused to be forgotten. Almost in the shadow of the courthouse, the Clark family held a reunion for more than fifty years, beginning in the 1930s, and for three years published the *Clark Clan Newsletter*, which bore the slogan *Uniting the Descendants of Nathaniel Miles Clark*. Others more quietly, if no less belligerently, maintained the social barriers raised by the Great Hanging.[24]

Gainesville in subsequent years became known for more pleasant distinctions. Perhaps the most notable appellation was "Circus Town, U.S.A.," a distinction earned because for almost thirty years its citizens produced a nonprofit community circus that won praise from professionals all over the United States.[25] In spite of this and other proud achievements, and the veneer of modernism obscuring much of the town's past, Gainesville has been unable to deny the Great Hanging and has remained partisan in its remembrance of that event. A simple stone slab commemorating the victims stands not on the courthouse lawn but in a roadside park away from the town center, on the far side of an interstate highway.

That an event begun over 125 years ago can still divide a community is a testament to the impact of vigilantism, and may provide some insight into the influence that the Confederacy has had on the nation as a whole. That regime, created during a period of great turmoil for southerners, promised security through insularity. When its promises proved to be illusions, many lost faith; but a majority of southerners continued to cling to the Confederacy as the source of order and security through extant authority, and they lashed out violently against those who, by their dissent, were disruptive, just as they had attacked suspected abolitionists. When the war ended, the concern for order and security continued unabated or even increased, impelling southerners to continue the suppression of disaffection and even to reshape their Confederate past. Although that practice has obscured grim events such as the Great Hanging, it cannot eradicate the scars left on the communities in which such affairs took place, nor the sectional divisions within the United States that have been deepened by the violence.

24. Scattered copies of the *Clark Clan Newsletter*, published fall 1978 to summer 1981, can be found in the Morton Museum.
25. Collins, *Cooke County*, 59–63.

APPENDIX A

Forty-Two Executed by the Citizens Court
at Gainesville

C. F. Anderson does not appear in the census record or the tax rolls for Cooke County, but on September 24, 1859, a man by that name and his wife, Nancy M., sold their preemption of 160 acres on Hickory Creek, a tributary of the Elm Fork of the Trinity, to a resident of Denton.[1]

George W. Anderson first appears in the Cooke County tax roll for 1862, when he paid taxes on $124 in property, including 1 horse and 4 cows.

Richard J. Anderson is listed in the 1860 Grayson County census (F.N. 1,178) as a twenty-eight-year-old farmer from Missouri with $750 in personal property and no real estate. His wife and their three children, the youngest of whom was six years old, were all born in Missouri.

William B. Anderson is listed in the 1860 Cooke County census (F.N. 451) as a twenty-seven-year-old farmer from Tennessee with $175 in personal property. His wife was from Arkansas, but their son, age eight, was born in Texas. Anderson first appears on the tax roll for Cooke County in 1859; he paid only a poll tax for that and the next few years, but in 1862 he was assessed for 2 horses and 7 cattle. He did serve for a period of time in a military unit, because the 1862 tax rolls for Cooke County found in the

---

The information presented in the appendixes, unless noted otherwise, is taken from: Census of 1850, Schedule 1 (Free Inhabitants), and Census of 1860, Schedule 1 and Schedule 2 (Slave Inhabitants), Family Numbers indicated by F.N., in Genealogy Division, TSL; County Tax Rolls, in TSL; and 1862 Tax Roll Manuscript for Cooke County, in UNT.

1. Edna H. McCormick, *William Lee McCormick: A Study in Tolerance* (Dallas, 1952), 104.

archives at UNT declare that his payment would be delayed because he had "gone to war."

Thomas O. Baker appears in the Cooke County tax rolls for the first time in 1862, when he was assessed for $150 in taxable property, including 5 cattle. He is listed in the 1850 Fannin County census (F.N. 277) as a farmer, age forty-one, from Tennessee, with $800 in real and personal property. His wife, Mary, was a native of Virginia, while their son, three years of age in 1850, was born in Texas.

Benjamin C. Barnes settled a preemption of 160 acres on Denton Creek, a tributary of the Elm Fork of the Trinity River in Denton County, on November 6, 1854. He filed another preemption on March 8, 1860, for 160 acres on Big Sandy Creek, which lay southwest of Decatur in Wise County. His widow, Sarah, filed for confirmation of the title in 1872, and testified that they moved to the tract on March 15, 1858, which is substantiated by the fact that they paid taxes in Wise County for the first time that year. Barnes is listed in the 1860 Wise County census (F.N. 166) as a farmer, age thirty-six, from Alabama with $1,020 in real and personal property. Sarah was also from Alabama, but their five children, the eldest ten years of age, were all born in Texas. In 1861, he paid taxes in Wise County for his land plus 2 horses and 15 cattle.

Barnibus Burch moved to Hood County, Texas, from Missouri about 1850, then to Cooke County by 1860. He was approximately seventy years of age, and crippled with arthritis, when he paid twelve cents in taxes on his personal property in 1862. His name is penciled in above that of "Thomas Burch" on the 1862 tax roll for Cooke County found in UNT.[2]

Samuel Carmichael is listed in the 1860 Cooke County census (F.N. 33) as a thirty-nine-year-old carpenter from Tennessee with $1,240 in real and personal property. He lived in Gainesville with his wife, Anna, a native of

2. Clorie A. Gibson to Harry Fogle, n.d., in Great Hanging File, Morton Museum, Gainesville, Tex.; B. D. Burch, "Statement," November 16, 1913 (MS in Lillian Gunter Papers, UNT); Sam Acheson and Julia Ann Hudson O'Connell, eds., *George Washington Diamond's Account of the Great Hanging at Gainesville, 1862* (Austin, 1963), 84; Michael Collins, *Cooke County, Texas: Where the South and the West Meet* (Gainesville, Tex., 1981), 14–15; A. Morton Smith, *The First 100 Years in Cooke County* (San Antonio, 1955), 31.

Illinois; Isaac Abelia, age fifteen, from Alabama; Josephus L. Wilson, a girl, age ten, from Norway; and William Gaston, a twenty-one-year-old Pennsylvanian with $150 in personal property. Carmichael paid a poll tax in Cooke County in 1859, but in 1862 he was assessed for 5 lots in Gainesville plus 7 horses and 2 cattle.

Ephraim Chiles, brother of Henry Chiles, is listed in the 1860 Wise County census (F.N. 37) as a farmer from Virginia, age thirty-four, with $200 in personal property. His wife, Margaret, and his elder son, age four, were also from Virginia, but his younger son, whom the census reported to be a year old, was born in Texas. Ephraim paid taxes for the first time in Wise County in 1861; the next year he again paid taxes on a 160-acre preemption, plus 1 horse and 20 cattle.

Henry Chiles, brother of Ephraim Chiles, was a physician about forty-two or forty-three years of age at the time of his execution. It is alleged that he immigrated to Texas from Missouri just before the Civil War.[3] He paid his first taxes in Cooke County in 1862 for 4 cattle, 2 horses, and a 200-acre survey, for which he signed a promissory note to Alexander D. Scott.

Nathaniel M. Clark was born in Kentucky on June 26, 1818. He immigrated to Texas from Arkansas in October, 1857, and established a farm seven miles southeast of Gainesville with his wife, Mahuldah, born in Tennessee, according to the 1860 Cooke County census (F.N. 96). They had seven children, four of whom were also born in Tennessee, one in Arkansas, and two in Texas.[4] In 1862 he paid taxes in Cooke County on 110 acres, 2 horses, and 18 cattle.

Henry Cockrum is listed in the 1850 Fannin County census (F.N. 1) as a nineteen-year-old farmer from Missouri; his wife, Elizabeth, was from Kentucky. He received a certificate for 640 acres from the Cooke County Commissioners' Court as a Peters Colonist, but his claim was later disallowed. He purchased 160 acres on July 3, 1858, and 100 acres five days

---

3. Acheson and O'Connell, eds., *Diamond's Account*, 53.

4. Lemuel D. Clark, ed., *The Civil War Recollections of James Lemuel Clark* (College Station, Tex., 1984), 16, 49, 50*n*; Frances T. Ingmire, comp., *Cemetery Records of Cooke County, Texas* (Gainesville, 1980), 45.

later, both in Cooke County, but sold the former property on October 8, 1859. By that time he operated a mill in Cooke County.[5]

John M. Crisp was born on June 23, 1824, in Kentucky. He moved from that state to Cooke County in 1855 with his father and brother. He filed a preemption on 160 acres located on Indian Creek east of Gainesville on February 2, 1855, and married Ailsey Stephens, from Missouri, in May, 1857. He tried herding sheep, but it proved fruitless, and he sold his homestead ten days before it was patented to him on July 21, 1859. The Cooke County census in 1860 (F.N. 407) recorded his occupation as blacksmith; in 1862 he paid taxes in Cooke County on 2 horses and 8 cattle.[6]

Arphax R. Dawson immigrated to Texas from Illinois; he is listed in the 1860 Grayson County census (F.N. 642) as a farmer from Georgia, age fifty-five, with $3,297 in real and personal property. His wife, Jane, was from Tennessee; their five children had been born in Illinois, Missouri, and Texas. Their oldest daughter, Mary Ann, married Rama Dye on June 27, 1861.[7]

Rama Dye and his brother Jacob settled with their family in the Peters Colony about 1846. The 1850 Cooke County census (F.N. 24) listed Rama as a farmer from Missouri, age twenty-nine, with $320 in real and personal property. On November 3 of that year he applied for 640 acres; he received a patent for this land, which he located on Cross Timbers Creek ten miles east of Gainesville on November 15, 1854, the same year in which he was elected a justice of the peace. By 1858 he had 320 more acres along Cross Timbers Creek and 320 acres on Brown's Creek. The 1860 Cooke County census (F.N. 296) recorded him as a forty-one-year-old farmer from Kentucky with $5,775 in property. He married Arphax R. Dawson's daughter

5. Cooke County, County Clerk, Deed Record, 1850–present, IV, 173, 190, 602, in Cooke County Courthouse, Gainesville, Tex.; Cooke County Commissioners' Court, "Minutes, 1857 to 1878," I, 33 (sheet 2), typescript in Works Progress Administration Historical Records Survey, BTHC; Seymour V. Connor, *The Peters Colony of Texas* (Austin, 1959), 222.

6. John M. Crisp, Jr., to George M. Crisp, October 20, 1921 (Typescript in Great Hanging File, Morton Museum); Frances T. Ingmire, comp., "Cooke County, Texas, Marriage Records, 1849–1879," p. 2, typescript in BTHC; Cooke Cty. Deed Record, IV, 527.

7. Frances T. Ingmire, comp., "Marriage Records of Grayson County, Texas, 1846–1877," p. 11; typescript in BTHC; Graham Landrum and Allen Smith, *An Illustrated History of Grayson County, Texas* (2d ed.; Fort Worth, 1967), 137.

Mary Ann on June 27, 1861, a few months after being appointed a road overseer for Cooke County.[8] In 1862 he paid taxes in Cooke County only on the tracts along Cross Timbers Creek, as well as 5 horses and 16 cattle.

Hudson J. Esman paid his first taxes in Cooke County in 1854; by 1860 he paid taxes on a 160-acre homestead. He was probably a brother-in-law of John M. Crisp, as he married Elizabeth Crisp in January, 1857.[9]

Henry S. Field is listed in the 1860 Collin County census (F.N. 115) as a shoemaker from Connecticut, age forty-five, with $800 in personal property. His wife Mary Ann's birthplace was "unknown," but their daughters, ages fourteen and six, were born in the Indian Territory, and their son, only a year old, was born in Texas. Another boy in the Field household, Thomas Baker, age three, was also born in the Indian Territory. Henry paid taxes in Cooke County in 1861 for 589 acres, 1 slave, 7 horses, and 2 cattle. The next year he no longer owned the slave and he had lost 3 horses, but his cattle had increased to 21. William H. McCool was his son-in-law, with whom his elder daughter, Lydia, allegedly had eloped.[10]

Thomas B. Floyd is listed in the 1860 Cooke County census (F.N. 91) as an illiterate farmer from Tennessee, age twenty-seven, with $300 in personal property. His wife, Clora, and his son, age eight, were also from Tennessee, but his daughter, age two, was born in Texas. He paid only a poll tax in Cooke County in 1860 and 1861, but had 2 horses and 10 cattle in 1862.

James T. Foster paid taxes in Cooke County in 1862 on a preemption of 160 acres, 1 horse, 2 cattle, and $365 money at interest.

Curd Goss paid his first Cooke County taxes in 1861 on 2 horses and 10 cattle. In 1862 he had 5 horses and 14 cattle.

8. Cooke Cty. Commissioners' Court, "Minutes," I, 79 (sheet 2), 80; Ingmire, comp., "Marriage Records of Grayson County," 11; Texas Secretary of State, Election Register 1848–1900, in Archives Division, TSL; William R. Strong, *His Memoirs*, ed. Pete A. Y. Gunter and Robert A. Calvert (Denton, Tex., 1982), 9; Collins, *Cooke County*, 6; Connor, *Peters Colony*, 243; Landrum and Smith, *Illustrated History of Grayson County*, 137.
   9. Ingmire, comp., "Cooke County Marriage Records," 2.
   10. Acheson and O'Connell, eds., *Diamond's Account*, 89.

Edward D. Hampton paid taxes in Cooke County in 1857 on 2 horses. He filed for a preemption of 160 acres in 1860 and paid taxes for it in 1861 and 1862, as well as 16 horses in the latter year according to the 1862 Cooke County tax roll, UNT.

M. D. Harper is listed in the 1860 Cooke County census (F.N. 250) as a thirty-one-year-old carpenter from Virginia with $245 in personal property. His wife, Elisa, was from Indiana, but three of their children were born in Illinois, Arkansas and Missouri. Their other children, the oldest six years of age, were born in Texas.

William W. Johnson paid a poll tax in 1859 in Cooke County; by 1862 he had a 160-acre homestead, 2 horses, 11 cattle, and 4 sheep.

C. A. Jones was referred to as a "hump back" in Diamond's account.[11] "C. Jones," an unmarried eighteen-year-old Louisiana native serving with a ranger company, was listed in the 1860 Clay County census (F.N. 802).

David M. Leffel paid only a poll tax in Cooke County in 1862.

Leander W. P. "Jacob" Lock is listed in the 1850 Lamar County census (F.N. 458) as a farmer from Tennessee, age twenty-nine, with $1,688 in real and personal property. His wife, Deannah, was an Illinois native; they had a daughter, age nine, born in Arkansas and another, age one, born in Texas. In 1860 the census again recorded him in Lamar County (F.N. 202), where he was reported as being forty-three years of age with an estate worth $3,250.

Abraham McNeese is listed in the 1860 Cooke County census (F.N. 663) as a thirty-year-old farmer from Indiana with $867 in real and personal property. His wife, Rebecca, was from Illinois, but their son, age five, had been born in Arkansas, and their daughter, age one, had been born in Texas. He applied for a 160-acre preemption on November 14, 1859, along Indian Creek seven miles southeast of Gainesville. The field notes were recorded on May 20, 1860, but a patent was never issued. He paid a poll tax in Cooke County in 1858, but by 1862 the taxes on his land, 3 horses, and 12 cattle

11. *Ibid.*, 76.

were in arrears. On April 14, 1862, he was elected captain of a militia company from the eighth precinct in the 21st Brigade, Texas State Troops, commanded by William R. Hudson.[12]

Richard N. Martin came with his parents from Wisconsin to the Peters Colony in July 1848. The census taker for Cooke County in 1850 (F.N. 35) recorded him as a twelve-year-old, born in Illinois, living in his father's household. In May, 1856, he married Cinthy J. Neely, from Illinois; they set up housekeeping that same year on 160 acres on Indian Creek. The couple did not fare well; he apparently lost this land and did not pay taxes in Cooke County again until 1860, when he paid taxes on 40 acres from his father's estate. The 1860 census for Cooke County (F.N. 108) records the couple's possessions as $417 in real and personal property. The next year he paid taxes in Cooke County on a 160-acre preemption for W. R. Martin; in 1862 he paid the taxes on his own property—1 horse and 20 cattle—as well as those of Jonathan Martin on his preemption of 160 acres and purchase of 80.5 acres. William Boyles was his brother-in-law.[13]

John B. Miller immigrated to the Peters Colony as a single man before July 1, 1845, and homesteaded 320 acres in Collin County. He paid a poll tax for the first time in Cooke County in 1858; by 1862 he paid taxes on 12 horses, 8 cattle, 20 sheep, and "$125 money at interest." He is listed in the 1860 Cooke County census (F.N. 183) as an illiterate thirty-nine-year-old carpenter from Kentucky with $2,160 in real and personal property. He was again single at that time but had three children; he married Mary Eubanks in Cooke County in September, 1860.[14]

John A. Morris is listed in the 1860 Montague County census (F.N. 724) as a farmer, age forty, from Arkansas, with $1,518 in real and personal property. His wife, Marguerite, was born in Indiana. Their eldest child, age

12. William R. Hudson to Jeremiah Y. Dashiell, May 20, 1862, in AGR; Texas Land Patent Records, Fannin S–1327.

13. Achenson and O'Connell, eds., *Diamond's Account*, 83; Ingmire, comp., "Cooke County Marriage Records," 2; Cooke Cty. Deed Record, I, 75; Texas General Land Office, Land Patent Records, Fannin 3–1588, in Archives and Records Division, Texas General Land Office, Austin; Connor, *Peters Colony*, 333.

14. Ingmire, "Cooke County Marriage Records," 4; Texas Land Patent Records, Fannin 3–1467; Connor, *Peters Colony*, 341.

sixteen, was born in the Indian Territory; the middle child, age eight, in Arkansas, and their youngest, age one, in Texas. Morris paid taxes in Cooke County in 1861 for $22 in personal property, and in 1862 for 1 horse and 10 cattle.

John W. Morris is listed in the 1860 Cooke County census (F.N. 608) as a farmer from Tennessee, age thirty, with $219 in personal property. His wife, Lucretia, and their sons, eleven and nine years of age, were born in Tennessee as well. He paid taxes in Cooke County in 1860 on 1 horse; in 1862 he had 3 horses.

M. W. Morris was a brother of William W. Morris. He paid only a poll tax in Cooke County in 1861 and 1862.

William W. Morris, brother of M. W. Morris, is listed in the 1860 Cooke County census (F.N. 369) as an illiterate farmer, age fifty, from Georgia, with $2,288 in real and personal property. His wife, Nancy, was from Alabama, and their three sons had been born in Tennessee, Alabama, and Arkansas. Morris paid his first Cooke County taxes in 1859 on 160 acres on Hickory Creek, 40 acres for which no location is given, and 200 acres on Cross Timbers Creek, which he purchased on April 26, 1858, from William W. Howeth.[15] In 1862 he paid taxes on the same land plus 3 horses, 35 cattle, and 24 sheep.

James A. Powers is listed in the 1860 Cooke County census (F.N. 259) as a "sawer" from Missouri, age twenty-seven, with $538 in real and personal property. His wife, Priscilla, and two of their children were also born in Missouri, but their youngest, age one, was born in Texas. Powers paid only a poll tax in Cooke County in 1859, but by 1862 he owned 160 acres. His sister, Dolly Jane, was married to Obediah B. Atkinson.[16]

William R. Rhodes came to Texas from North Carolina and preempted 320 acres in Cooke County. He doubled his property on December 24, 1856, by purchasing 320 acres, on which he paid his first taxes in Cooke County in 1857. The Cooke County census for 1860 (F.N. 177) lists him as

15. Abstract No. 1102, William W. Howeth's Land Title Office (photocopy) in Great Hanging File, Morton Museum; Clark, ed., *Recollections of James Clark*, 110.

16. Noel Parsons to author, April 25, 1989.

a forty-four-year-old farmer from Tennessee with $884 in real and personal property. His wife, Amanda, was from Alabama; all their children—the eldest of which was sixteen—were born in Texas. He joined the Frontier Regiment on March 11, 1862.[17]

Alexander D. Scott is listed in the 1860 Cooke County census (F.N. 389) as a thirty-nine-year-old farmer from Kentucky with $1,653 in real and personal property. Scott purchased 328 acres on Brown's Creek in Cooke County on December 10, 1858, then married Mary Woolsey, daughter of Elizabeth Woolsey, in August, 1859. He got behind in his taxes, but in 1862 paid both the current and back assessments on the unsold portion of his initial acquisition, 128 acres, plus 10 acres of another survey that he bought in 1860, 4 horses, and 14 cattle. He was appointed as a road overseer for Cooke County in February, 1861, but was not reappointed because he had enlisted in the 9th Texas Cavalry on October 14, 1861 for a year. There is no record that he remained with that unit after it was mustered into Confederate service.[18]

Elliot M. Scott is listed in the 1860 Cooke County census (F.N. 99) as a farmer from Tennessee, age forty-nine, with a wife, Maria, and six children born in Kentucky. He paid his first poll tax in Cooke County in 1857. His neighbor, James L. Clark, recalled that Scott came to Texas from California, but on June 1, 1858, Scott sold his possessions located in Scott County, Arkansas—5 horses, 50 or 60 cattle, 2 wagons, 8 to 10 sheep and some furniture—to F. M. Scott, a woman, for $800.[19] He purchased 220 acres soon thereafter, because he paid taxes in Cooke County on this land in 1861 and 1862, when he also paid taxes on 8 horses and 9 cattle.

Gilbert Smith, age twenty-three, is listed as being in a militia company from Fannin County mustered on July 7, 1861. Although the unit was accepted into Confederate service on October 10, 1861, there is no record of Smith's presence.[20] He paid taxes in Cooke County in 1862 on 2 cattle, worth a total of $12.

17. Card Index to Confederate Muster Rolls, in Archives Division, TSL; Clark, ed., *Recollections of James Clark*, 109.

18. Card Index to Confederate Muster Rolls; Cooke Cty. Commissioners' Court, "Minutes," I, 79 (sheet 2), 80; Ingmire, comp., "Cooke County Marriage Records," 4.

19. Clark, ed., *Recollections of James Clark*, 109; Cooke Cty. Deed Record, V, 577.

20. Card Index to Confederate Muster Rolls.

William B. Taylor is listed in the 1860 Cooke County census (F.N. 424) as a thirty-two-year-old farmer from Tennessee with $600 in personal property. His wife, Martha, was from Missouri, but their year-old son had been born in Texas. Taylor came to Cooke County in 1854 and bought 12 lots in Gainesville on October 2 and 3. In 1857 he paid taxes in Cooke County on a 160-acre preemption along Denton Creek; apparently he had lost or sold the town lots. He married Martha Ann Welch in September, 1858; in 1860 they still lived on his preemption, and he had acquired 4 horses.[21]

Eliott S. Thomas is listed in the 1860 Cooke County census (F.N. 387) as a physician from Ohio, age thirty-seven, with $10,400 in real and personal property. His wife, Mary, was from Kentucky; their six-year-old son was born in Iowa, and their nine-year-old daughter in Texas. Thomas paid a poll tax in Cooke County in 1861.

James A. Ward paid taxes in Cooke County for the first time in 1855 on a preemption of 160 acres on Islebury Creek; the tax roll in 1859 records his homestead as lying on Timber Creek. His only other taxable property in 1859 was 4 horses; he did pay his taxes on them and his land in 1862 according to the 1862 Cooke County tax roll, UNT.

William W. Wernell is listed in the 1850 Panola County census (F.N. 76) as a farmer, age thirty-four, from Ohio, with $250 in real and personal property. His wife, Elizabeth, was from Tennessee, and they had five children, ranging in age from nine years to one month, born in that state. Wernell bought 160 acres of Obediah B. Atkinson's survey from him on February 24, 1862.[22]

21. Ingmire, comp., "Marriage Records of Grayson County," 6; Cooke Cty. Deed Record, II, 88–89.
22. Cooke Cty. Deed Record, V, 483.

Members of the Citizens Court Jury at Gainesville

Thomas Barrett, born June 21, 1809, in North Carolina, was a self-taught physician, Christian Church minister—ordained in 1833 in Tennessee—and farmer. Although he obtained a land grant from the Republic of Texas in 1839, he moved from Tennessee to Missouri in 1842, then to Hopkins County, Texas, in 1848. He lived for a time in Titus County, then moved to Cooke County about 1860. He purchased 160 acres in May, 1861, and paid taxes in 1862 on this land plus another 56-acre tract, 1 slave, 3 horses, 60 cattle, and 400 sheep.[1]

Newton J. Chance, brother of Joseph C. Chance, was a twenty-nine-year-old blacksmith from Illinois living in the Valetta Ranch community in Denton County in 1860 (F.N. 613). His wife, Margaret, and their son, age four, were born in Illinois, but they had a two-year-old daughter born in Kansas, so they probably moved to Texas from that territory sometime after 1858. He reported no land, but in 1863 he paid taxes in Cooke County on $228 in personal property. He allegedly resigned as lieutenant colonel of a Tarrant County regiment of volunteers in October, 1861, then organized a company for the 14th Texas Cavalry. Official records indicate that he enrolled as a private in the 9th Texas Cavalry in October, 1861, was mustered out for a disability, then joined a "Spy Company," from which he was again discharged for a disability in August, 1862.[2]

1. Missouri Ann Barrett Dustin, "The Early Days of Cook County, Texas" (Typescript in BTHC); William R. Strong, *His Memoirs*, ed. Pete A. Y. Gunter and Robert A. Calvert (Denton, Tex., 1982), 18; Texas General Land Office, Land Patent Records, Republic Certificate #1,618 . . . 232, Court of Claims File 402, Fannin 2-632, all in Archives and Records Division, Texas General Land Office, Austin; *Biographical Souvenir of the State of Texas* (Chicago, 1889), 50; Frances T. Ingmire, comp., *Cemetery Records of Cooke County, Texas* (Gainesville, 1980), 484.

2. CSR, 9th Tex. Cavalry and Capt. Alfred Johnson's Spy Company; Joe T. Roff, *A Brief*

Samuel C. Doss, a stockraiser from Virginia, in 1860 was age thirty-five and living in Gainesville with $64,150 in real and personal property, including 8 slaves, 4,500 cattle, and 1,200 milch cows. He had immigrated with his father to Red River County, Texas, in 1836, then married and moved to Cooke County in 1853 to establish the "Hog Eye" ranch, where he and his wife, Sarah, a Tennessee native, were found by the census taker in 1860 (F.N. 12). He filed for a preemption of 136 acres along the Red River in Cooke County on October 2, 1854; in 1862 he paid taxes on 1,890 acres in Cooke County and, as executor of an estate, on 7 additional slaves.[3]

John W. Hamill, a native of South Carolina, became a minister in the Tennessee Conference of the Methodist Church in 1831. He remained with the southern branch after the 1844 schism, serving primarily as a missionary to Indians. He was in Texas as early as 1850, when the Fannin County census (F.N. 429) listed him as a forty-one-year-old minister, but just prior to his arrival in Cooke County he had been superintendent of the Colbert Institute in the Chickasaw District of the Indian Territory. He bought 320 acres in Cooke County on November 12, 1861.[4]

William W. Howeth is listed in the 1850 Rusk County census (F.N. 28) as a farmer, age thirty-two, from Tennessee, with $4,000 in real and personal property and four children—the oldest seven years of age—born in Texas. He paid his first taxes in Cooke County in 1854 on 3,709 acres on the Elm Fork of the Trinity River and 320 acres on the Red River, all within the county; 2,390 acres outside the county—154 acres in Grayson County, the rest in Hunt County; and two slaves. The tax rolls for 1860 show that he reported an estate of $19,500 to the census taker and that his wife, Mary,

History of Early Days in North Texas and the Indian Territory (Roff, Okla., 1930), 8; William H. Griffin to Jeremiah Y. Dashiell, November 20, 1861, in AGR; Dallas *Herald*, January 29, February 12, 1862; Marcus J. Wright, *Texas in the War*, ed. Harold B. Simpson (Hillsboro, Tex., 1965), 26, 116.

3. Texas Land Patent Records, Fannin 3–1747; Buckley B. Paddock, ed., *A Twentieth Century History and Biographical Record of North and West Texas* (2 vols.; Chicago, 1906), I, 669–70.

4. Cooke County, County Clerk, Deed Record, 1850–present, V, 506; Walter N. Vernon, *Methodism Moves Across North Texas* (Dallas, 1967), 82–83; Carole Ellsworth and Sue Elmer, comps., "1860 Census of the Free Inhabitants of Indian Lands West of Arkansas (Oklahoma Indian Territory)," typescript in Genealogy Division, TSL.

from Tennessee, had separate assets worth $2,000 (F.N. 41)—she owned 960 acres inside and 160 acres outside Cooke County, as well as their slaves, now increased to 3 by the birth of a girl. He paid taxes on just 851 acres that year, all in Cooke County.

Jeremiah E. Hughes is listed in the 1860 Cooke County census (F.N. 25) as the postmaster for Gainesville, a position he held through the Civil War. He was a native of New Jersey, age forty-three, with $1,210 in real and personal property. He paid his first taxes in Cooke County in 1853 on a horse and some hogs; by 1862 he had 4 lots in Gainesville, 1 horse, and 4 cattle. He married Sophronia Sparks, a native of Virginia, in Cooke County in March, 1857. He was elected tax assessor and collector for Cooke County in 1854, justice of the peace in 1855, and county clerk in 1856, 1858, and 1860.[5]

James Jones is listed in the 1860 Cooke County census (F.N. 137) as a farmer from North Carolina, age forty-eight, with $4,205 in real and personal property. His wife, Adeline, and their children, the youngest of whom was only ten months old, were born in Missouri. Jones paid taxes on a headright of 320 acres on Islebury Creek in Cooke County in 1855; in 1858 he was assessed for 320 acres registered under another man's name on the same stream. In 1862 he paid taxes on 205 acres of the latter survey, 14 horses, 20 cattle, and 15 sheep.

Reason Jones was born on October 10, 1813, in Tennessee. He came to Texas during the Republic period as he is listed in the muster rolls of "Captain Clapp's" company, organized at Mustang Prairie on September 10, 1836, but the notation "Never mustered nor done any duty" accompanies his name. He moved to Cooke County in June, 1855, and filed for a 160-acre preemption on November 25, 1856, located on the Elm Fork of the

5. Jeremiah E. Hughes to Andrew Johnson, August 25, 1865, in Amnesty Files; Frances T. Ingmire, comp., "Cooke County, Texas, Marriage Records, 1849–1879," 2; Texas Secretary of State, Election Register, 1848–1900, in Archives Division, TSL; *Register of the Officers and Agents, Civil, Military and Naval in the Service of the United States for the Year 1859* (Washington, D.C., 1859), 369; *Register of the Officers and Agents, Civil, Military and Naval in the Service of the United States for the Year 1861* (Washington, D.C., 1861), 237; *Register of the Officers and Agents, Civil, Military and Naval in the Service of the United States for the Year 1865* (Washington, D.C., 1865), 249.

Trinity River 15 miles southeast of Gainesville, in the Eastern Cross Timbers. This land was patented to him on December 16, 1860, a few months after he married Malinda Sowers, from Missouri. The 1860 Cooke County census lists him (F.N. 129) as an illiterate farmer with $13,225 in real and personal property, and six children; the elder, ages seventeen, fifteen, and nine, were born in Missouri, but the rest were born in Texas. In 1862 he paid taxes in Cooke County on 16 horses, 200 cattle, 45 sheep, and 860 acres.[6]

Wiley Jones, born November 8, 1803, in North Carolina, is listed in the 1860 Cooke County census (F.N. 568) as having $17,940 in real and personal property, including 10 slaves. His wife, Anna, was from South Carolina. He paid his first taxes in Cooke County in 1860 on 160 acres on Clear Creek, 10 slaves, 9 horses, and 30 cattle; in 1862 he had the same land and slaves, 8 horses, 70 cattle, and 260 sheep. He was elected a commissioner for Cooke County in 1860 and 1862, and a legislator in 1863.[7]

J. Pope Long, born in Kentucky in 1815, moved with his parents to Missouri, then studied medicine and enlisted in John C. Fremont's regiment as a surgeon during the Mexican War. He never practiced medicine as a civilian, apparently preferring to make his living as a farmer. He immigrated to Texas in 1859, but did not come to Sivell's Bend of the Red River in Cooke County until May 19, 1861, with his family and 5 slaves. By 1863 he had acquired 1,300 acres along the Red River.[8]

James W. McPherson is listed in the 1860 Cooke County census (F.N. 111) as a thirty-four-year-old farmer from Indiana, with $356 in personal

6. Ingmire, comp., "Cooke County Marriage Records," 4; Texas Land Patent Records, Fannin 3–3269; Texas General Land Office, Muster Roll Book, Army of the Republic of Texas, 203, in Archives and Records Div., Texas General Land Office; Ingmire, comp., *Cemetery Records of Cooke County*, 168.

7. Secretary of State, Election Register; Cooke County Commissioners' Court, "Minutes 1857 to 1878," I, 100, in Works Progress Administration Historical Records Survey, BTHC; A. Morton Smith, *The First 100 Years in Cooke County* (San Antonio, 1955), 31; Ingmire, comp., *Cemetery Records of Cooke County*, 167.

8. Willie Russell, "Sivell's Bend Community History" (Typescript in Cooke County Historical File, Cooke County Library, Gainesville, Tex.); Bettie L. Gunter, "Recollections of an Early Cooke County Settler" (Typescript in Morton Museum, Gainesville); *Biographical Souvenir of Texas*, 531; Smith, *First 100 Years*, 32.

property. His wife, Nancy, was from Kentucky, but their son, age ten, was born in Missouri and their daughter, four years of age, was born in Texas.

Daniel Montague was born in Massachusetts on August 22, 1798. Educated as a surveyor and engineer, he moved to Louisiana in 1820, where he practiced his profession, purchased slaves, and established a plantation. He came to Texas in 1836 but returned to Louisiana to sell his holdings, and then in 1837 settled near old Warren in the Fannin Land District; as the first surveyor for that district, he amassed a large estate. During the Mexican War he was a captain in the 3d Texas Mounted Volunteers, commanded by William C. Young. Afterward he moved to Cooke County, where the census taker in 1850 listed him (F.N. 1) as a farmer with $5,000 in real and personal property. His estate increased substantially during the ensuing decade, according to the 1860 Cooke County census (F.N. 374), which also recorded that his wife, Jane, was from Virginia. In 1862 he paid taxes on 1 slave, 1,440 acres along the Elm Fork of the Trinity River, and 4,026 acres scattered in Grayson, Collin, Fannin, and Montague counties, the last one named in his honor. He was elected as district surveyor in 1854, Cooke County commissioner in 1858 and 1862, and state senator in 1863.[9]

Benjamin Scanland is listed in the 1860 Cooke County census (F.N. 521) as a farmer, age forty-two, from Tennessee, with $10,625 in real and personal property, including a female slave. Elizabeth, his wife, was also born in Tennessee, as were five of their six children; the youngest was born in Texas. In 1853 he paid taxes in Cooke County for the first time on a horse; in 1858 he was assessed for a 160-acre preemption along the Red River and bought a slave girl from his brother on March 2. By 1863 he had supplemented his preemption by acquiring 3,980 acres on Fish Creek, where he was active in developing the Sivell's Bend community.[10]

9. Secretary of State, Election Register; Sam Acheson and Julia Ann Hudson O'Connell, eds., *George Washington Diamond's Account of the Great Hanging at Gainesville, 1862* (Austin, 1963), 27–28; Rex W. Strickland, "History of Fannin County, Texas, 1836–1843," *SWHQ*, XXXIII (1930), 270–71; Zachary T. Fulmore, *The History and Geography of Texas As Told in County Names* (Austin, 1915), 86–87; Graham Landrum and Allen Smith, *An Illustrated History of Grayson County, Texas* (2d ed.; Fort Worth, 1967), 10; *Members of the Texas Legislature 1846–1981* (Austin, 1981), 40; Charles D. Spurlin, *Texas Veterans in the Mexican War* (Victoria, Tex., 1984), 57.

10. Russell, "Sivell's Bend Community History"; Gunter, "Recollections of an Early Cooke County Settler"; Cooke Cty. Deed Record, IV, 16; Charles N. Jones, *Early Days in Cooke County* (Gainesville, 1936), 17.

William J. Simpson is recorded in the 1860 Cooke County census (F.N. 525) as a farmer from Tennessee, age forty-eight, with $2,330 in real and personal property. His wife, Jemima, was a Tennessee native as well, but two of their children were born in Alabama and three in Mississippi. He paid his first taxes in Cooke County in 1858 on 260 acres on Fish Creek; in 1862 he had the same land, 4 horses, and 20 cattle.

Thomas Wright is listed in the 1860 Cooke County census (F.N. 441) as a farmer from North Carolina, age forty-eight, with $5,291 in real and personal property, including 7 slaves. His wife, Julia, a Georgia native, was many years his junior—she was only twenty-two in 1860—but they had three daughters. The oldest, four years of age, was born in Arkansas, and the younger two in Texas. He paid only a poll tax in Cooke County in 1857; in 1862 he paid taxes on 160 acres along the Red River, 220 acres in another tract, 8 slaves, 27 horses, 30 cattle, and 27 sheep.

APPENDIX C
Other Participants at Gainesville

Obediah B. Atkinson is recorded in the 1860 Cooke County census (F.N. 169) as a farmer from Illinois, age twenty-nine, with $1,481 in real and personal property. His wife, Dolly, the sister of James A. Powers, was born in Missouri, as was their eldest son, but the other five children were born in Texas. He first appears on the Cooke County tax rolls in 1854, when he paid a poll tax. He filed for a preemption of 320 acres on Wolf Creek, adjoining William R. Rhodes's and Hudson J. Esman's tracts, on January 26, 1854. A patent was granted on June 20, 1859, but he soon sold most of it; in 1862 he paid taxes on only 60 acres of his own homestead, 160 acres of another survey, 1 horse, 18 cattle, and 4 sheep.[1]

A. G. Birdwell paid taxes in Wise County in 1862 on 160 acres, 3 horses, and 40 cattle.

James G. Bourland was born in South Carolina on August 11, 1801. He married in Kentucky on June 16, 1822, then moved to Tennessee, where he traded in slaves and horses. Immigrating to the Republic of Texas in 1837, he settled in present-day Lamar County. He led a company of volunteers in a punitive expedition against hostile Indians along the Forks in 1841, then served as second-in-command to William C. Young in a second foray later that year. Bourland served as a deputy surveyor until appointed collector of customs for the Red River District on February 4, 1842. When he clashed with the crew of a United States steamship that had unloaded its cargo on Texas soil without paying duties, they bound him and left him for

1. Texas General Land Office, Land Patent Records, Fannin 3–2746, in Archives and Records Division, Texas General Land Office, Austin; Noel Parsons to author, April 25, 1989.

several hours. For that indignity he was awarded $26,000 by a United States court in 1848. He was lieutenant colonel of the 3d Regiment, Texas Mounted Rifles, commanded by William C. Young, during the Mexican War, and was elected to the senate of the first and second state legislatures of Texas. In 1851 he moved to Cooke County, where he established a plantation on the Red River. The 1860 Cooke County census (F.N. 439) reported that he had $56,260 in real and personal property, including 23 slaves. By 1862 he had 2,316 acres in Cooke County, as well as 4,918 acres in Clay, Hunt, Fannin, Montague, and Wise counties.[2]

William W. Bourland, eldest son of James G. Bourland, is listed in the 1860 Cooke County census (F.N. 438) as a single farmer, age thirty-three, born in Tennessee, with $5,800 in real property and $800 in personal property. Later that year, he acquired land from his father, who also transferred title to a slave. In 1862 William paid taxes in Cooke County on the land and 3 slaves, as well as 2 horses and a small herd of 50 cattle.[3]

Alexander Boutwell was born in Arkansas in 1824, and immigrated with his parents to Fannin County, Texas, in 1843. He married and moved to Cooke County sometime before 1848—when he served as a member of a Cooke County ranger company—and filed a claim for 640 acres on the Elm

2. Bourland Family File in Sherman Municipal Library, Sherman, Tex.; Frederick W. Sumner, "Written by F. W. Sumner During the Civil War 1860–1865" (Typescript in Sherman Historical Museum, Sherman, Tex.); James G. Bourland to Andrew Johnson, September 18, 1865, in Amnesty Files; George P. Garrison, ed., *Diplomatic Correspondence of the Republic of Texas* (3 vols.; Washington, D.C., 1908–1911), II, 181–85, 342–46; Amelia Williams and Eugene C. Barker, eds., *The Writings of Sam Houston* (8 vols.; Austin, 1943), IV, 127–28; Texas Land Patent Records, Red River 2–16, Fannin 2–292, Lamar 2–112, Lamar S–9, 635, 8894 and 5468; Texas Secretary of State, "Register of Elected and Appointed Officials for the Republic of Texas," I, 455, II, 159, typescript, 2 vols., n.d., in TSL; Rex W. Strickland, "History of Fannin County, Texas, 1836–1843, II," *SWHQ*, XXXIV (1930), 40–47; *Biographical Souvenir of Texas* (Chicago, 1889), 98; John H. Brown, *History of Texas from 1685 to 1892* (2 vols.; St. Louis, 1893), I, 419–21; John H. Brown, *Indian Wars and Pioneers of Texas* (St. Louis, 1893), 85–87; *Members of the Texas Legislature 1846–1980* (Austin, 1981), 1, 4; John H. Brown and William S. Speer, eds., *Encyclopedia of the New West* (Marshall, Tex., 1881), 233–34; James T. DeShields, *Border Wars of Texas* (Tioga, Tex., 1912), 353–59; Charles D. Spurlin, *Texas Veterans in the Mexican War* (Victoria, Tex.), 54.

3. Cooke County, County Clerk, Deed Record, 1850–present, IV, 560, in Cooke County Courthouse, Gainesville, Tex.; *Biographical Souvenir of Texas*, 98–99; Graham Landrum and Allen Smith, *An Illustrated History of Grayson County, Texas* (2d ed.; Fort Worth, 1967), 61.

Fork of the Trinity River under the Peters Colony grant on April 17, 1850. He paid taxes on his property, located north of Gainesville, in 1852, but sold it the next year and moved onto the townsite. The 1860 Cooke County census (F.N. 11) lists him as a merchant with $5,000 in real and personal property; in 1862 he paid taxes in Cooke County on 100 acres in the far western portion of the county, on Elm Fork, plus 7 lots in Gainesville. He was Cooke County's first sheriff, and was elected a justice of the peace in 1854.[4]

William Boyles came to Peters Colony as a single man before July 1, 1848. He served in ranger companies during 1846 and 1848, then married in May, 1849. The 1850 Grayson County census (F.N. 14) lists him as a farmer, age twenty-four, from Kentucky, and his wife, Elizabeth, as being from Ohio. The census taker in 1860 found him in Cooke County (F.N. 184) with $730 in personal property. He had three children—ages seven years, five years, and seven months—born in Texas, and a three-year-old born in Arkansas. His father died in October, 1857, and William, then in Crawford County, Arkansas, inherited his land in Cooke County. He paid taxes in Cooke County in 1861 on 311 acres of the "James" Boyles grant on the Red River, but in 1862 he was assessed for only a third of this grant, 4 horses, 20 cattle, and 4 sheep.[5]

John K. Bumpass was born in North Carolina in 1828, and came to Texas in 1857. The 1860 Collin County census (F.N. 1,096) lists him as a farmer,

4. CSR, 11th Texas Cavalry; Lemuel D. Clark, ed., *The Civil War Recollections of James Lemuel Clark* (College Station, Tex., 1984), 102; William R. Strong, *His Memoirs*, ed. Pete A. Y. Gunter and Robert A. Calvert (Denton, Tex., 1982), 24; Texas Secretary of State, Election Register, 1848–1900, in Archives Division, TSL; *Biographical Souvenir of Texas*, 99; John H. Brown, *History of Dallas County from 1837 to 1887* (Dallas, 1887), 50–51; Seymour V. Connor, *The Peters Colony of Texas* (Austin, 1959), 197; A. Morton Smith, *The First 100 Years in Cooke County* (San Antonio, 1955), 28. A copy of Boutwell's land grant certificate, dated May 22, 1854, is in the Cooke County Historical File, Cooke County Library.

5. Frances T. Ingmire, comp., "Marriage Records of Grayson County, Texas, 1846–1877," p. 1, typescript in BTHC; Cooke County Deed Record, V, 377; Texas Land Patent Records, Fannin 3–1569; Dorman H. Winfrey and James M. Day, eds., *The Indian Papers of Texas and the Southwest* (4 vols.; Austin, 1960–1966), III, 66–67, 70–71; Brown, *History of Dallas County*, 50–51; Connor, *Peters Colony*, 198; Roy F. Hall and Helen G. Hall, *Collin County: Pioneering in North Texas* (Quanah, Tex., 1975), 21; Jacob L. Stambaugh and Lillian J. Stambaugh, *A History of Collin County, Texas* (Austin, 1958), 255.

age thirty, reporting $11,000 in real and personal property. His wife, Elizabeth, and the first four of their five children were natives of North Carolina as well; the last child was born in Texas. In 1862 he paid taxes in Collin County on 560 acres, a town lot in Sulphur Springs, 7 slaves, 2 horses, and 157 cattle.

Joseph C. Chance, Newton J. Chance's brother, is listed in the 1860 Wise County census (F.N. 342) as a twenty-five-year-old farmer from Illinois with $800 in real and personal property. He moved to Texas by way of Kansas and Missouri, arriving in Texas from the latter state within the previous year. He owned no land, but paid taxes in Cooke County in 1862 on 3 horses and 6 cattle.[6]

James B. Davenport, Jr., is recorded in the 1860 Cooke County census (F.N. 469) as a twenty-one-year-old farmer from Missouri living with H. Lander, a childless forty-five-year-old farmer born in Georgia. Davenport had immigrated to Texas from Missouri in 1857 with his father, who is listed in the 1860 Cooke County census (F.N. 9) as a farmer from Kentucky with $8,000 in real and personal property, including 9 slaves. The younger Davenport was a deputy sheriff in Gainesville for several years, served on the county patrols organized in 1861, and was elected sheriff of Cooke County on August 1, 1862.[7]

John Davidson is listed in the 1860 Cooke County census (F.N. 279) as a farmer, age forty-one, from Alabama, with $2,922 in real and personal property. His wife, Lucinda, was from Alabama, too, but their six children, whose ages ranged from seventeen years to six months, were all born in Texas.

James A. Dickson, born in Tennessee on September 23, 1826, is recorded in the 1860 Cooke County census (F.N. 560) as a thirty-two-year-old farmer with $5,275 in real and personal property, including a slave. In 1861

6. Joe T. Roff, *A Brief History of Early Days in North Texas and the Indian Territory* (Roff, Okla., 1930), 8.

7. Cooke County Commissioners' Court, "Minutes, 1857 to 1878," I, 102, typescript in Works Progress Administration Historical Records Survey, BTCH, Texas Secretary of State, Election Register; *Biographical Souvenir of Texas*, 233–34; Smith, *First 100 Years*, 32.

he inherited the property of his father and paid taxes on holdings in Cooke County that included 160 acres on Clear Creek, 7 town lots, and 6 slaves.[8]

Robert O. Duncan is listed in the 1860 Wise County census (F.N. 331) as a day laborer for Henry R. Maple, a miller. Duncan was twenty-three years of age, from Illinois, unmarried, with $500 in personal property. He paid taxes in Cooke County in 1862 on a horse.

Jonathan Edmiston is listed in the 1860 Cooke County census (F.N. 364) as a twenty-six-year-old farmer, born in Tennessee, with $1,245 in real and personal property. His wife, Ann, whom he had married in October, 1854, in Cooke County, was also from Tennessee, but their children were all born in Texas. Edmiston purchased 120 acres in Cooke County on May 3, 1853, another 120 acres from the same man on August 21, 1854, and another 25 acres on February 5, 1856. In 1858 Edmiston paid taxes for the first time in Cooke County on 90 acres along Elm Creek; in 1862 he had this same land, on which he pastured 3 horses and 14 cattle. He served as a road overseer for Cooke County in 1861 and 1862.[9]

Hydeman P. Garrison is listed in the 1860 Wise County census (F.N. 416) as a farmer from Tennessee, thirty-six years of age, with $1,600 in real and personal property. His wife, Gelse, was born in Tennessee as well, but their older children, ages seven and three, were born in Illinois and their youngest, only four months old, was born in Texas. He paid taxes in 1862 in Cooke County on 2 horses and 8 cattle.

Harry Gilman moved to the Peters Colony before July 1, 1848, and married Jane Boggs in December, 1849. The 1850 census taker found them in Grayson County (F.N. 152), listing him as a farmer from New York and recording her state of birth as Kentucky. Gilman filed a claim for 320 acres on October 29, 1850; the certificate was issued on May 20, 1854, for land located on Cross Timbers Creek in Cooke County. The Cooke County census taker in 1860 (F.N. 237) recorded that Gilman was thirty-eight years

8. Sue Wood and Ronnie Howser, comps., *Fairview Cemetery, Gainesville, Cooke County, Texas* (Gainesville, 1982), 19.

9. Cooke Cty. Commissioners' Court, "Minutes," I, 79 (sheet 2), 80, 93; Frances T. Ingmire, comp., "Cooke County, Texas, Marriage Records, 1849–1879," p. 1, typescript in BTHC; Cooke County Deed Record, I, 79, II, 70, 296.

of age, with $1,829 in real and personal property and four children born in Texas. He paid current and back taxes in 1862 on his 320 acres, 80 acres of an adjoining survey, and 34 cattle.[10]

Aaron Hill, born August 15, 1796, in South Carolina, is listed in the 1850 Grayson County census (F.N. 159) as a farmer with $1,970 in real and personal property. He moved in 1850 to Cooke County, where he was elected district clerk and tax assessor that same year, and filed a claim on April 23 for 640 acres as he had come to the Peters Colony before July, 1848, with a wife and child. The land, patented to him on May 22, 1854, was located on the Elm Fork of the Trinity River south of Gainesville. The census taker for Cooke County in 1860 (F.N. 70) recorded that he was still the district clerk, a post he retained until after the Civil War, and had $7,500 in real and personal property. His first wife died on August 15, 1858, and he married Menta C. Rodgers in April, 1861. In 1862, Hill paid taxes on his grant plus 1,220 more acres along Elm Fork, on which he pastured horses, cattle, and sheep. He was an elder of the Southern Methodist church.[11]

Harvey Howeth was a native of Tennessee, born on October 1, 1821. He immigrated with his parents to present-day Rusk County in 1839, then fought in the Mexican War. In 1847 he married, and in 1852 he moved to Cooke County, where he rented Alexander Boutwell's farm. The 1860 Cooke County census (F.N. 310) lists him as a farmer, thirty-four years of age, with $2,471 in real and personal property. In 1862 he paid taxes in Cooke County on a 320-acre preemption, 10 acres of another survey, 8 horses, and 40 cattle. He served one term as a county commissioner.[12]

William R. Hudson, born in South Carolina on December 6, 1829, served in the army of the Republic of Texas from October 1, 1836, to June 3, 1837.

10. Ingmire, comp., "Cooke County Marriage Records," 1; Texas Land Patent Records, Fannin 3–1686; Connor, *Peters Colony*, 259.

11. Ingmire, comp., "Cooke County Marriage Records," 5; Texas Secretary of State, Election Register; Sam Acheson and Julia Ann Hudson O'Connell, eds., *George Washington Diamond's Account of the Great Hanging at Gainesville, 1862* (Austin, 1963), 37–38; Texas Land Patent Records, Fannin 3–1173; Connor, *Peters Colony*, 282; Smith, *First 100 Years*, 10; Frances T. Ingmire, comp., *Cemetery Records of Cooke County, Texas* (Gainesville, 1980), 287; Walter N. Vernon, *Methodism Moves Across North Texas* (Dallas, 1967), 91.

12. Cooke County Deed Record, II, 28; Texas Secretary of State, Election Register; *Biographical Souvenir of Texas*, 421–22; Vernon, *Methodism Moves Across North Texas*, 91; Wood and Howser, comps., *Fairview Cemetery*, 15.

For his military service he received a patent for 960 acres in Navarro County on April 9, 1847. An itinerant surveyor, Hudson ᴎoved to Cooke County in July, 1854, and formed a lucrative partnership with attorney James M. Lindsay that lasted twenty-five years. Hudson filed several pre-emptions and in 1862 paid taxes in Cooke County on four Gainesville lots; 4,150 acres on Clear and Fish creeks in Cooke County; 1,976 acres in Wise County, some of which had been purchased from James G. Bourland; 3,537 acres in Montague County; and 1,800 acres in Clay County. The Cooke County census of 1860 (F.N. 10), the year Hudson was elected as county commissioner, reported him as a resident of Gainesville, with $32,700 in real and personal property including 3 slaves. He married Mary J. Fletcher, a native of Missouri, in Cooke County during October, 1858.[13]

William H. Jasper was described as being a farmer, age forty-two, five feet six inches tall, and darkly complected at the time of the mustering out of his company on January 15, 1863, by which date he had already accepted a commission in the regular Confederate army. He was a resident of Denton County in 1862, and paid taxes on 908 acres, 2 horses, and 30 cattle. He paid his first assessment in Denton County, a poll tax, in 1861.[14]

Jonas B. McCurley is recorded in the 1860 Denton County census (F.N. 172) as a farmer from Tennessee, age forty-eight, with $3,000 in real and personal property. His wife, Sarah, was from Indiana, but two of their children, ages eleven and nine, were born in Illinois, and two others, ages two years and six months, were born in Texas. In 1861 he paid taxes in Denton County on 320 acres, a town lot in Denton, 3 horses, and 35 cattle.

Abner M. Marshall is listed in the 1860 Wise County census (F.N. 350) as an attorney, age twenty-five, from Illinois, with $250 in personal property. His wife, Elizabeth, was from Ohio. He paid a poll tax in Wise County in

13. Price M. Cheaney, "William R. Hudson" (Typescript in Price M. Cheaney Papers, Morton Museum, Gainesville); Ingmire, comp., "Cooke County Marriage Records," 2; Texas General Land Office, Muster Roll Book, Army of the Republic of Texas, 193, in Archives and Records Division, Texas General Land Office, Texas; Texas Land Patent Records, Bounty & Donation 240, Fannin 3–2790; Texas Secretary of State, Election Register; Smith, *First 100 Years*, 28, 33; Brown and Speer, eds., *Encyclopedia of the New West*, 355–56.

14. Muster Roll of William H. Jasper's Mounted Company C, January 7, 1863, and of Theodore J. Dorsett's Mounted Company C, January 15, 1863, in AGR.

1857; five years later he was assessed for a 160-acre preemption near Prairie Point, 3 horses, and 50 cattle.

Jackson H. Mounts was an Illinois native, born in 1823. He came to Peters Colony before July 1, 1844, and received a land patent, but he sold it unlocated. In 1850, Mounts was listed in the Collin County census (F.N. 302) as a farmer; in 1860 he was recorded by the census taker for Jack County (F.N. 630) as an innkeeper with $4,300 in real and personal property. He voted against secession in Jack County on February 23, 1861, and paid taxes there on 1,000 acres and a horse. The next year he had moved to Cooke County, where he was assessed for taxes on 187.5 acres there plus 1,457 acres he had in Jack County.[15]

Samuel P. C. Patton is listed in the 1860 Denton County census (F.N. 715) as a master carpenter, age thirty-six, from North Carolina, with $1,600 in real and personal property. His wife, Janet, was a native of England, while their nine-year-old son was born in Texas. Patton first appears in the Denton County tax rolls in 1858, when he was assessed for a town lot in Denton. In 1862 he paid taxes on 160 acres in Tarrant County, 2 horses, and 12 cattle.

James M. Peery was born May 1, 1830, in Missouri. In 1855 he came with his parents to Cooke County, where he married a daughter of William Bean in April, 1857. The Cooke County census taker in 1860 (F.N. 14) listed him as a surveyor living in Gainesville, with $17,000 in real and personal property, which included two slaves—a mother and her infant son. He paid taxes in Cooke County for the first time in 1856 on 3,640 acres along the Little Wichita River; by 1863 he and his two brothers, both of whom were also surveyors, paid taxes on 6,127 acres along Fish, Elm, and Pecan creeks, and on another 4,085 acres located in Wise, Clay, and Montague counties.[16]

William Peery, the father of James M. Peery, was born in Kentucky on February 19, 1800. He immigrated to Missouri in 1818, then to Fannin

15. Texas Land Patent Records, Fannin 3–2060; Edward F. Bates, *History and Reminiscences of Denton County* (Denton, Tex., 1918), 115; Connor, *Peters Colony*, 347; Ida L. Huckaby, *Ninety-Four Years in Jack County, 1854–1948* (Austin, 1949), 77.

16. Ingmire, comp., "Cooke County Marriage Records," 2; Strong, *Memoirs*, 9, 21, 29; Charles N. Jones, *Early Days in Cooke County* (Gainesville, 1936), 18–19; Smith, *First 100 Years*, 28; Ingmire, comp., *Cemetery Records of Cooke County*, 290.

County, Texas, in 1851. He moved to Cooke County about 1855, but did not pay taxes until 1859, when he was assessed for 320 acres on Fish Creek. The Cooke County census in 1860 (F.N. 531) recorded him as a sixty-year-old farmer from Kentucky with $36,570 in real and personal property, including 4 slaves. By 1863 he paid taxes in Cooke County on 5 slaves and 820 acres in that county, as well as 2,210 acres in Fannin County, 3,200 acres in Wise County, and 320 acres in Clay County.[17]

Ralph G. Piper came to Cooke County from Kansas City, perhaps as early as 1856, and settle just north of Gainesville. He bought 173 acres along Elm Creek on April 29, 1858, and paid his first taxes in Cooke County the next year. He taught school, then was elected chief justice on August 1, 1861, and later mayor. He is listed in the 1860 Cooke County census (F.N. 623) as a farmer from Virginia, age forty-five, with $2,366 in real and personal property. By 1862 he had added 50 more acres to the holdings, and paid taxes on 7 horses and 100 cattle as well.[18]

Cincinnatus Potter immigrated to Cooke County in October, 1858, from Mississippi. He paid taxes in 1859 on 1 horse, 2 cattle, and a carriage worth $100; in 1862 he was assessed for a preemption of 160 acres, 80 acres of another survey, 6 horses, 25 cattle, and 160 sheep. Potter is inexplicably recorded in the 1860 Cooke County census (F.N. 489) as "Cincinnati Jones," a thirty-two-year-old farmer from Georgia with $1,720 in real and personal property. His wife, Melissa, was from Georgia, but six of their seven children were born in Mississippi and the youngest, only four months old, was born in Texas. It is interesting to note that their twelve-year-old son was named after Henry Clay, while their six-year-old son was named for John C. Calhoun, perhaps indicating a shift in political orientation by their father. In 1862, Potter was elected tax assessor and collector for Cooke County.[19]

17. Acheson and O'Connell, eds., *Diamond's Account*, 28n; *Biographical Souvenir of Texas*, 664; Ingmire, comp., *Cemetery Records of Cooke County*, 290.

18. Cooke County Deed Record, IV, 108; Texas Secretary of State, Election Register; Samuel W. Geiser, "Men of Science in Texas," *Field and Laboratory*, XXVII (1959), 173.

19. Cooke Cty. Commissioners' Court, "Minutes," I, 102 (sheet 2); Texas Secretary of State, Election Register; Brown, *Indian Wars and Pioneers of Texas*, 692–93; Brown and Speer, eds., *Encyclopedia of the New West*, 396; Buckley B. Paddock, ed., *A Twentieth Century History and Biographical Record of North and West Texas* (2 vols.; Chicago, 1906), I, 669–70.

Moses Powers is listed in the 1860 Cooke County census (F.N. 318) as a stonemason from Missouri, age forty-seven, with $1,010 in real and personal property. His wife, Lucy, was from Kentucky but their children were all born in Missouri. He was the uncle of James A. Powers and of Dolly Jane Powers, who married Obediah B. Atkinson. In 1860 he paid a poll tax in Cooke County; two years later he paid taxes on 1 horse and 9 cattle.[20]

Charles L. Roff was born in Virginia on July 19, 1817, and came to Texas in 1860 by way of Ohio and Missouri. He paid taxes in Cooke County for the first time in 1861 on 2 slaves, 5 horses, and 20 cattle.[21]

John Russell was born January 27, 1808, in Pennsylvania. He moved to Grayson County on November 1, 1856, from Illinois. The census taker in 1860 listed him in Grayson County (F.N. 572) as a wagon maker, age fifty-two, with $2,215 in real and personal property. His wife was from Pennsylvania also, but their three children had all been born in Illinois. In 1861, Russell paid taxes in Grayson County on 320 acres and 7 cattle.[22]

Bob Scott, a slave, was born in Tennessee on August 25, 1825. He came to Texas with the Rufus F. Scott family in 1855, settling in Gainesville, and worked as a jack-of-all-trades, earning a pittance as a carpenter, teamster, and horse breaker.[23]

James E. Sheegog is listed in the 1860 Cooke County census (F.N. 553) as a farmer from Dublin, Ireland, age fifty-three, with $10,140 in real and personal property, including 5 slaves. In 1857 he paid a poll tax in Cooke County; by 1863 he owned 800 acres along Clear Creek. In 1859, the year in which he was elected county commissioner and the only one for which

20. Parsons to author, April 25, 1989.

21. CSR, Bourland's Border Regiment; Muster and Pay Rolls for Charles L. Roff's Minute Company, Frontier Battalion, Texas State Troops, Commanded by Colonel William C. Twitty, January 7, 1863, and Muster Roll of Roff's Company, April 8, 1863, in AGR; Acheson and O'Connell, eds., *Diamond's Account*, 18n; Roff, *A Brief History of Early Days*, 5–6; *Biographical Souvenir of Texas*, 729–30; Ingmire, comp., *Cemetery Records of Cooke County*, 133.

22. Landrum and Smith, *Illustrated History of Grayson County*, 168.

23. Gainesville *Register*, February 2, 1926; James Smallwood, *A Century of Achievement: Blacks in Cooke County, Texas* (Gainesville, 1975), 3, 10.

detailed information is available on him, he was assessed for 4 slaves, 6 horses, 12 cattle, and sheep worth $1,500.[24]

S. Snodgrass is recorded in the 1860 Denton County census (F.N. 529) as a farm laborer, age thirty-three, from Illinois, with $200 in personal property. His wife, Louisa Jane, and their elder daughter were also from Illinois, but their younger daughter, age two, was born in Texas.

James B. Stone is listed in the 1860 Cooke County census (F.N. 505) as a physician from Virginia, thirty-seven years of age, with $24,875 in real and personal property, including 15 slaves. His elder son, age seven, was born in Texas, his daughter, age three, was born in Missouri, and his younger son, age one, was born in the Chickasaw District of the Indian Territory. In 1859, Stone paid taxes in Cooke County for the first time on 758 acres, purchased from James G. Bourland, along the Red River. Two years later he had added 576 more acres and owned 16 slaves, 60 horses, and 320 cattle. He lived in the Sivell's Bend community.[25]

William C. Twitty, born in Kentucky on October 14, 1820, came to Texas about 1836 and by 1850, according to that year's census in Cooke County (F.N. 1), was living with his father-in-law, Daniel Montague, under whom he had served as second lieutenant in the 3d Regiment of Texas Mounted Volunteers during the Mexican War. Twitty married two of Montague's daughters: Rebecca in 1842, then Elizabeth in September 1851, after his first wife died in 1849. Twitty prospered as a land locator, having been elected as surveyor for the district that included Denton County in 1846, 1848, and 1850. The 1860 Cooke County census (F.N. 28) reveals that he had $20,500 in real and personal property, including 2,984 acres on the Red River and the Elm Fork of the Trinity River in Cooke County. He built his home within a mile of Montague's near the present town of Lindsay in Cooke County.[26]

24. Texas Secretary of State, Election Register.

25. Willie Russell, "Sivell's Bend Community History" (Typescript in Cooke Cty. Historical File); Bettie L. Gunter, "Recollections of an Early Cooke County Settler" (Typescript in Morton Museum).

26. CSR, 11th Tex. Cav., Bourland's Border Regiment; Card Index to Confederate Muster Rolls, in TSL; Ingmire, comp., "Cooke County Marriage Records," 1; Bates, *Denton County*, 140; Smith, *First 100 Years*, 20; Ingmire, comp., *Cemetery Records of Cooke County*, 196, 205; Spurlin, *Texas Veterans in the Mexican War*, 58.

John Ware, a Missouri native, first paid taxes in Cooke County in 1855 on 320 acres on Timber Creek; in 1861 he paid taxes on that tract, 640 acres elsewhere along that stream, 8 horses, and 60 cattle. His house served as a polling station during the secession referendum. His descendants still owned the "Ware Ranch" in 1975, which had been in continuous operation since its founding in 1854.[27]

Isham W. Welch, born in Missouri on February 9, 1826, immigrated to Grayson County on August 24, 1856. The 1860 Grayson County census (F.N. 641) lists him as a farmer from Missouri, age thirty-four, with $2,578 in real and personal property. His wife, Mary, was from Missouri, too, as were their four older children. Their fifth child, only a year old, was born in Texas.[28]

William C. West is listed in the 1860 Cooke County census (F.N. 401) as a farmer, age forty-two, from Kentucky with $928 in personal property. His wife and nine of their children, the youngest three years of age, were born in Missouri. Their tenth child, only six months old, was born in Texas.

John M. Wiley is reported in the 1860 Grayson County census (F.N. 640) as a farmer from Tennessee, age forty-five, with $5,391 in real and personal property. His wife, Lizzie, and all of their children were born in Missouri. He paid taxes in Cooke County in 1855 for $230 in livestock.

Nicholas Wilson first paid taxes in Denton County in 1858, when he was about twenty-four years of age, on a lot in Pilot Point, 1 slave, 2 horses, and 2 cattle; in 1862 he was assessed for 4 town lots in Pilot Point, 1 slave, 2 horses, and 20 cattle.[29]

Elizabeth Woolsey is listed in the 1860 Cooke County census (F.N. 376) as a single woman from Tennessee, age fifty-four, working as a farmer, with $1,525 in real and personal property. She had seven children born in North

27. Cooke Cty. Commissioners' Court, "Minutes," I, 67 (sheet 2); Dallas *News*, July 20, 1975.
28. *Biographical Souvenir of Texas*, 876; Landrum and Smith, *Illustrated History of Grayson County*, 173.
29. CSR, 29th Texas Cav.

Carolina, including four sons who were of military age in 1862. She paid taxes in 1862 on 160 acres, 2 horses, 4 cattle, and 4 sheep.

William C. Young was born in Tennessee on May 12, 1812, and came to Texas in 1837, settling in Red River County. He served as sheriff of that county from 1837 to 1838, then as attorney for the Seventh Judicial District from 1844 to 1854. He was a delegate to the annexation convention in 1845, then led the 3d Regiment, Texas Mounted Volunteers in the Mexican War. He moved to Grayson County in 1854, and accepted an appointment as United States marshal for the Western District of Texas, a position he held until 1861. He married Ann D. Black, the widow of a prominent Grayson County planter, in 1858, and they built a plantation on Horseshoe Bend of the Red River in Cooke County. Their joint holdings included 4,966 acres in Cooke County, 10,780 more in Davis, Denton, Ellis, Fannin, Grayson, Hunt, and Red River counties, 53 slaves, and 2,000 cattle. An inventory filed after Young's death revealed that the property in Cooke, Fannin, and Davis counties belonged to his wife, while the rest of the land and 24 slaves were his. Young County, created in 1856, was named for him.[30]

30. CSR, 11th Tex. Cav.; Ingmire, comp., "Marriage Records of Grayson County, Texas," 5; Cooke County, County Clerk, Probate Record and Minutes, I, pp. 332–33, 338, 341–43, 358, 376, 382, 395, 397–99, 400–401, in Cooke County Courthouse, Gainesville; Cooke County, County Clerk, Probate Papers, 1849–present, Box 19, in Cooke Cty. Courthouse; "Register of Elected and Appointed Officials for the Republic of Texas," I, 283, II, 144; Bates, *Denton County*, 8–9; *Biographical Souvenir of Texas*, 937; Collins, *Cooke County*, 10; Landrum and Smith, *Illustrated History of Grayson County*, 181; E. R. Lindley, *Biographical Dictionary of the Texan Conventions and Congresses, 1836–1845* (Austin, 1942), 196–97; Ingmire, comp., *Cemetery Records of Cooke County*, 12; Spurlin, *Texas Veterans in the Mexican War*, 54; Carrie J. Crouch, *A History of Young County, Texas* (Austin, 1956), 28; Mattie D. Lucas and Mita H. Hall, *A History of Grayson County, Texas* (Sherman, Tex., 1936), 65, 68; Francis W. Johnson, *A History of Texas and Texans*, ed. Eugene C. Barker (5 vols.; Chicago, 1914), IV, 1688.

Index

Index